A CAT
OF YOUR OWN

White and Red Tabby British Shorthair kittens

A Blue Tortoiseshell-and-white (Dilute Calico) Persian (Longhair)

A CAT
OF YOUR OWN

DOROTHY
SILKSTONE RICHARDS

American Consultant
CHARLENE BEANE

Veterinary Consultant
MICHAEL FINDLAY

Illustrated by
JOHN FRANCIS

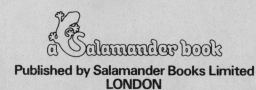
a Salamander book
Published by Salamander Books Limited
LONDON

A Salamander Book

Published by Salamander Books Ltd.,
Salamander House,
27 Old Gloucester Street,
London WC1N 3AF,
United Kingdom.

© Salamander Books Ltd 1981

ISBN 0 86101 093 0

Distributed in the United Kingdom
by New English Library.

Credits

Editors: Geoff Rogers, Valerie Noel-Finch
Designer: Roger Hyde
Colour and monochrome reproductions: Bantam Litho Ltd.,
Essex, United Kingdom
Filmset: Modern Text Typesetting Ltd.,
Essex, United Kingdom.
Printed in Belgium by Henri Proost & Cie, Turnhout.

A Lilac-point Siamese

Part Two
PRACTICAL SECTION
Essential information for everyone with a cat or thinking
of buying one.

A Chocolate Tortie Shaded Silver Oriental Shorthair

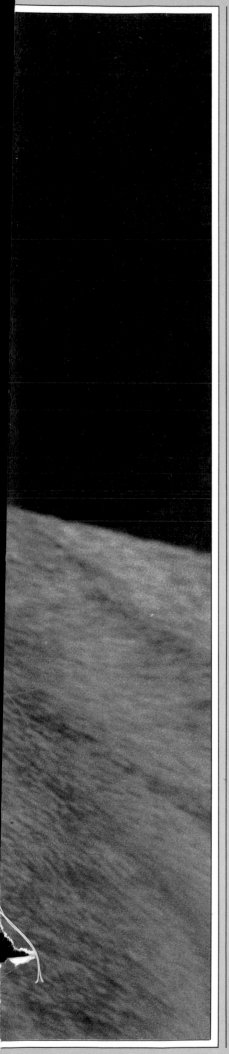

Part One
PROFILE SECTION

Detailed profiles of all major breeds, divided into longhairs and shorthairs.

Part One of this book aims to provide the potential cat owner with a comprehensive guide to choosing the most suitable cat. Beautiful full-colour illustrations show typical examples of each breed and detailed drawings show the distinctive shape of the head in each case. Alternative coat colours and patterns are featured in accompanying colour photographs.

There are two body types in cats: the powerfully built cat with a round head, as typified by the Persian (Longhair) and the Exotic and British Shorthairs; and the more lightly built cat with a wedge-shaped head, as typified by the Balinese longhair, Siamese and other 'Foreign' breeds. Likewise, there are five coat types: longhair, shorthair, curly, wirehair and hairless. (The last is really a misnomer as the cat has very fine hair on several parts of its body.) The various coat colours and patterns are reviewed on pages 10-15.

In the breed profiles each breed, and sometimes each colour, of cat is individually considered. Its *Good points* are listed and under the heading *Take heed* the buyer is warned of any possible drawbacks that ought to be considered in making a choice. The temperament and personality are at least as important as the cat's looks.

The *Grooming* requirements of each breed are outlined: it is foolish to choose a show-quality Persian unless time is set aside for grooming its long coat (perhaps an hour every day for 20

years). For people with less time available there are many other lovely cats that need hardly any grooming at all to keep them looking smart.

The paragraph devoted to the *Origin and history* of each cat explains which are so-called 'natural' breeds and which have been developed by selective breeding according to the science of genetics. Under *Breeding* and *Kittens* the would-be breeder can discover how to achieve the desired results.

The *Show summary* lists the standard points of each breed under headings such as Coat, Body, Tail, Head and Eyes. This detailed description outlines what is expected of a top show specimen. Each breed profile is concluded by a list of *Colours* and coat patterns available within the breed.

There is something about cats that makes people either want to be their undying slave or dislike them intensely; indifference is rare. Some people are prevented from owning a cat because they have a hay-fever type reaction to fur. Do not give a kitten as a present to a household without first making sure that it will be welcome and that no one is allergic. It is wiser to make sure before buying a kitten.

The cats in this section are from the show benches of the world; all may not be available in each country. If you choose a breed that suits your tastes and temperament then you should enjoy up to 20 years of devotion, delight and companionship from your pet.

SELF (SOLID) AND BICOLOUR CATS

Self- or solid-coloured cats and bicolours have been well known for centuries. Some colours are more prolific than others in the wild because they are dominant genetically and obscure the recessive colours to a large extent.

1 Black Black is one of the earliest known coat colours and is shown here by a sleek American Shorthair. Blacks may be fully longhaired as in the Persian, Angora, Norwegian Forest, Maine Coon and Cymric (longhaired Manx, pronounced kum-rick); or shorthaired as in the American, British and Exotic Shorthairs, Scottish Folds, Manx, American Wirehair, Cornish and Devon Rex, and Sphynx (not really hairless but with closely cropped fur on parts of its body). In the foreign-shaped cats black appears in the Bombay, Oriental (Foreign) Shorthair and the Japanese Bobtail. In Australia black Russians are now being bred.

2 Blue The Blue Persian shown here is one of the most aristocratic of cats. Blue—a recessive colour genetically—is rarely seen in free-roaming cats and so is much prized on the show bench. The colour is selectively bred among cat fancy breeders. Longhaired cats in blue may be Persian, Norwegian Forest, Angora, Maine Coon or Cymric; shorthaired cats may be British Blues, Chartreuse, Wirehair, Manx, Scottish, Sphynx or Exotic Shorthair; foreign-shaped cats may be Russian Blues, Korats, Oriental (Foreign) Blues or Blue Burmese (not strictly a self-coloured cat).

3 Red The Red Cornish Rex shown here is a very handsome animal. Red is often sex-linked and consequently in some breeds red females are rare or non-existent: the males are red and the females tortoiseshell. Solid red longhaired cats may be Persian, Peke-faced Persian, Angora, Cymric, Maine Coon or Norwegian Forest. In shorthaired cats red appears in American and Exotic Shorthairs, Scottish Folds, Sphynx, Manx, American Wirehairs and Rex. Among the foreign-shaped cats red occurs in Oriental (Foreign) Shorthairs, the Japanese Bobtail and the Red Burmese, although the latter is not strictly a self-coloured cat. The deep red required on the show bench is very different from the ginger colouring of non-pedigree cats and is obtained by selective breeding. Apricot, a dilution, is one of the new self-coloured Orientals now appearing on the show bench.

4 Cream The beautiful British Cream Shorthair shown here represents the dilute form of red. Cream is a recessive colour and is obtained only by selective breeding; it is not seen frequently among free-roaming cats. Longhaired cream cats may be Persians, Peke-faced Persians, Cymric, Maine Coon or Norwegian Forest. Shorthaired creams are British, American and Exotic Shorthairs, Scottish Fold, Manx, Sphynx, American Wirehair and Cornish and Devon Rex. Foreign-shaped cats may be Oriental (Foreign) Creams, Japanese Bobtail or Cream Burmese (not truly a self-coloured cat). Beige is a new shade of Oriental now coming onto the show bench.

5 White The Oriental (Foreign) White shown here looks like porcelain but despite appear-

1 Black
American Shorthair

2 Blue
Persian (Longhair)

3 Red
Cornish Rex

4 Cream
British Shorthair

ances it is not a fragile breed. With the white coat pattern comes a linked gene for deafness and in many breeds blue-eyed whites may be deaf. Longhaired white cats may be Persian, Angora, Maine Coon, Norwegian Forest or Cymric. Shorthaired whites are American Wirehair, Rex and Sphynx. White also appears in the Japanese Bobtail. In Australia and some other countries White Russians are being bred.

6 Chocolate Genetically the Havana represents the true chocolate self-coloured cat. The chocolate colour is a dilute form of black, as is brown. Because this is a recessive colour it is not generally seen in the wild. The longhaired chocolate cats are the Chocolate Persian, the Self-Chocolate Himalayan or Kashmir, and the Chocolate Angora. In

shorthaired cats only the foreign breeds recognize the brown or chocolate self-colouring, namely the Havana and the Chocolate (Champagne) Burmese, which is not truly a self-coloured cat. The Brown (Sable) Burmese is genetically black, although the appearance is that of a brown cat because of a gene restricting coat colour. Other self-coloured Oriental dilutions coming onto the show bench are Cinnamon and Caramel.

7 Lilac Lilac (lavender) is genetically a dilute form of chocolate (brown) and is a very beautiful colour, as shown here in a Lilac Angora. Another lilac longhaired breed is the Self-Lilac Himalayan or Kashmir. The shorthaired lilac breeds are the Oriental (Foreign) Lilac (Lavender) and the Lilac (Platinum) Burmese,

which although not a true self-coloured breed has the appearance of a self-coloured lilac cat.

8 Bicolour The bicolour coat pattern may be black-and-white, blue-and-white or red-and-white and should be mostly white on the underparts and ideally symmetrical elsewhere, with an inverted 'V' covering the nose. It is a very old coat pattern, known for centuries. Shown here is a Black-and-white Maine Coon. Longhaired bicolours may be Maine Coon, Persian, Ragdoll (in one of its colour variations), Norwegian Forest and Cymric. Shorthaired cats include the American, British and Exotic Shorthairs, the Scottish Folds, Manx, American Wirehair and Sphynx (if symmetrical). Cornish Rex may be bicolour if symmetrical, but not Devon Rex.

None of the foreign breeds at present accept bicolours, except the Japanese Bobtail.

9 Piebald An almost white cat with colour restricted to odd patches on the head and tail. It features in many ancient Chinese and other Oriental paintings, and is sometimes known as Harlequin. This piebald kind of white spotting is very common in non-pedigree cats as shown here. In America, cats with this coat pattern but with more white on the body, are known as Van, the patches being self coloured, or tortie or blue-cream. In the Van pattern (more white than illustrated), Persian, Turkish and Turkish Angora may display it in the longhairs; and American and Exotics in short-hairs. Also the Japanese Bobtail. The Van pattern or piebald is not accepted in the UK at present.

5 White
Oriental (Foreign) Shorthair

6 Chocolate
Havana (UK)

7 Lilac
Angora

8 Bicolour
Black-and-white Maine Coon

9 Piebald
Black-and-white Household pet

TIPPED AND PARTICOLOUR CATS

Tipped cats
Genetically the genes for a white undercoat are dominant; this is how it was possible to develop the tipped cats, which are among the most beautiful.

1 Light tipping Shown here is a Cymric (longhaired Manx) with chinchilla coat pattern. These are coat patterns where the guard hairs are tipped with a darker colour for about $\frac{1}{8}$ of their length ($\frac{1}{32}$ in the USA), giving a sparkling effect over the underlying white or paler colour. Black tipping is called Chinchilla; if the tipping is blue, we get the Blue Chinchilla; if brown, Golden Chinchilla; and if red, the Shell Cameo or Red Chinchilla. Despite their fairy-like appearance, these cats are very sturdy. It is also possible to get tortoiseshell tipping or blue-cream tipping, or even cats lightly tipped in a tabby pattern. This coat pattern is found in Maine Coon and Persian longhairs and in the American, British and Exotic Shorthairs, the Scottish, Manx and Wirehair, and in the Orientals.

2 Medium tipping Shown here is a Red Shaded American Shorthair, a very lovely animal. Coats in which the tipping on the guard hairs is restricted to approximately $\frac{1}{4}$ of the length ($\frac{1}{3}$ in USA) are known as Shaded cats, and this gives the effect of the cat wearing a mantle over the underlying white or paler coat. If the tipping is black, the coat is called Shaded Silver; tipping can also be brown, tortoiseshell, red, chocolate or lilac. This coat pattern is found in Persians, Maine Coon and Cymric in longhairs. In shorthairs it can be found in the Rex, American, British, Exotic, Wirehair, Scottish Fold, Manx and Orientals.

3 Heavy tipping Shown here is a magnificent Blue Smoke Persian. Where the coat is very heavily tipped, ie approximately half its length or more ($\frac{3}{4}$ in USA), the cats are known as Smokes. Tipping may be black, blue, red or tortoiseshell. Longhairs that have this coat pattern may be Persians, Maine Coon or Cymric. Shorthairs may be British, American, Exotic, Scottish Fold, Manx, American Wirehair or Rex. There are also Oriental Smokes.

Particolour cats
4 Tortoiseshell Shown here is a very pretty British Shorthair Tortoiseshell. The tortoiseshell coat pattern is very old and has been reported for centuries from every country in the world. It is a female-only pattern, the males that produce this coat pattern in their offspring being solid or self-coloured. In nature the black and red or cream coats are intermingled rather than patched (but more patched as white is added to the coat). In longhaired cats this coat pattern can be found in Persians, Norwegian Forest, Maine Coon, Angora and Cymric; and in the shorthairs in British, American, Exotic, Scottish, Manx, Wirehair, Sphynx and Rex. The foreign-shaped cats include Oriental Torties and the Japanese Bobtail. The dilution of tortie is blue-cream.

5 Chocolate tortoiseshell This colouring is shown to perfection in this lovely Chocolate Tortoiseshell Longhair Persian, where the brightly coloured patches are distinct and well-broken on the

1 Light Tipping
Chinchilla Cymric (Longhaired Manx)

2 Medium Tipping
Shaded Red American Shorthair

4 Tortoiseshell
Brown Tortoiseshell British Shorthair

3 Heavy Tipping
Blue Smoke Persian (Longhair)

face and body. This is one of the newer coat colours that appeared during selective breeding programmes, where the black pigment has been replaced by chocolate but with red and cream. This colouring can be found in the Burmese and in Orientals. The dilute form of chocolate tortie is lilac-cream/lilac tortie. Both are female-only.

6 Blue-cream (Blue Tortoiseshell)
The Scottish Fold, a very different looking cat, here demonstrates the blue-cream patched coat. This is a dilute form of the tortoiseshell colouring and consists of blue and cream mingled (UK) or patched (USA). The natural form would be mingled (but patched when combined with white). It is a female-only variety, the males being blue or cream. Genetically blue is a dilute of black; and

cream the dilute of red. A lot of cats share this kind of colouring: in the longhairs, Persian, Maine Coon, Cymric and Norwegian Forest; in shorthairs, American, British, Exotic, Scottish, Manx, Wirehair, Rex and Sphynx; in the foreign cats, there are Blue Tortie Orientals, Blue Tortie Burmese

7 Lilac-cream (Lilac Tortoiseshell)
Here is a pensive Lilac Tortie Burmese. Lilac tortie is the dilute form of the chocolate tortoiseshell where the chocolate colour has been replaced by lilac, with cream. There are not many cats with this colouring at present, but with our modern knowledge of genetics we shall be able to produce this coat colour in many other types of cats within a few years. The chocolate and lilac colours are still rare. The Persian comes in Lilac Tortie (Lilac Cream)

in the UK. The Oriental Lilac Tortie (Lavender Cream) has the same coloured coat.

8 Tortoiseshell-and-white (Calico) This fascinating American Wirehair cat shows off the tortie-and-white coat to perfection. This is a very old coat pattern, known for centuries all over the world. Before selective breeding took place, those cats with white in the coat as well as black and red had large well-defined patches of colour, compared with the mingled colours of black and red without white. The pedigree tortie-and-white (calico) cat must have mainly white on the underparts and a nose blaze of white is preferred. Longhairs with this colouring may be Persian, Maine Coon, Cymric or Norwegian Forest. Shorthairs may be British, Manx, Wirehair, Rex or Sphynx.

The Japanese Bobtail is also found in this colouring, although its coat usually has more white than in the other pedigree cats of this particular colouring.

Dilute Tortoiseshell-and-white
The dilute form of tortoiseshell-and-white is the blue-cream and white or dilute tortoiseshell and white, or dilute calico. The black in the coat is replaced with blue and the red is replaced with cream and these two colours are combined with white. This produces a lovely combination.

If you like the colours and coat patterns of the cats on this page, you will be able to turn to the breeds in which they appear and read more about them. There will probably be a cat that is suitable for you in your choice of colour.

5 Chocolate Tortoiseshell
Persian (Longhair)

7 Lilac-cream
Lilac Tortie Burmese

6 Blue-cream
Scottish Fold

8 Tortoiseshell-and-white (Calico)
American Wirehair

TABBY AND HIMALAYAN CATS

The tabby coat pattern has been around for centuries. In fact thousands of years ago tabby cats were depicted in Egyptian paintings and Pompeiian relics and in Far Eastern mythology. Sometimes the cats were striped, sometimes spotted (broken stripes), and many of today's wild cats still have this coat pattern.

1 Classic tabby (Blotched tabby) The classic tabby coat pattern is shown here on a very striking British Shorthair Silver Tabby, but the classic pattern can be silver, brown, blue, red or cream in almost any breed of cat except the 'one colour' or 'one coat pattern' breeds. The ground colour should be a good contrast with the over-lying pattern colour, and the pattern shows up best in the shorthairs, although longhaired tabbies are very beautiful. In the longhairs we find Persians, Peke-faced Persians (Red only), Maine Coon, Norwegian Forest and Cymric. In shorthairs, British, American, Exotic, Scottish, Manx, Sphynx, Rex and Wirehair. There are very lovely Oriental tabbies in the above colours and in some of the newer colours that have recently been arriving on the cat scene. The full classic tabby pattern is described on page 50.

2 Mackerel tabby Illustrated here is a Cream Tabby Persian. As opposed to the classic or blotched tabby, the mackerel tabby has vertical stripes down the flanks. These stripes are less visible in a longhair, particularly on the paler varieties. Mackerel tabbies can be of all the same breeds as the classic or blotched tabbies. The full mackerel tabby coat pattern is described on page 50.

3 Spotted tabby Shown here is a beautiful Oriental Cameo Tabby cat. With its off-white ground colour and deep rich red markings and green eyes, it makes an unusual and attractive combination. In the spotted tabby the stripes have broken up into spots, giving a very beautiful coat pattern like a miniature leopard. The full coat pattern is described on page 50. Spotted tabbies are usually British Shorthairs, Manx or Rex. Foreign spotted cats may be Oriental, the Ocicat or the elegant Egyptian Mau.

4 Ticked tabbies The cat chosen to illustrate this class is a Blue Abyssinian, one of the newest colours in this breed. The ticked coat of the wild rabbit occurs in the Somali (a longhaired Abyssinian) and in Angoras. The shorthaired Singapura, where the ticking is brown and the ground colour bleached linen, is one of the latest among pedigree cats. There are also Oriental ticked tabbies. This type of ticked coat is known genetically as agouti.

5 Patched tabby (Torbie) The patched tabby coat is admirably seen here on a Brown Exotic Patched Tabby (Torbie) Shorthair. A torbie is a tabby with tortie patches. It has become a recognized coat pattern, as it is very prolific and often seen in the wild. Torbies may be brown, blue or silver tabby with bold patches of red and/or cream. Patched tabbies (torbies) occur in Persians, Norwegian Forest and Cymric in the longhairs; American and Exotic Shorthairs, Rex and Manx. Oriental torbies come in standard and silver tabby coat patterns in black, blue, chocolate and lilac.

2 Mackerel Tabby
Cream Persian (Longhair)

4 Ticked Tabby
Blue Abyssinian

1 Classic Tabby
Silver Tabby
British Shorthair

3 Spotted Tabby
Cameo Tabby
Oriental Shorthair

6 Combination coats

Demonstrating the combination coat is a Japanese Bobtail in pure glistening white with bold patches of coal black, and brown tabby. Many cats have a combination of one of the above coats with white, and these are called combination coat patterns. In longhairs these coats may be seen on Maine Coon, Norwegian Forest and Cymric, although in the latter, combinations with chocolate or lilac are not allowed. In the shorthairs the Sphynx may have a combination coat if symmetrical. The Wirehair and the Japanese Bobtail may also have combination coats. The Manx may not have combinations with chocolate or lilac.

7 Himalayan coat pattern
(Pointed coat pattern) Shown here is a Seal-point Siamese, one of the most dramatic colourings among cats. The Himalayan coat pattern is one in which the colour is concentrated in the points, ie the mask, ears, legs and tail. The points may be seal, chocolate, blue, lilac, tortie, blue-cream, tabby, torbie, red (flame) or cream according to breed. Longhairs with the Himalayan coat pattern are the Colourpoint Longhair, the Balinese and the Ragdoll in its colourpoint form. Shorthairs cover the large range of Siamese cats, Colourpoint Shorthairs and the Devon Si-Rex. To a lesser extent the Burmese show this coat pattern, particularly in kittens. They are not true self-coloured cats as they show vestigial points. The points are more obvious in the Tonkinese, which is a cross between Siamese and Burmese. Longhaired Burmese are known as Tiffany. The Himbur is a cross between the Colourpoint (Himalayan) and the Burmese, and has a coat similar in colouring to the Tonkinese but longhaired.

8 Himalayan combination coats

The illustration shows a very lovely Lilac Birman, similar to the Colourpoint but with four symmetrical white feet. These coats combine the Himalayan pattern with white, produced genetically by a gene for white spotting. Other longhairs in this coat pattern are the Mitted Ragdoll; and chocolate and lilac bicolours are being produced by the breeders of the Self Chocolate and Lilac Longhairs (Kashmirs.) Normally bicolour does not include combinations with chocolate and lilac. In shorthairs there is the Snowshoe, which is a Siamese coloured cat with white feet and sometimes a white muzzle; this is a relatively new breed, still awaiting recognition in many places, including the UK.

Summary

Pages 10 to 15 illustrate the range of cat coats, patterns and coat types. The patterns are solid colours; bicolours; piebald (van); particolours; tabbies; combination coats; Himalayan; and Himalayan combinations.

The coat types are shorthair, longhair, curly coat, wirehair and hairless.

Choose the coat colour, pattern and coat type you find most attractive, then look in the Breed Profiles for the breeds listed under each coat pattern. Choose for temperament and availability as well as good looks. One will be just right for you and will respond to your loving care with a lifetime's devotion and companionship.

7 Himalayan Pattern
Seal-point Siamese

6 Combination Coat
Japanese Bobtail

5 Patched Tabby (Torbie)
Brown Torbie
Exotic Shorthair

8 Himalayan Combination
Lilac-point Birman

15

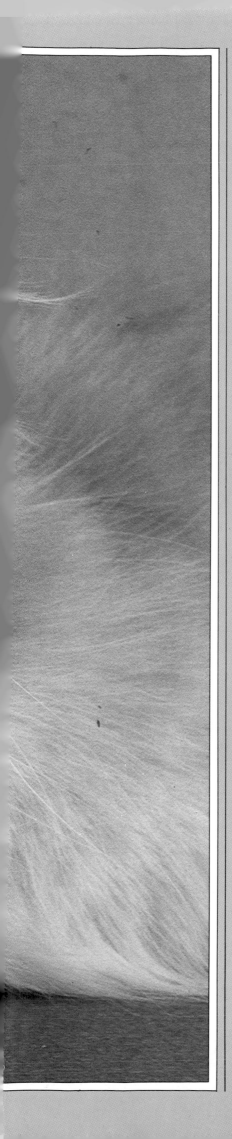

LONGHAIRED CATS

Longhaired cats are really very beautiful creatures but some of them do need a lot of attention. If you favour a longhaired cat do make sure, in advance, that you or someone in your household will groom it every day. In particular, the show quality Persians with their very long coats need a good half-hour grooming session night and morning, every single day; not only to keep them looking beautiful but to prevent them swallowing their fur and getting the coat knotted up, with painful consequences. Some of the other longhaired breeds, such as the beautiful Balinese or the rugged Maine Coon, are easier to groom than Persians and I would make this one of the deciding factors when choosing a kitten. You will find many lovely cats in this section and there will be one just for you. The Persians are firm favourites and are available in over 30 colour varieties. You may like to consider the distinctively marked Colour-points or the stately Birman. For an outdoor life the Norwegian Forest Cat is ideal and for adaptability and grace the Angora is hard to beat. Perhaps the tail-less Cymric or the charming Somali are more to your taste. Whichever breed you choose, do make sure that its temperament and personality are exactly what you are looking for; do not judge by looks alone.

Left: An elegant and beautifully groomed Shaded Cameo Persian.

PERSIAN
(Longhair)

Good points
- *Beautiful and elegant*
- *Affectionate*
- *Companionable*
- *Undemanding*
- *Quiet*
- *Docile*
- *Suitable for apartment life*

Take heed
- *Needs daily grooming*
- *Vulnerable*
- *Moults*
- *Does not like to be teased*

The Persian makes an attractive, sweet and undemanding pet. It is docile, quiet, companionable and elegant. It likes being with people and is generally good tempered, unless teased. However, it must be protected from dogs and traffic because, with its short legs and rather heavy body, it cannot always escape quickly.

However, the Persian is quieter and less adventurous than some of its shorthaired cousins, and can often be kept in a fenced area of the garden from which a longer legged cat would escape, though the cat should not be permanently penned up on its own. A Persian will also live happily in an apartment, provided it is given the run of the place and plenty of fresh air.

The Persian's main disadvantage for a busy person is that it *must* be groomed daily. The cat will moult all year, but especially in the summer months, and if it swallows large quantities of hair, fur balls may form and cause an obstruction in the stomach that, in extreme cases, would have to be removed surgically. When it runs free outside, because of its short legs, leaves and debris may be caught up in the long fur, and if left, will knot up into hard balls. Their removal will then be very painful for the cat.

Consequently, owning a Persian is quite a responsibility, but if you have plenty of time to look after one, then you will be sure to find it an excellent, loving and devoted companion.

Persians are not as prolific as some of the shorthaired or foreign varieties, and therefore may cost more to buy. However, if you want a pet rather than a show champion, it is possible to purchase a non-show class kitten, which will make a super pet, much more cheaply.

Grooming
Daily grooming is essential and involves removing any knots and tangles (which may not always be readily visible) with a wide-toothed comb, then using a fine-toothed comb to remove dead hairs and finally giving the coat a good brush with a long-handled pure bristle brush (as this gives rise to less static electricity than brushes with synthetic fibres). The tufts between the toes should be combed carefully, as mats here would be very uncomfortable for the cat. The eyes should be checked regularly, as Persians are prone to blocked tear ducts and any discharge from the eyes will discolour the fur around the nose.

If destined for show, the paler-coloured Persians will benefit from a bath a week before the show, followed by a powdering with fuller's earth or a proprietary non-toxic grooming powder to remove grease marks from the coat. The powder should be rubbed in well down to the roots, then brushed out thoroughly. Pre-show preparation for the darker colours involves the application of bay rum to the coat — not powder, as this may mar the colour. The hair is whipped up with the brush so that every hair stands up away from the body, and frames the face in a most appealing way.

Origin and history
Longhaired cats have been known in Europe since the sixteenth century, but their precise origin remains obscure. Records show that there were two types of longhaired cat, one from Turkey — the Angora — and the other from Persia (now Iran), although it is likely that both these types originated in Russia and were brought by traders to Europe via Asia Minor. Whereas cats with long hair are found today in both Turkey and Iran, they are still much more common in parts of Russia, and it is possible that the harsh climate there may have favoured the evolution of the long coat.

The so-called Persian cats had broader, rounder heads, smaller ears, shorter bodies and plushier coats than the Angoras, and were undoubtedly the forerunners of the modern Persian type. Selective breeding of these cats over the years, particularly in the last 100 years, has produced the typical Persian type and the numerous colour varieties known today. The Persian is one of the oldest and most popular show breeds, and many fine cats bred in the United Kingdom have been exported to form the foundations of breeding lines in Europe, the United States, Australia and New Zealand.

SHOW SUMMARY
General appearance. The show Persian is a sturdy cat of gently curving lines. It is a medium to large cat with a long, flowing coat, an ethereal look and a pretty face.
Coat. Long and thick (up to 15cm/6in in length), but fine, soft and silky, standing away from the body, ideally with every hair separate. The coat should shine with glowing good health. There is a very full ruff forming a halo around the head, and a long frill between the front legs.
Body. Cobby, solid and rounded, low lying on the legs. Deep in the chest; massive across the shoulders and rump. Legs short, thick and strong with straight forelegs. Feet large, firm, rounded and well tufted.
Tail. Short and full, especially at the base. No kinks.
Head. Broad, round and massive on a short, thick neck. Face round and pretty, with no hint of wedginess. Jaw broad. Chin strong, not undershot. Cheeks full. Nose almost snub, short and broad with a good break or stop where it meets the forehead. The stop is particularly pronounced in American Persians. Ears tiny, rounded at the tips, set wide apart and tilted forward, set low on the head, with long ear tufts.
Eyes. Large, round and set wide apart. Full, brilliant and wide-awake, with a sweet expression. Slanted, oval or deep-set eyes are faults. Eye colour may fade with age.

PERSIAN COLOURS
There are at least 30 colour varieties of Persian at present, although not all are recognized for competition in all countries. In the United Kingdom, each colour variety is regarded as a separate breed, and classified by the name 'Longhair' rather than Persian, whereas in the United States, colours are listed simply as varieties of Persian.

WHITE PERSIAN

White Persians are very beautiful cats and one of the oldest varieties. They were often regarded as status symbols in London drawing rooms at the turn of the century. White Persians have been known in Europe for about 300 years, but the earliest Whites had blue eyes and long, pointed faces, and were frequently deaf. White cats began to attract attention in the late 1800s and were first shown in London in 1903, at which time they were also becoming popular in the United States.

Today there are three varieties — Blue-eyed White, Orange-eyed White and Odd-eyed White (one of each colour) — due to outcrossing to other Persians, notably blues. It seems difficult to breed the good Persian type with blue eyes, and the Blue-eyed Whites on the show bench still have slightly longer ears and faces, although they usually have better coats than Orange-eyed Whites.

One disadvantage of white cats is that many of the Blue-eyed Whites are deaf from birth and some of the odd-eyed cats are deaf on the blue-eyed side. Deafness may be difficult to detect at first, because the cat's other senses may compensate. It is quite a responsibility to own a deaf cat, because it must be protected from traffic and other dangers. It is best to confine such a cat to your property to avoid any unforeseen accidents.

Grooming
To keep the cat's coat really white, dust with talcum powder or a proprietary chalk-based grooming powder daily, then brush and comb out thoroughly. Any grease in the coat of a White Persian will show up as yellowish marks, particularly on the tail, and especially in male cats. To remove these stains, the tail should be washed in warm water to which a little borax has been added, and rinsed thoroughly afterwards.

For a show cat, a bath a few days before a show will probably be essential to set the coat off to its full advantage. Sunlight is unlikely to spoil the coat, so there is no need to keep the cat indoors.

Breeding
Blue-eyed Whites have smaller litters, which may account for the fact that they are not as numerous as the Orange-eyed Whites. Their deafness may also account for their lack of popularity and unfortunately two cats with normal hearing may produce deaf kittens. Unless you are experienced, it is advisable not to use a deaf cat for breeding. A deaf queen requires more supervision than a normal cat because she cannot hear the cries of her kittens. She should be placed on a hard surface covered with newspaper, so that she can feel her kittens and the vibrations of their cries.

Kittens
All the kittens are born with blue eyes and it may be some weeks before you can tell whether there are blue-eyed, orange-eyed or odd-eyed kittens in the litter. The depth of the eye colour also takes some months to develop. Orange eyes should be deep orange or copper, and if a kitten does not have the deep eye colour by the time it is six or seven months old, then it is unlikely that it will intensify later in life. When born the kittens are pinkish in colour, but this baby coat soon disappears and they become covered in lovely fluffy white fur. Some kittens are born with a smudge of black hairs on top of their head. This is an indication that they will have normal hearing, at least in one ear. The spot disappears as the adult coat starts to grow at about nine months.

SHOW SUMMARY
The coat must be pure white throughout, with no shadow markings or black hairs. Nose-leather and paw pads are pink. Eyes deep blue; orange or copper; or one orange or copper and one deep blue. Pale or green tinged eyes are faults.

BLACK PERSIAN

The Black Persian is a very old variety; it is one of nature's original breeds. It is still quite rare, however, probably because a perfect black is very difficult to obtain.

As with other black cats, the Persian is seen in some countries as a 'lucky' cat, notably in the United Kingdom; but in others it is considered 'unlucky' instead. As with other longhaired cats, Blacks were known in Europe at the end of the sixteenth century, but no one knows exactly where they came from, as there are no reliable early records. It can be said with certainty, however, that they first appeared on the British show

Persian
(Longhair)

Black Persian

Blue-eyed White Persian

19

bench in 1871. The early black cats were more like Angoras than Persians, with long noses and big ears, but these features have now been bred out, and the current champion will have the typical snub nose, round head and tiny ears.

Grooming
Daily grooming with brush and comb is essential. Bathing before a show may not be necessary, except to make the coat more fluffy, but the addition of bay rum to the coat will enhance the shine. Do not use powder, as it will be impossible to brush it all out, and it will deaden the colour. Dampness and strong sunlight will produce a rusty tinge on the coat, so a show cat should be kept away from these two conditions whenever possible.

Breeding
Mating two Black Persians will produce black kittens, but to improve type it is also necessary to outcross to some of the other colours, notably Blue or White. In this case only the females from such crosses are used for further breeding. Black males from Black-to-Black matings are used to produce Tortoiseshells, Tortoiseshell-and-white (Calicos), Whites, Smokes, Creams and Bicolours.

Kittens
All kittens are born with blue eyes, which gradually change to copper. The kittens are born black but they often have rusty coats or some white hairs until the full adult jet black coat appears. In fact, the worst kitten coats at six months old often become the densest black adults at 12 to 18 months.

SHOW SUMMARY
The coat must be a solid even black all over, and each hair must be black from its tip down to its root. A real jet black is required, with no tinge of rustiness, no white hairs and no tabby markings. Noseleather and paw pads black. Eyes brilliant orange or deep copper.

BLUE PERSIAN

Blues have always been the most popular of the longhaired cats, with their long, flowing coats, delicate looks and sweet little faces.

It is said that they come from Persia (now Iran), Turkey, China, Burma, Afghanistan and Russia! They have featured in artists' impressions for several centuries, but they were largely unknown in Europe before the end of the sixteenth century. They were certainly known in Italy during the Renaissance, however, and were prized in India. First bred principally in France and England, where they enjoyed the patronage of Queen Victoria, they were later exported to the United States.

The blue colour is a dilution of black genetically, probably a result of crossing a black with a white cat

originally, but blue cats did not appear in a separate class on the British show bench until 1889, although before that they may have been shown in mixed classes with Blue Tabbies and Blue-and-white Bicolours. Since hitting the show scene they have reigned supreme. They even have a show entirely to themselves in the United Kingdom, so numerous have they become.

Grooming
Daily grooming with brush and comb is essential. Bathing before a show is not usually necessary. Any grease marks can be removed by dusting the coat with grooming powder, taking care that it reaches the roots, and then brushing it well out.

Breeding
Blues are often used to produce Blue-creams and, because they seem to excel in Persian type, to improve the type of eye colour of other Persians.

Kittens
When born, the kittens may have tabby markings, but these usually disappear as the adult coat develops. In fact, the more heavily marked kittens often become the cats with the best all-over blue coats. The kittens are born with blue eyes, which change to deep orange over the next few months.

SHOW SUMMARY
The coat should be an even pale grey-blue all over, the same depth of colour from root to tip, with no sign of a paler undercoat and no tabby markings or white hairs. Generally the paler blue coats are preferred. Noseleather and paw pads slate blue. Eyes brilliant copper or deep orange with no green tinge.

RED PERSIAN

The Red Persian is an outstanding-looking cat with a flame-coloured, flowing coat. The name 'red' is misleading, as the coat colour is much more orange than scarlet, more flame than crimson. Although red cats have appeared at shows since the beginning of the century, a really good specimen is very rare. In fact, it is almost impossible to produce without some tabby markings in the coat.

Grooming
Daily grooming is essential. Powder before a show or the application of a little bay rum will enhance the coat for a show appearance.

Breeding
Despite the predominance of male red cats (in the wild), red females do occur and can be obtained by mating a Red male with either a Tortoiseshell or a Blue-cream female (providing the male does not carry the blue colour factor in his genetic make-up). It is unwise to mate Reds to Red Tabbies, as this will reintroduce tabby markings. It is best to outcross to other self-

coloured cats, such as Blacks. Reds are used to breed Tortoiseshells and Tortoiseshell-and-whites (Calicos).

Kittens
Red kittens are usually born with tabby markings, which they may or may not lose when the adult coat is grown. Often, therefore, it is difficult to tell whether there are Red or Red Tabby kittens in the litter, and breeding for Red Persians presents quite a challenge.

SHOW SUMMARY
The coat should be a deep, rich red without markings of any kind or white hairs. Noseleather and paw pads brick red. Eyes deep copper.

CREAM PERSIAN

Cream Persians are not as numerous as some of the other Persian varieties, perhaps because they have small litters as a rule. They are very beautiful cats and quite ethereal-looking with their pale cream fur.

The Cream was first recorded in the United Kingdom in 1890, but at first such cats were generally regarded as Reds that were too pale to meet the show standard and many were sold as pets. Others were exported to the United States, where breeders have always been more interested in Cream Persians, and they are very popular there today. In the United Kingdom serious breeding for Creams in their own right did not start until the 1920s.

It is possible that Cream kittens first appeared in litters born to Tortoiseshells mated to Red Tabby males. Tortoiseshells have red, black and cream in their coats, and so this mating could produce some all-cream kittens. Any breeder who found this colour attractive could then proceed to isolate it by selective breeding.

Below: Red and Cream Persian kittens; the faint tabby marking may fade at about nine months.

Grooming
Daily grooming is essential. A bath may be necessary a few days before a show, and grooming powder will fluff the coat into show condition.

Breeding
Continuous like-to-like matings between Cream Persians produce gradual loss of type, and therefore outcrosses to other coloured varieties are necessary. Cream is genetically a dilution of the red colour and is, in fact, much easier to achieve than the solid red. Creams are produced most reliably from matings between Blues and Creams. A Cream female mated to a Blue male will produce Cream male and Blue-cream female kittens; a Cream male mated to a Blue female will produce Cream kittens of either sex, Blue males and Blue-cream females.

Kittens
Cream kittens are often born with faint tabby markings, but these usually disappear when the adult coat starts to develop at about nine months of age.

SHOW SUMMARY
The cream coat should be sound throughout, without markings of any kind and without a darker area down the spine. A medium depth of colour is preferred in the United Kingdom; American associations prefer a paler buff cream; too red ('hot') a colour is a fault. There should be no sign of a paler undercoat; the hair should be the same colour from root to tip. The coat colour may be darker in older cats or just before moulting. Noseleather and paw pads pink. Eyes brilliant deep copper.

BICOLOUR PERSIAN

Two-coloured cats have been known since early times but are relative newcomers to the show bench, due to the fact that they were originally regarded as alley cats without known parentage. They can be Black-and-white, Blue-and-white, Red-and-white or Cream-

Persian
(Longhair)

Blue Persian

Black-and-white
Bicolour Persian

Cream Persian kitten

Red Persian

Above: This Shaded Golden shows the typical seal brown tipping over the warm cream undercoat.

and-white, although the latter are more rare. In pedigree breeding it has been difficult to meet the standard, which requires that the coat pattern should resemble that of the Dutch rabbit, with symmetrical patches of colour on the head and body; the symmetry seems to be an elusive characteristic, and few perfect Bicolours are seen. However, when achieved the cat is sure of adulation on the show bench. The 1979 Cat Fanciers' Association's Cat of the Year was in fact a Black-and-white female Persian of exceptional merit, which is no mean achievement in a country where the feline population exceeds 45 million (USA).

Grooming
Daily grooming is essential. For showing, a bath may be necessary, but powder should not be used on the coat as this tends to deaden the contrast between the colour and the white.

Breeding
Bicolours may be obtained from mating two Bicolours, a Bicolour with a Tortoiseshell-and-white, a Bicolour with a solid colour, or a solid colour with a White. They are accepted as being the best sires for producing Tortoiseshell-and-white kittens. Bicolour queens make excellent mothers, and the litters usually contain a colourful assortment of three or four kittens, of all the above patterns.

Kittens
Bicoloured kittens are robust and hardy and if kept for breeding can produce almost any coloured kitten, depending on their own ancestry and that of their mating partner. The kittens are large and mature early.

SHOW SUMMARY
The show Bicolour Persian must have a patched coat with not more than two-thirds of the body coloured and not more than one half white. The pattern should be symmetrical, with patches of colour on the face, head, back, flanks and tail. Accepted colours are Black-and-white (Magpie), Blue-and-

white, Red-and-white and Cream-and-white (rare). Tabby markings and brindling (white hairs) within the colour patches are faults. White is desirable on the underparts, chest, feet, legs, chin and lips, and a facial blaze is preferred. A white collar is permitted. Noseleather and paw pads generally pink, otherwise in keeping with the coat colour. Eyes deep brilliant copper to orange in colour.

CHINCHILLA & SHELL CAMEO PERSIAN

The Persian Chinchillas and Cameos belong to a group that contains some of the most beautiful of all longhaired cats, which can conveniently be described as having a 'tipped' coat pattern. The characteristic feature of such cats is that the undercoat is one colour (usually white, but sometimes cream), and the guard hairs are tipped to varying extents with a different, contrasting colour. These cats are classified further according to whether the colour tipping is light (Chinchillas and Shell Cameos), medium (Shaded Silvers and Shaded Cameos) or heavy (Smokes).

In the Chinchillas and Shell Cameos, the undercoats are usually pure white, and the ends of some of the guard hairs, for approximately one-eighth of the hair length, are lightly tipped with a contrasting colour, giving a shimmering, sparkling effect to the coat.

The name Chinchilla is misleading, as the South American rodent whose name was given to this cat has fur that is dark at the roots and white at the tips — the opposite of the cat's coat. Despite this discrepancy, Chinchilla Persians have been so named since the 1890s, although the early Chinchillas were much more heavily marked, and probably rather more like today's Shaded Silvers. They are believed to have been developed from cats with silver genes, probably Silver Tabbies, whose markings were indistinct or almost absent, mated to Blue Persians or Smokes; further selective breeding used only the palest kittens or non-tabby

kittens mated to White Persians with blue eyes. Early Silver Tabbies would have had hazel or golden eyes, and the first Chinchillas also had hazel eyes; when these were mated to Blue-eyed White Persians, some of the kittens had green or blue-green eyes. These were considered an immediate success, and thereafter affected the standard. After the Second World War there was a shortage of all types of pedigree cats in Europe, and American Chinchillas were imported to improve the stamina of the variety. In Europe and Australia Chinchillas are, and have always been, fairy tale cats, finer-boned than other Persians, but in the United States, they are larger and conform more closely to the general Persian standard.

Their delicate appearance belies their hardy nature; they are not in fact fragile cats, but very robust and healthy. Their sweet baby faces and ethereal looks have made Chinchillas among the most popular of cats. Patronized before the Second World War by Queen Victoria's grand-daughter, Princess Victoria, and being particularly photogenic, they are known worldwide, helped, no doubt, by their numerous appearances on television and in magazines.

Although the name Chinchilla traditionally conjures up a picture of a cat with a coat of black silk on white velvet, in recent years the name has been extended to cats of similar appearance and coat pattern but of different colour, notably the Chinchilla Golden, a lovely brown tipped variety now becoming popular in the United States and Europe.

The beautiful Shell Cameos are similar to the Chinchilla in coat pattern, and were developed in the late 1950s, mostly in the United States, by selective breeding of Silver Persians with Red cats. (In the United Kingdom, Creams were also used.) Using Chinchillas, the kittens were green-eyed, which was not desired, so Smokes with copper eyes were then introduced and mated to Reds or Tortoiseshells In general, tabbies of any colour are not used (except to produce the Cameo Tabby), so as not to reintroduce any tabby markings. Such mixed breeding produces a wide variety of coloured Cameos, from the Red to the Tortoiseshell and the Blue-cream.

All Cameo varieties enjoyed immediate popularity because they are so beautiful, and they are now widely bred and appreciated in the United States, Europe, Australia and New Zealand.

Grooming
For showing, Chinchillas and Cameos should be bathed a week before the show, then powdered with baby powder every day for four or five days to give back the body to the coat. Daily combing thereafter is essential to prevent the formation of knots. The day before the show, all traces of powder must be removed and each hair will stand out from the body. This is true show condition:

every hair separate and the coat beautifully fluffy.

Sunlight affects the white fur and tends to give it a yellow tinge, so if showing the cat, try to keep it out of direct sunlight.

Breeding
Female Persians develop relatively slowly, and it is usually advisable not to arrange the first matings until the cats are 12 to 18 months old. This gives the females time to develop fully before bearing kittens. Once mated they usually become good mothers. To preserve the variety as it is, Chinchillas are now mated only to other Chinchillas, and it is advisable to mate the queen to a stud possessing all the qualities missing or less than perfect in the queen. For example, if the queen has poor eye colour, a stud must be chosen that excels in the colour of his eyes.

Breeding for Cameos is more complex. First crosses of Copper-eyed Smokes to Red or Cream Persians preferably without blue in their backgrounds, or to Tortoiseshells, will produce Cameo males, which when mated to the Blue-cream, Tortoiseshell, Shaded Tortoiseshell or Shaded Blue-cream cats also produced from this mating, will give Shell Cameo females. Alternatively, Blue-cream and Tortoiseshell females can be mated to Red or Cream males. An exchange of blood lines (mating cats of different parents) will be better than brother and sister matings in some instances, if these can be found, and will also save waiting for two years until the kittens from the first mating mature.

The average Chinchilla and Cameo litter contains three or four kittens, though there was once a Chinchilla litter of 10.

Kittens
Chinchilla kittens are born with dark markings and tabby markings, particularly on the tail, but these disappear by the time they are four to six weeks old. If a kitten still shows markings after 10 weeks of age, then it is not destined for showing. Cameo kittens are born white, the tipping gradually appearing. They are particularly appealing when the colour develops, resembling balls of pink tinsel or vanilla ice-cream topped with orange sherbet!

SHOW SUMMARY
Chinchilla. Type to conform to the standard for Persians (United States), or to be slightly lighter boned and larger eared (United Kingdom). The undercoat should be pure white, the last one-eighth of each hair on the back, flanks, legs, head and tail tipped with black, giving a sparkling silver appearance to the coat. The chin, ear tufts, stomach and chest are pure white. The lips, nose and eyes are outlined in black and deep brown. Whiskers should be white, but may be black nearest the face. Noseleather brick red: a pale noseleather is considered a fault. Paw pads black. Eyes emerald green to blue-green.

Cameo Tabby Persian
(Shown in moult)

Shell Cameo Persian

Persian
(Longhair)

Chinchilla Persian

23

Masked Silver Persian. A Chinchilla with a pure white undercoat and top coat tipped lightly with black on the back, flanks and tail, but with darker, heavier tipping on the face and paws. Noseleather brick red. Paw pads black or deep brown. Eyes green or blue-green.

Chinchilla Golden. The undercoat should be a rich, warm cream. The coat on the back, flanks, head and tail is lightly tipped with seal brown to give a sparkling golden appearance. The legs may be very lightly tipped. The chin, ear tufts, stomach and chest should be cream. The lips, nose and eyes should be outlined with seal brown. Noseleather deep rose. Paw pads seal brown. Eyes green or blue-green.

Shell Cameo. (Red Chinchilla). The undercoat should be pure white with the coat on the back, flanks, legs and tail lightly tipped with red (and/or cream in United Kingdom) to give an enchanting sparkling pink tinsel effect. The chin, ear tufts, stomach and chest are pure white. Tabby markings are a fault. Noseleather and paw pads rose. Eyes brilliant copper, outlined in rose.

Shell Tortoiseshell. (Tortoiseshell Cameo, Tortie-cream Cameo). Females only. The undercoat should be pure white, lightly tipped with red, black and cream in well-defined patches, and well broken on the face. The chin, ear tufts, stomach and chest are white. A blaze of red or cream tipping on the face is desirable. Noseleather and paw pads black, pink or a combination of the two. Eyes brilliant copper.

Blue-cream Particolour Cameo. Females only. The undercoat should be pure white. The coat on the back, flanks, legs and tail is lightly tipped with blue and cream, softly intermingled, to give the effect of a mantle of mother of pearl. Noseleather and paw pads blue, pink or a combination of the two. Eyes deep copper.

Cameo Tabby. Undercoat should be off-white, lightly tipped with red in either classic or mackerel tabby coat pattern. Noseleather and paw pads rose. Eyes brilliant copper.

SHADED PERSIAN

Similar to the Chinchillas and Shell Cameos, the Shaded Persians also have pale (usually white) undercoats, but approximately a quarter of the hair length is tipped with a contrasting colour to give the effect of a coloured mantle over the body.

Shaded kittens appear in the same litters as Chinchillas and Cameos, and the information given about breeding also applies to the Shaded Persians (see page 22). In the early days of pedigree cat breeding, when Chinchillas were darker than they are today, it was difficult to distinguish between the two types. It is only recently that interest in the shaded cats has been revived and a standard introduced for them. They are very much loved in the United States and Australia and are now bred in several colours, although the original variety was Silver. There is no reason why, with well-regulated outcrossing to other coloured Persians, they should not be bred in any coat colour or pattern.

Grooming
Daily grooming is essential. Show preparation requires the same treatment as for Chinchillas and Shell Cameos.

SHOW SUMMARY
Shaded Silver. The undercoat should be pure white, the top coat tipped in black to give the effect of a black mantle overlying the undercoat, on the back, flanks, face, legs and tail. Generally darker than the Chinchilla. Noseleather and paw pads brick red. Eyes green or blue-green, rimmed with black.

Shaded Cameo. (Red Shaded). The undercoat should be pure white, with the top coat tipped in red to give the effect of a red mantle overlying the undercoat, on the back, flanks, face, legs and tail. Generally darker than the Shell Cameo. Noseleather and paw pads rose. Eyes brilliant copper, rimmed with rose.

Shaded Golden. The undercoat should be a rich, warm cream, with the top coat tipped in seal brown to give the effect of a golden overcoat. Generally darker than the Chinchilla Golden. Noseleather deep rose. Paw pads seal brown. Eyes green or blue-green, rimmed in seal brown.

Shaded Tortoiseshell. The undercoat should be pure white, with the top coat tipped in black, red and cream in well-defined patches of the tortoiseshell pattern. Generally much darker than the Shell Tortoiseshell. A blaze of red or cream on the face is desirable. Noseleather and paw pads black, pink, or a combination of the two. Eyes brilliant copper.

Pewter. The undercoat should be white, with the top coat tipped in black, giving the effect of a black mantle overlying the undercoat. Generally darker than the Chinchilla but similar to the Shaded Silver. Lips, nose and eyes outlined in black. Noseleather brick red. Paw pads black. Eyes orange or copper, with no green tinge.

SMOKE PERSIAN

Like the Chinchillas and Shaded Persians, the Smokes are also characterized by their white undercoats and contrasting tipped top coats. But these hairs are tipped for at least half their length with colour and at first glance, Smoke Persians may look like solid-coloured cats until they move,

Above: A Black Smoke Persian with the pale undercoat showing through.

when the beautiful pale undercoat shows through. The ruff and ear tufts are generally of the paler colour, making these cats among the most striking of the Persians.

Smoke-coloured cats have been recorded in the United Kingdom since the 1860s, and appeared originally as the result of chance matings of Chinchilla, Black, Blue, and White Persians. Very good Smokes were shown in England in the first 20 years of this century, but then, oddly, their popularity declined, until interest was revived again in the 1960s. Now several colours are being bred, but so far not all are recognized for competition in all countries.

Grooming
More than most varieties, Smoke Persians require frequent and expert grooming to look their best. In fact, it may take many weeks of dedication before the contrasting coat is ready to be shown to perfection.

Apart from a bath a week before the show to remove grease, the undercoat must be well brushed up to show through the dark top coat. This is a job that requires patience and skill; too much brushing may pull out the undercoat. Strong sunlight tends to bleach the coat, so Smokes are best shown during the winter months.

Breeding
Outcrosses to improve type can be made to Black, Blue or Tortoiseshell Persians, giving Black, Blue or Tortoiseshell Smokes; this will preserve the copper eyes. Silver Tabbies should not be used, because they would reintroduce the green eye and tabby markings, neither of which is desirable, although there was a time in the United Kingdom when green eyes were permitted. Another good cross is to a Chinchilla, to improve the undercoat, though again this may introduce the green eye colour.

In order to produce all-Smoke kittens, the parents must have a Smoke in their backgrounds; but Black is dominant over Smoke, and therefore Black-to-Smoke matings will produce all-Black kittens. Even Smoke-to-Smoke matings may produce some all-Black kittens. Unfortunately mating Smokes with Smokes repeatedly results in loss of Persian type.

Kittens
Smokes are difficult to distinguish at birth from their solid-coloured counterparts, except that Smoke kittens sometimes have white around the eyes and a paler stomach. It may take some months to distinguish which will be Smokes, and the full coat colour and pattern is sometimes not seen until the adult coat is grown at about two years of age. Kittens whose undercoats get paler quickest usually become the best adult Smokes. The undercoat begins to show through at about three weeks, and by six to eight weeks old the cats have a mottled appearance. At six months they are ready to be shown. Kittens with unsatisfactory coats can be sold as pets and will make affectionate, even-tempered companions.

SHOW SUMMARY
Black Smoke. The undercoat should be white, heavily tipped on the back and flanks with black to give the effect of a solid coloured cat, until the animal moves. The coat shades to silver on the lower flanks. The face and feet are black, with no markings (colour solid to the roots in the United Kingdom; white at the roots in the United States). The ruff and ear tufts are silver. Noseleather and paw pads black. Eyes brilliant copper or orange.

Blue Smoke. The undercoat should be white, heavily tipped with blue on the back and flanks to give the appearance of a solid blue cat, until the animal moves. The face and feet are blue, without markings (colour solid to the roots in the United Kingdom; white at the roots in the United States). The ruff and ear tufts are silver. Noseleather and paw pads blue. Eyes brilliant orange or copper.

Cameo Smoke. (Red Smoke). The undercoat should be white, heavily tipped with red on the back and flanks to give the appearance of a solid red cat, until the animal moves. The face and feet are red, without markings (colour solid to the roots in the United Kingdom; white at the roots in the United States). The ruff and ear tufts are

Shaded Cameo Persian

Shaded Silver Persian

Persian
(Longhair)

white. Noseleather and paw pads rose. Eyes brilliant orange or copper.

Smoke Tortoiseshell. The undercoat should be white, heavily tipped with black, red and cream in clearly defined patches on the back and flanks to give the appearance of a tortoiseshell cat, until the animal moves. Face and feet solid red, black and cream, with preference given to a facial blaze of red or cream. (Colours solid to the roots in the United Kingdom; white at the roots in the United States.) Ruff and ear tufts white. Noseleather and paw pads charcoal, rose, pink or a combination of these colours. Eyes brilliant copper.

TORTOISESHELL PERSIAN

Despite the fact that tortoiseshell shorthaired cats have been domesticated in Europe since the days of the Roman Empire, the longhaired Tortoiseshell was not recorded before the end of the nineteenth century.

Tortoiseshells first appeared at cat shows in the early 1900s, and became popular on both sides of the Atlantic, although because they are difficult to breed, they are still relatively rare. As a result, the demand for a Tortoiseshell kitten invariably exceeds the supply and they may be more expensive than other Persians.

Grooming
Daily grooming with brush and comb throughout the year is essential to keep the coat in good condition. Grooming powder should not be used as it will deaden the colour.

Breeding
As this is a female-only variety, and the rare male seems invariably sterile, like-to-like mating is not possible and breeding is difficult and unpredictable. Mating Tortoiseshells to various self-coloured males—Black, Blue, Red or Cream —or to Bicolours cannot be relied upon to produce a single Tortoiseshell kitten! It is more by luck that one appears as an occasional kitten in a litter. Tabby sires should not be used as they would introduce unwanted bars and markings.

Kittens
When Tortoiseshells are mated to males of different colours, a very colourful assortment of kittens usually results, and they are not difficult to find homes for.

SHOW SUMMARY
The coat should be evenly patched with red, cream and black. All colours should be clear and brilliant rather than mingled. Black should not predominate, and over large patches of any one colour are considered a fault. A red or cream blaze from the forehead the nose is desirable. The colour should be well broken up on the

head and ears and the fur should be particularly long on the ruff and tail. White hairs and tabby markings are faults. Noseleather and paw pads pink or black. Eyes copper or deep orange.

BLUE-CREAM PERSIAN

The Blue-cream is a female-only variety, genetically a dilute form of the Tortoiseshell, and a most attractive and popular cat. Although relatively slow to gain championship status, achieving official recognition in the United Kingdom only in 1930, they had appeared in litters resulting from Blue and Cream matings ever since pedigree cat breeding began, and were first shown in the United States as Blue Tortoiseshells in the early 1900s.

It is now generally recognized that they are very valuable as breeding stock for Blues, Creams and Blue-creams. The crossing of two longhaired varieties has given stamina to both Blues and Creams and the Blue-creams themselves are a very healthy and robust variety of good Persian type.

The British and American standards are quite different. The former calls for evenly intermingled blue and cream throughout the coat, but the latter requires well-broken patches of blue and cream.

Grooming
Daily grooming with brush and comb is essential. A bath may be necessary before a show, and a little grooming powder to fluff the coat into show condition.

Breeding
If a Blue-cream is mated to a Cream sire, the resulting kittens will be everything except Blue females. If a Blue-cream is mated to a Blue sire, the resulting kittens will be everything except cream females. Similarly, a Blue female mated to a Cream male will produce Blue-cream female and Blue male kittens, whereas a Blue male mated to a Cream female will produce Blue-cream female and Cream male kittens.

Kittens
The kittens are very pretty and colourful, and there may be Blues, Creams and Blue-creams in any litter. Those with the palest coats will probably develop into the best adults from a competition point of view. Often a very fine Blue-cream will look much like pale blue in the first few weeks, so breeding Blue-creams can be quite exciting.

TORTOISESHELL -AND-WHITE PERSIAN (Calico)

The Tortoiseshell-and-white (Calico) Persian is another female-only variety, with a delightfully patched coat of black, red and cream with white. Beautiful cats, they are always in demand.

Although shorthaired Tortoiseshell-and-white cats have been known in Europe for centuries, the origin of the longhaired variety is obscure. Like the Tortoiseshell, it is said to have no distinct history, and probably arose by chance in litters of solid-coloured Persians with mixed colour backgrounds.

The colour is sex-linked genetically to produce females only, and when the rare male occurs, it is invariably sterile. Cats with this coat pattern were known in the past as 'chintz' cats, because of the bright, bold colour patches.

On the show bench, the pedigree variety is relatively new, attaining recognition only in the 1950s. More recently, the dilute variety, Blue Tortoiseshell-and-white (Dilute Calico), has also attained recognition in Europe and the United States. Such cats often appear in the same litter as Tortoiseshell-and-whites, and have patched coats of blue and cream with white.

In the United Kingdom, the standard requires the colour patches to be interspersed with white, but in the United States, the preference is for white to be concentrated on the underparts. One American association describes the cat as a Tortoiseshell that has been dropped into a pail of milk, the milk having splashed up onto the face and neck.

Grooming
This cat's coat is said not to mat as much as most Persian varieties, but a daily brushing and combing is still advisable. If it is being prepared for a show, a little Fuller's earth can be rubbed into the lighter parts of the coat and then thoroughly brushed out.

Breeding
Like Tortoiseshells, Tortoiseshell-and-whites are also renowned for producing kittens in a lovely assort-

ment of colours, but it appears that more Tortoiseshell-and-white kittens are born when sired by Red-and-white or Black-and-white Bicoloured cats. Those producing the best patched coats are males with too much white in their own coats, according to the Bicolour standard. Tabbies should not be used as they might introduce bars and markings, which are rather undesirable.

Kittens
The kittens often have patches of dull blue, dark cream or drab white when young, but these usually turn into jet black, bright red and pure white patches in the adult. Blue Tortoiseshell-and-white kittens, which often appear in the same litter, are generally paler in colour. In both cases, however, it is difficult to assess the quality of the coat colouring when the kittens are young.

SHOW SUMMARY
Tortoiseshell-and-white (Calico). The cat should be strikingly patched with black, red and cream, interspersed with white. The patches should be equally distributed, bright and clear, without white hairs (brindling) or tabby markings, and should be evenly spread over the body with white on the legs, feet, chest and face. Too much white is a fault. The American standard requires white to be concentrated on the underparts. A cream or white blaze from the top of the head to the nose is desirable, especially when it sharply divides the black side of the face from the red side. Noseleather and paw pads pink, black or a combination of the two. Eyes brilliant copper.

Blue Tortoiseshell-and-white (Dilute Calico). Coat should be patched with blue and cream. Patches should be evenly distributed over the body, clear and unbrindled, with white on the legs, feet, chest and face, and concentrated on the underparts (US). A cream or white blaze on the face is desirable. Noseleather and paw pads pink. Eyes brilliant copper or orange.

Below: A fine example of a Blue Tortoiseshell-and-white Persian.

Persian
(Longhair)

Tortoiseshell-and-white
(Calico) Persian

Tortoiseshell
Persian

Blue-cream Persian (UK)

27

CHOCOLATE TORTOISESHELL & LILAC-CREAM PERSIAN

New varieties developed from the Colourpoint (Himalayan) breeding programme, with outcrossing to Tortoiseshell and Cream Persians respectively. In the United States they are regarded as Himalayan hybrids (see page 32) and cannot be shown. In the UK, however, they have received official recognition as varieties of Persian (Longhair).

SHOW SUMMARY
Chocolate Tortoiseshell. The coat should be patched with chocolate, red and cream. The colours should be bright and rich, and well broken on the face. Noseleather and paw pads brown. Eyes copper.

Lilac-cream. Throughout the coat shades of lilac and cream should be softly intermingled, with no white hairs. Noseleather and paw pads pink. Eyes copper.

TABBY PERSIAN

Persian Tabby cats are creatures of great beauty. They make excellent pets for people who have the time to devote to their grooming and well-being. Generally they are healthy, docile and rather more independent and outdoor loving than other Persian varieties.

The name 'tabby' is said to have come originally from the similarity of the cat's coat pattern to tabby or plain woven watered silk or taffeta, which was known as tabbisilk in England. This type of weaving produces a striped or ridged effect on the cloth. The word itself probably derives from Attabiya, a district in Baghdad where this material was made.

The tabby pattern is very common among domestic cats, although longhaired tabbies were not recorded in Europe until the end of the sixteenth century. Judging from the markings of many wild felines, the original domestic tabby was probably a striped cat, resembling the Mackeral Tabby of today. It appears that the classic or blotched pattern, more common now in pedigree cats, is a mutation of the striped form that first appeared in Europe among domestic and feral cats and was already common by the middle of the seventeenth century.

Although the original tabby colours are likely to have been brown and red, or rather, ginger, selective breeding over the last 100 years has produced several others, of which the striking Brown Tabby is not a common variety in pedigree circles, possibly because it is extremely difficult to breed a cat to the required colour standard. Affectionately known as 'brownies', they are noted for their health, strength and longevity, and deserve a larger following.

The Red Tabbies are particularly popular in the United States, as are the Silver Tabbies, which always attract attention at shows in all countries. Silver Tabbies were bred in the United States long before there were organized cat shows.

The Blue Tabby is a variety more recently recognized for competition in the United States and Europe. As blue is a dilution of black genetically, kittens with this colouring appear from time to time in Brown Tabby litters, especially if there is a blue cat in the ancestry.

The clearly defined tabby markings required by the show standards are difficult to achieve in all the tabbies, but especially so in the Cream Tabby. Genetically a dilute form of the Red, it shows very little contrast between the ground colour and the markings, and as a result a good specimen is rare. This variety is recognized for competition in the USA only, at present.

Grooming
To show a Tabby Persian to perfection the coat must be brushed to enhance the markings. This entails brushing and combing only from head to tail, with no forward brushing to fluff up the coat as can be done with some of the self-coloured varieties. The use of powder on the coat is not recommended as it tends to deaden the contrast between the ground colour and the markings. Some bay rum to remove grease is beneficial before a show.

Breeding
Mating two Tabbies of the required colour together will give several generations of good type but eventually outcrossing to a solid colour will be necessary, using in each case the solid colour of the overlay coat pattern, or, alternatively, a Tortoiseshell. Thus in the Brown Tabby, this will mean an outcross to a solid Black Persian; in the Red Tabby to a Red or a Tortoiseshell; in the Silver Tabby to a Black; in the Blue Tabby to a Blue Persian; and in the Cream Tabby to a Cream. In the case of the Silver Tabby this may introduce the golden eye colour, which is undesirable, and consequently a Chinchilla can be used.

Kittens
Tabby kittens are very colourful balls of fluff, with the markings showing even as they are being born. Often the darker striped they are at birth, the clearer the adult coat pattern will be. Imperfectly marked kittens unsuitable for showing will make excellent colourful pets. These include those with white hairs in the darker markings, white patches, a white tip to the tail or a white chin, too solid a colour down the back and incorrect eye colour; also, in Silver Tabbies a brown or yellow tinge to the fur.

SHOW SUMMARY
Classic Tabby pattern. All markings should be clearly defined from the ground colour. The characteristic head marking is a letter 'M'

Above: An extremely attractive Blue Classic Tabby Persian.

resembling frown marks on the forehead. Unbroken lines run from the outer corners of the eyes towards the back of the head. There are other pencil-thin lines on the face, especially in the form of swirls on the cheeks. Lines extend back from the top of the head to the shoulder markings, which are shaped in a butterfly pattern. Three unbroken lines run parallel to each other down the spine from the shoulder markings to the base of the tail. A large blotch on each flank is circled by one or more unbroken rings; these markings should be symmetrical on either side of the body. There should be several unbroken necklaces on the neck and upper chest, and a double row of 'buttons' running from chest to stomach. Both legs and tail should be evenly ringed.

Mackerel Tabby pattern. (Rare in Persians, but recognized in the United States.) Head is marked with the characteristic 'M', and there is an unbroken line running from the outer corner of the eyes towards the back of the head. There are other fine pencil markings on the cheeks. A narrow unbroken line runs from the back of the head to the base of the tail. The rest of the body is marked with narrow unbroken lines running vertically down from the spine line. These lines should be as narrow and numerous as possible and, ideally, clearly defined from the ground colour. There should be several unbroken necklaces on the neck and upper chest, and a double row of 'buttons' on the chest and stomach. The legs should be evenly barred with narrow bracelets and the tail evenly ringed.

Brown Tabby. Ground colour rich tawny sable to coppery brown. Markings jet black. No white hairs. Noseleather brick red. Paw pads black or dark brown, the dark colour extending up the backs of the hind legs from paw to heel. Eyes brilliant copper or hazel.

Red Tabby. Ground colour rich red. Markings dark rich red. Lips and chin red. No white hairs or patches. Noseleather brick red. Paw pads pink. Eyes brilliant copper or gold.

Silver Tabby. Ground silver. Markings jet black and clearly defined. Noseleather brick red. Paw pads black. Eyes green or hazel.

Blue Tabby. Ground colour, lips and chin pale bluish ivory. Markings very deep slate blue. Noseleather deep rose pink. Paw pads rose pink. Eyes brilliant copper.

Cream Tabby. Ground colour, lips and chin very pale cream. Markings rich cream, not too red, but sufficiently dark to afford a contrast with the ground colour. Noseleather and paw pads pink. Eyes brilliant copper.

Cameo Tabby. Ground colour, lips and chin off white. Markings red. Noseleather and paw pads rose. Eyes brilliant copper to gold.

Patched Tabby (Torbie) pattern. Markings classic or mackerel tabby with red and/or cream patches. Facial blaze preferred.
Brown. Ground colour coppery brown. Markings jet black, with red and/or cream. Noseleather brick red. Paw pads black or brown. Eyes brilliant copper.
Silver. Ground colour pale silver. Markings jet black with red and/or cream. Noseleather and paw pads rose pink. Eyes copper or hazel.
Blue. Ground colour pale bluish ivory. Markings deep slate blue with red and/or cream. Eyes brilliant copper.

VAN PERSIANS

Mostly white cats with patches of colour on head, legs and tail. Noseleather and paw pads in keeping with coat colour or pink. Eyes copper/gold.
Van Bicolour. Patches of black, blue, red or cream.
Van Calico. Patches of black/red.
Van Blue-cream. Patches of blue and cream.

Brown Classic
(Blotched) Tabby Persian

Silver Classic
Tabby Persian

Persian
(Longhair)

Red Mackerel Tabby Persian

PEKE-FACED PERSIAN

Good points
- *Affectionate*
- *Intelligent*
- *Quiet*
- *Suitable for an apartment*

Take heed
- *Needs daily grooming*
- *May suffer breathing difficulties*
- *May have feeding problems*

From time to time in Red Self and Red Tabby Persian litters, there appears spontaneously a different-looking kitten with a face resembling that of a Pekingese dog. Such a cat has a much shorter nose and an obvious indentation between the eyes, and because of this is known as a Peke-faced Persian. It is just as sweet and companionable as other Persians, but because of its very large jowls and very snub nose, it may suffer from snuffles and other breathing problems, and also from feeding problems if the upper and lower teeth do not meet in an even bite.

Although the Peke-faced Persian has appeared occasionally elsewhere, at present it is virtually unknown outside the United States.

Grooming
Like all Persians, the Peke-faced requires daily grooming with brush and comb to remove knots and tangles·from the long coat. Attention must also be paid to the eyes, as the tear ducts may become blocked. Any mucus that collects in the corners of the eyes should be sponged away with warm water. The ears and teeth should be examined regularly.

Origin and history
Peke-faced Persians have been bred in the United States for many years. They have been shown there since the 1930s, and are popular cats. However, the breed has attracted criticism, especially from veterinarians, because its extreme characteristics may cause breathing and feeding difficulties.

Breeding
Two Peke-faced cats mated together do not necessarily produce Peke-faced kittens. The best ones come from Red Tabby and Peke-faced matings.

It is not immediately obvious whether there are any Peke-faced kittens in a litter of Red Selfs or Red Tabbies, as the characteristics do not show for some weeks. Special care has to be taken by breeders to make sure that the extreme physical features that are known to cause problems are reduced, as it is these features that have limited the breed's popularity in the past.

Kittens
There is a high mortality rate among Peke-faced kittens due to the difficulties encountered in feeding and breathing in cats with extremely snub noses (over-typed). The kittens often try to feed with their paws, bringing the food to their mouths. If they do not have an even bite, they may not be able to get enough to eat. They develop slowly and seem to remain kittens for longer than other Persians.

Kittens with just sufficient facial characteristics to be recognized as Peke-faced, but without the problems associated with over-typing, develop normally.

SHOW SUMMARY
The Peke-faced Persian is a solid, cobby cat of Persian type, but with a distinctive face, which resembles that of a Pekingese dog.
Coat. Long, flowing, silky and soft with a large ruff around the neck.
Body. Short, cobby and massive. Legs short. Paws large and well tufted.
Tail. Short, well plumed and especially full at the base.
Head. Large, round and heavy with a very short snub nose, indented between the eyes, giving an obvious nose break. The muzzle is wrinkled and there is a fold of skin running from the corner of the eye to the mouth. The forehead bulges out above the nose and eyes. The neck is short and thick. The ears are small, although slightly larger than other Persians.
Eyes. Very prominent, almost bulging, round and full.

PEKE-FACED COLOURS
Only two colours are recognized for competition at present, although Peke-faced cats also appear in dilute red (cream).

Red. Body colour an even deep, rich red throughout with no markings or white hairs. Noseleather and paw pads brick red. Eyes brilliant copper.

Red Tabby. Ground colour red. Markings, in either classic or mackerel tabby pattern, deep rich red. Noseleather and paw pads brick red. Eyes brilliant copper.

RAGDOLL

Good points
- *Gentle and affectionate*
- *Quiet*
- *Playful*
- *Intelligent*
- *Suitable for an apartment*

Take heed
- *Vulnerable*
- *Has a high tolerance of pain*

The Ragdoll is a large cuddly cat and fun to have around. It has lots of fur, which is said not to mat. It is a quiet, loyal and affectionate cat and very dependent on its owner. Because it is supposed not to feel pain, the Ragdoll is vulnerable and any injury may go unnoticed. Anyone contemplating owning a Ragdoll should therefore expect to be entirely responsible for it, as this cat, more than any other, requires mothering.

The Ragdoll has another unique feature: when picked up and carried it relaxes completely, becoming limp like a ragdoll or bean bag. Although this has given the breed its name and a large press coverage, scientific tests have shown that, physiologically, this cat is no different from others.

Grooming
Because the Ragdoll has a very long coat, it will need daily grooming, if not to remove knots and tangles, then to remove dead hairs. As it moults heavily in the summer, thorough grooming at this time is particularly important. The tangles should be combed out using a wide-toothed comb, then the coat brushed gently but thoroughly using a long-bristled brush.

Origin and history
The Ragdoll originated in California and its ancestors are very mixed. The foundation stock seems to have involved a white Angora, a Birman and a non-pedigree Burmese. This mixed blood has resulted in large and vigorous descendants. Within the accepted colours, Ragdolls breed true, so that today Ragdolls are mated only to Ragdolls, although in the early days of the breed there were many back crosses to the foundation sires. The breed was first recognized for competition in the United States in 1965. At present Ragdolls are unknown outside the USA.

Breeding
To preserve the distinguishing features of the breed, Ragdolls are mated only to Ragdolls. It is possible to produce Ragdoll kittens in one of the desired coat patterns and colours in every litter.

Kittens
Like all Himalayan-patterned cats, the kittens are born all-white, the point colours and coat shading developing gradually. Ragdoll kittens are slow to mature and it may be three years before the full adult coat is developed.

SHOW SUMMARY
The Ragdoll is a large, heavily built cat with a long flowing coat and a characteristic limpness when held.
Coat. Exceptionally long, full and silky. Non-matting. Luxuriant ruff and extra-long fur on the chest and stomach; shorter on the face. The coat is likely to be longer in cold than in warm climates and will moult considerably during the summer months.
Body. Very large and heavy with strong heavy bones. Males 6.8-9kg (15-20lb); females 4-5.4kg (9-12lb) and shorter in body than males. Hindquarters are heavy and there is a furry loose-muscled stomach pad. As broad across the shoulders as across the rump, with a deep chest. Legs medium in length and fairly heavy with hind legs slightly longer than forelegs. Paws large, round and firm with tufts between the toes.
Tail. Long and furry. Medium thick at the base with a slight taper towards the tip. A short or kinked tail would be a fault.
Head. Medium in size with a modified wedge; wider in the male than in the female. The skull between the ears is flat. The cheeks are full and taper to a full round chin. There is a gentle nose break, which, with the flat head, gives a distinctive profile. Neck is strong, short and thick. Ears are medium in size, broad at the base, tilted forward, rounded at the tips and furnished with ear tufts. Very large, very small or pointed ears are faults.
Eyes. Very large, oval, set wide apart. Round or almond-shaped eyes or squints are faults.

RAGDOLL COLOURS
Ragdolls are bred in three coat patterns—colourpoint, mitted and bicolour—and in seal, chocolate, blue and lilac point colours within these patterns. All are recognized for competition in the United States.

Colourpoint. Body colour should be an even shade down to the roots. Points (ears, mask, legs and tail) darker providing a distinct contrast with the body colour. Chest, bib and chin a much lighter shade of the body colour. Ticking and white spotting not accepted.

Mitted. Body colour should be an even shade down to the roots. Points (ears, mask, legs and tail) darker, providing a distinct contrast with the body colour. Chest, bib and chin white. A white stripe runs from the bib between the forelegs to the base of the tail. White mittens on both front paws should be evenly matched and scalloped. White boots on hind legs also to match. Coloured spots in white areas or ticking on coloured areas are faults.

Bicolour. Body colour should be an even shade down to the roots. The ears, mask (with the exception of an inverted 'V' down the nose, which is white) and tail are darker and clearly defined. Chest, stomach and legs white. The symmetrical inverted 'V' on the face starts between the ears, covers the nose, whisker pads, neck and bib. It should not extend beyond the outer edge of the eyes. There should be no coloured spots on the white areas. The body areas may have small spots of white.

Seal-point. Body colour a pale fawn shading to pale cream on the underparts. Points dense seal brown. Noseleather dark brown. Paw pads dark brown or black. Eyes deep blue.

Chocolate-point. Body colour an even ivory all over. Points warm milk-chocolate. Noseleather rose. Paw pads salmon. Eyes deep blue.

Blue-point. Body colour an even platinum grey-blue, shading to lighter blue on the underparts. Points deep blue-grey. Noseleather and paw pads dark blue-grey. Eyes deep blue.

Lilac-(Frost-)point. Body colour an even milk white all over. Points frosty grey-pink. Inside ears very pale pink. Noseleather lilac. Paw pads coral pink. Eyes deep blue.

Ragdoll

Lilac-point Bicolour
Ragdoll kitten

Chocolate-point
Bicolour Ragdoll

Peke-faced
Persian

Red Tabby Peke-faced Persian

COLOURPOINT

(Himalayan)

Good points
- Beautiful
- Affectionate
- Devoted
- Intelligent
- Provocative
- Quick to learn
- Good with children

Take heed
- Needs daily grooming
- Does not like to be caged

A Colourpoint is essentially a Persian with Siamese (Himalayan) colouring. It is rather more demanding and more enterprising than many of the Persians, although more docile and less demonstrative than the Siamese. As with all cats, the Colourpoint likes to choose its own activities and will be happiest if given the run of the house or garden.

It would not be advisable to have a Colourpoint as a pet unless you are prepared to devote a lot of time to its grooming. Well cared for, the Colourpoint, or 'Himmy' as it is affectionately known, is an extremely beautiful cat, and makes a very affectionate and devoted pet.

Show cats will be expensive but kittens that do not quite meet the standard for showing can be obtained more reasonably and will make excellent and charming companions just the same.

Grooming

As for all longhaired cats, daily grooming is essential for the Colourpoint. If neglected, the undercoat will become matted into tight knots that in an extreme case might have to be cut out under anaesthetic. Despite regular attention mats do sometimes form, particularly if the cat spends a lot of time outside, and in experienced hands a mat cutter, designed for dogs, can be used to cut through a mat to remove it rather than cutting it out and leaving a bare spot. But be careful not to cut the cat!

A wide-toothed comb can be used to remove knots, followed by a medium-toothed comb to remove dead hairs. Finally, the coat should be brushed with a long-handled, pure-bristle brush. Repeated daily, this will ensure a healthy coat and the cat will enjoy the process. A little dry grooming powder dusted into the coat before brushing will usually help to untangle the fur, but it should be brushed out thoroughly afterwards. Inspection of the eyes for blocked tear ducts and the ears for mites completes the daily routine.

Origin and history

The Colourpoint or Himalayan is a 'manufactured' breed, specifically produced by breeders. It is not a Siamese with long hair, but a Persian with Siamese (Himalayan) colouring. The name Himalayan derives from the coat pattern of the Himalayan rabbit, where the darker colour is confined to the face, legs and tail (as in the Siamese), and not because of any pretensions to a Himalayan origin, geographically. Its production involved complex scientific breeding and took years to perfect into the correct Persian type. Breeders had been crossing Siamese with Persians for many years but had been getting only self-coloured shorthaired kittens as a result. Eventually, in the 1940s, a series of scientific experiments was made, crossing Siamese with longhaired Blacks and Blues. The resulting shorthaired self-coloured kittens proved very useful for breeding as they carried the genes required to produce the Colourpoint. They were mated together and back to their parents until Colourpoint kittens were produced. Further selective breeding back to longhaired Blacks and Blues to develop Persian type was carried out and the resulting cats, when mated back to Colourpoints, produced excellent, new generation Colourpoints. Eventually, after 10 years of selective breeding, the long noses and large ears of the Siamese were bred out, but the Himalayan coat pattern, blue eyes and Persian type were fixed, and the lovely Colourpoints had arrived. The breed was recognized for competition in 1955 in the United Kingdom, and independently as the Himalayan in the United States in 1957.

Breeding

Colourpoint-to-Colourpoint breeding produces 100 percent Colourpoint kittens, but to preserve type, outcrosses are still made to self-coloured Persians and the offspring mated back to the original Colourpoints. With outcrossing to other coloured Persians, all point colours are possible. The mixed breeding has rendered the Colourpoint a particularly hardy breed, and litters containing six kittens are not uncommon.

Kittens

The kittens are born with creamy white fur and pink paw pads, noses and ears. The point colouration gradually develops over the first few weeks. They are charming little balls of fluff with plenty of energy and enterprise.

SHOW SUMMARY

The Colourpoint (Himalayan) is essentially a Persian-type cat, although slightly larger, with the Himalayan coat pattern: the main colour is confined to the mask, legs and tail. The British standard has been accepted for all countries.
Coat. Long, thick, soft and silky, standing well away from the body. The ruff is very full and extends to a frill between the front legs.
Body. Cobby and low on the legs. Deep in the chest. Massive across the shoulders and rump, and short and rounded in between. Long, svelte Siamese lines are a fault. The legs are short and thick, straight and strong. The paws are large, round and firm with long toe tufts.
Tail. Short, very full and carried low. A long or kinked tail is a fault.
Head. Broad and round with width between the ears. The neck is short, and thick. The face is well rounded. The nose is short and broad with a definite nose break in profile. The ears are small, rounded at the tips, tilted forward and not too open at the base. They are set far apart and low on the head, and are well furnished with long tufts.
Eyes. Large, round, brilliant and full, wide apart, with a sweet expression.

COLOURPOINT COLOURS

All point colours are possible, as in the Siamese, though not all are recognized everywhere at the present. The more recently developed varieties include the female-only Chocolate Tortie-point and Lilac-cream point; the Smoke-points; and the Tabby-(Lynx-) points now recognized in Europe.

Coat pattern. Body should be an even pale colour, with the main contrasting colour confined to the points (mask, ears, legs and tail). The mask should cover the whole face, but not the top of the head, and be connected to the ears by tracings.

Seal-point. Body colour an even pale fawn to warm cream, shading to a lighter cream on the chest and stomach. Points deep seal brown. Noseleather and paw pads seal brown. Eyes deep vivid blue.

Chocolate-point. Body colour ivory all over. Points warm milk-chocolate colour. Noseleather and paw pads cinnamon-pink. Eyes deep vivid blue.

Blue-point. Body colour glacial, bluish white, shading to a warmer white on the chest and stomach. Points slate blue. Noseleather and paw pads slate blue. Eyes deep vivid blue.

Lilac-point. Body colour magnolia (UK) or glacial white (USA) all over. Points frosty grey with a pinkish tone (lilac). Noseleather and paw pads lavender-pink. Eyes deep vivid blue.

Red-(Flame-) point. Body colour creamy white. Points delicate orange to red. Noseleather and paw pads flesh or coral pink. Eyes deep vivid blue.

Cream-point. Body colour creamy white. Points buff cream. Noseleather and paw pads flesh or coral pink. Eyes deep vivid blue.

Tortie-point. Body colour and basic point colour as appropriate to Seal- and Chocolate-point. Points patched with red and/or cream. A blaze of red or cream on the face is desirable. Noseleather and paw pads in keeping with the basic point colour and/or pink. Eyes deep vivid blue.

Blue-cream point. Body colour bluish white or creamy white, shading to white on the chest and stomach. Points blue with patches of cream. Noseleather and paw pads slate blue and/or pink. Eyes deep vivid blue.

Lilac-cream point. Body colour magnolia (UK) or glacial white (US) all over. Points frosty pinkish grey, patched with pale cream. A facial blaze is desirable. Noseleather and paw pads lavender-pink and/or pink. Eyes deep vivid blue.

Tabby-(Lynx-) point. Body colour as appropriate to the point colour, which can be seal, chocolate, blue, lilac or red. Points should carry characteristic 'M' marking on forehead, bars on face and fainter rings on legs and tail, in the appropriate solid colour, well defined from a paler background. Noseleather and paw pads in keeping with point colour. Eyes deep vivid blue in colour.

HIMALAYAN HYBRIDS

Outcrossing to other Persians made to improve type in colourpoint breeding resulted in the appearance of other coloured longhaired kittens in the litters. In the United Kingdom some of these cats have now been granted official recognition as varieties of Persian (Chocolate Tortie and Lilac-cream; see page 28). In the United States, however, such cats are regarded as Himalayan Hybrids. They are useful for breeding Himalayans as they carry the appropriate genes, but they cannot be shown. They look just like Persians, but are usually much less expensive to buy and so would make excellent pets for people wanting a Persian-type cat, but not intending to show.

KASHMIR

(Self-coloured Himalayan)

The self-coloured chocolate and lilac cats that appeared during the Colourpoint breeding programme are classed as Self-coloured Persians in the United Kingdom, but as Solid-coloured Himalayans or Kashmirs (a separate breed) in the United States.

They first appeared in Colourpoint litters or in hybrid litters, where an outcross to a Persian had been made to improve type, and it has taken several years to achieve an even body colour throughout with the long flowing coat required by the standard. The Lilac is a dilute form of the Chocolate.

The show standard is the same as Colourpoint (Himalayan).

SHOW SUMMARY

Chocolate. Coat colour medium to dark chocolate brown all over, with the same depth of colour from the root to the tip of each hair and no sign of a paler undercoat. Noseleather and paw pads brown. Eyes deep orange or copper.

Lilac. Coat colour pinkish dove grey all over with no sign of a paler undercoat. Noseleather pink. Paw pads very pale pink. Eyes pale orange.

Lilac Kashmir

Tortie-point
Colourpoint

Colourpoint
and Kashmir

Seal-point Colourpoint

BALINESE
(Longhaired Siamese)

Good points
- *Quieter than Siamese, vocally*
- *Lively*
- *Affectionate*
- *Good with children*

Take heed
- *Dislikes being left alone*
- *Needs daily grooming*

A Balinese makes an excellent pet: it wants to enjoy fun and games with the family and loves people. In fact a longhaired Siamese, it resembles the Siamese in its graceful beauty, but is quieter in voice and temperament and less boisterous. It is easy to care for.

Although still rather a rare breed, the Balinese is becoming increasingly popular because of its delightful personality. A Balinese would be a good choice of pet for the person who likes the Siamese look, but prefers a less over-whelming personality!

Grooming
The Balinese is easy to groom. Although the coat is fairly long, it is very silky and non-matting. It does need daily grooming, however, to remove dead hairs and to keep the coat in good condition, but this is not the chore that it may be with a Persian. A few minutes' gentle brushing with a soft brush is all that is required.

Origin and history
The Balinese is a natural mutation derived from Siamese parents with a mutant gene for long hair. A few longhaired kittens first appeared in Siamese litters in the United States. They were soon recognized by breeders as potentially beautiful cats, and selectively bred together. First recognized as a breed in 1963, by 1970 the Balinese was recognized by all governing bodies in the United States. They have reached Europe only recently.

The name is unconnected with their origin: they were so named because of their graceful agility, their movements resembling those of Balinese dancers.

Breeding
Longhaired Siamese kittens appear from time to time in Siamese litters. When two are mated together they breed true, producing all-Balinese kittens. Outcrossing to Siamese is necessary occasionally to improve type. Balinese litters normally contain five or six kittens.

Kittens
The kittens are born white, the point markings gradually appearing over the first few weeks.

SHOW SUMMARY
The Balinese is a medium-sized svelte and dainty cat, yet lithe and muscular, with long, tapering Siamese lines and a long silky coat.
Coat. Ermine-like, soft, silky and flowing, 5cm (2in) or more in length (although it may be shorter in summer). No downy undercoat and no ruff around the neck.
Body. Medium sized, long and svelte. Fine boned but well muscled. Males may be larger than females. Legs long and slim, hindlegs longer than forelegs. Feet dainty, small and oval.
Tail. Long, thin and tapering to a point, but well plumed.
Head. Long, tapering wedge, making a straight-edged triangle from the jaw to the ears. There should be no whisker break. The nose is long and straight with no nose break. Neck long and slender. Ears wide at the base, large and pointed. Not less than the width of an eye between the eyes.
Eyes. Medium sized, almond shaped and slanted towards the nose. No squints allowed.

BALINESE COLOURS
In the United Kingdom all colours recognized in the Siamese are now being bred. In the United States only Seal, Chocolate, Blue and Lilac are recognized for competition as Balinese; cats with other Siamese colours are known as **Javanese** but carry the same standard for type as the Balinese.

Coat pattern. Body should be an even pale colour with the main contrasting colour confined to the points (mask, ears, legs and tail). The mask should cover the whole face, but not the top of the head, and be connected to the ears by tracings. Older cats may have darker body colour.

Seal-point. Body colour an even pale fawn to warm cream, shading to a lighter cream on the chest and stomach. Points deep seal brown. Noseleather and paw pads seal brown. Eyes deep vivid blue.

Chocolate-point. Body colour ivory all over. Points warm milk-chocolate colour. Noseleather and paw pads cinnamon-pink. Eyes deep vivid blue.

Blue-point. Body colour glacial, bluish white, shading to a warmer white on the chest and stomach. Points slate blue. Noseleather and paw pads slate blue. Eyes deep vivid blue.

Lilac-point. Body colour magnolia (UK) or glacial white (US) all over. Points frosty grey with a pinkish tone (lilac). Noseleather and paw pads lavender-pink. Eyes deep vivid blue.

Red-point. Body colour creamy white. Points delicate orange to red. Noseleather and paw pads flesh or coral pink. Eyes deep vivid blue.

Cream-point. Body colour creamy white. Points buff cream. Noseleather and paw pads flesh or coral pink. Eyes deep vivid blue.

Tortie-point. Body colour and basic point colour as appropriate to Seal- and Chocolate-point. Points patched with red and/or cream. A blaze of red or cream is desirable. Noseleather and paw pads in keeping with the basic point colour and/or pink. Eyes deep vivid blue.

Blue-cream point. Body colour bluish white or creamy white, shading to white on the chest and stomach. Points blue with patches of cream. Noseleather and paw pads slate blue and/or pink. Eyes deep vivid blue.

Lilac-cream point. Body colour magnolia (UK) or glacial white (US) all over. Points frosty pinkish grey, intermingled (UK) or patched (US) with pale cream. A facial blaze is desirable. Noseleather and paw pads lavender-pink and/or pink. Eyes deep vivid blue.

Tabby-(Lynx-)point. Body colour as appropriate to the point colour, which can be seal, chocolate, blue, lilac or red. Points should carry characteristic 'M' marking on forehead, bars on face and fainter rings on legs and tail, in appropriate solid colour, well defined from a paler background. Noseleather and paw pads in keeping with point colour. Eyes deep vivid blue.

BIRMAN
(Sacred Cat of Burma)

Good points
- *Charming*
- *Intelligent*
- *Adaptable and easy to train*
- *Good with children*
- *Quiet*

Take heed
- *Needs daily grooming*
- *Does not like to be caged*

Birman cats are as individual in their personalities as in their looks and have a quiet, gentle charm. Intelligent and companionable, a Birman will enjoy being part of the family and mixes well with other animals. It is adaptable and playful.

However, a Birman likes freedom to roam about the house and garden, and as it is not as prone to climb as the longer legged cats, is easier to confine to your property.

Grooming
Although the Birman's coat is said never to mat, it must be brushed and combed daily to remove dead hairs, so that these are not swallowed in large quantities and a fur ball formed in the stomach. For a show cat, a little grooming powder dusted into the paler areas of the coat will remove any grease marks.

Origin and history
The Birman, or Sacred Cat of Burma, is said to have originated in the temples of Burma. If it did, it was probably developed by natural crosses between Siamese and bicoloured longhaired cats. In France it was established in the 1920s and first recognized there in 1925. At about the same time another line was established in Germany. In 1959 the first Birmans arrived in the United States; in 1965 British breeders began to establish the breed in the UK.

Breeding
Birmans breed true to type, and litters usually contain four kittens.

Kittens
Birman kittens are large and healthy, and seem to maintain their playful behaviour long into adulthood.

SHOW SUMMARY
The Birman is a large, longhaired cat with the Himalayan coat pattern, but with four white paws.
Coat. Long and silky with a tendency to wave on the stomach. Non-matting. Thick and heavy ruff around the neck.
Body. Medium long, but stocky and low on the legs. Legs heavy, medium in length; paws round, firm and very large with toes close together.
Tail. Medium in length and bushy. No kinks allowed.
Head. Strong, broad and rounded. Cheeks full. Roman nose with low nostrils. Ears wide apart, as wide at the base as tall, and rounded at the tips.
Eyes. Almost round.

BIRMAN COLOURS
Only four colours occur naturally within the breed: Seal-point, Chocolate-point, Blue-point and Lilac-point. All have the characteristic white feet or 'gloves'.

Coat pattern. Body should be an even pale colour with the main contrasting colour confined to the points (mask, ears, legs and tail). The mask should cover the whole face, including the whisker pads, and is connected to the ears by tracings. The white foot markings should be symmetrical. Front paws have white gloves ending in an even line across the paw over the knuckles; in the hind paws the white glove covers the whole paw and extends up the backs of the legs to a point just below the hocks known as the 'laces' or 'gauntlets'.

Seal-point. Body colour an even pale beige to cream, warm in tone with a characteristic golden glow over the back, especially obvious in adult males. Underparts and chest are slightly paler. Points (except gloves) dark seal brown. Gloves pure white. Noseleather deep seal brown. Paw pads pink. Eyes deep violet blue.

Chocolate-point. Body colour even ivory all over. Points (except gloves) warm milk-chocolate colour; gloves pure white. Noseleather cinnamon-pink. Paw pads pink. Eyes deep violet blue.

Blue-point. Body colour bluish-white, cold in tone, becoming less cold on the stomach and chest. Points (except gloves) deep blue; gloves pure white. noseleather slate grey. Paw pads pink. Eyes deep violet blue.

Lilac-point. Body colour cold glacial white. points (except gloves) frosty grey-pink; gloves pure white. Noseleather lavender-pink. Paw pads pink. Eyes deep violet blue.

Balinese

Blue-point Balinese

Seal-point Birman

Birman

NORWEGIAN FOREST CAT

(Norsk Skogkatt)

Good points
- *Beautiful*
- *Athletic*
- *Waterproof coat*
- *Good hunter*
- *Playful*

Take heed
- *Needs daily grooming*
- *Prefers an outdoor life*
- *Moults heavily in spring and summer*

The Norwegian Forest Cat is an outdoor-loving, active cat with a robust, hardy disposition. An amusing cat, it loves to climb high trees and comes down spirally head first! It has a unique water-proof coat that dries in about 15 minutes after heavy rain. It loves to show off in front of an audience and is affectionate, intelligent and extremely playful.

The Norwegian Forest Cat is used to a rough life and makes a good mouser. This cat would be happiest given an outdoor life where it is free to roam; confined in an apartment it might soon become bored.

Grooming
The Norwegian Forest Cat has a double coat: an undercoat that is tight and woolly, and a water-resistant silky top coat. The coat does not mat, but it needs careful daily grooming if the cat is destined for showing. To prevent fur ball, even the non-show cat should be groomed daily with a brush and comb, especially during the early summer months when the undercoat is being shed. After this, less attention is necessary until the full coat is grown again in the autumn.

Origin and history
Despite its name, which suggests a wild origin, the Norwegian Forest Cat has always been more or less domesticated in Norway, and has lived with or near man for several centuries. Even today cats of this type are frequently kept on farms.

The breed is believed to have arisen as a result of the harsh Scandinavian climate. It is likely that the cat's ancestors were both shorthaired cats from Southern Europe and longhaired cats from Asia Minor, brought into Scandinavia with traders and travellers. As domestic cats were usually kept as mousers and not as pets, they led an outdoor life; and the harsh climate may have meant that only cats with heavier coats would survive the winters.

In recent years, pedigree breeding lines of Norwegian Forest Cats have been established, and today there are about 500 registered. The breed was dignified with recognition by FIFE (Fédération Internationale Féline d'Europe) in 1977 and is now accepted for competition at all European shows. At present, however, the breed is little known outside Europe, and most cats are bred in Norway.

Breeding
Naturally robust, the queens kitten easily and make attentive mothers.

Kittens
Norwegian forest kittens are healthy and playful. The first adult coat begins to grow at three to five months of age.

SHOW SUMMARY
The Norwegian Forest Cat should give the impression of strength, being well built and muscular, with a long body and long legs. The characteristic feature is the shaggy weather-resistant coat.
Coat. Very long top coat; guard hairs are smooth and oily, making the coat water-repellent. Tight woolly undercoat. In autumn a ruff grows around the neck and chest, but this is shed the following summer. Coat quality may vary with living conditions: cats kept indoors for much of the time have softer, shorter coats.
Body. Long, large and heavily built. Legs long; hind legs longer than forelegs. Feet wide, with heavy paws. Slender type is a fault.
Tail. Long and well furnished.
Head. Triangular in shape, with a long, wide, straight nose without a nose break. Neck long. Cheeks full. Chin heavy. Ears long, set high on the head, upright and pointed, well furnished inside with long ear tufts. Whiskers prominent and long. Faults include a short nose, small or wide-set ears.
Eyes. Large, open and set wide apart.

NORWEGIAN FOREST CAT COLOURS
Any coat colour or pattern is permitted, with or without white. Commonly white appears on the chest and paws. Tabby cats generally have heavier coats than the solid and bicoloured varieties. Eye colour should be in keeping with the coat colour.

MAINE COON

Good points
- *Hardy*
- *Active*
- *Fun-loving*
- *Quiet, unique voice*
- *Adaptable*
- *Good with children*
- *Even-tempered*
- *Easy to care for*
- *Good mouser*

Take heed
- *No drawbacks known*

The Maine Coon is a large cat, very hardy and active, and good with children, but shy. It is good-tempered, easy to groom and to care for. It loves playing and performing tricks, and has a delightful quiet, chirping voice; no two Maine Coons will sound alike. Distinctive in appearance, the cat is almost shorthaired in front and longhaired along the back and stomach. Used to harsh climates and to living rough, the Maine Coon is apt to sleep in strange positions and in peculiar places. Although adaptable to indoor or outdoor life, this cat would prefer plenty of space to roam.

Requiring little grooming, it makes an ideal pet for the person who likes the beauty of a long-haired cat, but does not have the time to devote to daily grooming.

Grooming
The Maine Coon's undercoat is slight, so the cat is easy to groom and a gentle brushing and combing every few days will suffice to remove dead hairs.

Origin and history
Like many breeds of cat, the Maine Coon's origin is largely unknown. Most likely, it developed from matings between domestic shorthaired cats and longhaired cats brought to Maine and other parts of New England, long before records of cats were kept.

It is possible that in its early days, the Maine Coon may have roamed free, and was given the name 'coon cat' because of its similarity in appearance and habits to the native raccoon. Both have long fur, climb trees and, as tabby is the common pattern among non-pedigree cats, have fur of a similar colour and ringed tails.

Although no early records were kept, the Maine Coon was well known in the East Coast states by the end of the nineteenth century. They were kept as mousers long before they became show cats, but were one of the earliest breeds seen at cat shows: many Maine Coons were exhibited at the first New York cat show in 1860, and a Maine Coon was Best Cat in Show at a Madison Square Garden show in New York in 1895. After that time, however, interest in the breed almost died out until the formation of the Maine Coon Cat Club in 1953 revived interest, and held regular one-breed shows for them.

The Maine Coon is no longer confined to the state from which it takes its name, but is well known and bred throughout the United States, and now even in Europe.

Below: Healthy Maine Coon kittens taking an active interest in life.

Breeding
Maine Coons usually have only one litter per year and make good mothers. Because of the breed's mixed background, the litters often contain a colourful assortment of kittens.

Kittens
The large, robust kittens mature slowly and may take up to four years to develop their full beauty.

SHOW SUMMARY
The Maine coon is a tough, large and rugged cat, solidly built, with a smooth, shaggy coat.
Coat. Heavy and shaggy, yet silky in texture, lustrous and flowing. Short on the face and shoulders, but longer on the stomach and hind legs, where it forms long, shaggy breeches.
Body. A long-bodied cat with a broad chest and level back, giving a rectangular appearance. Males 4.5-5.4kg (10-12lb); females smaller, 3.6-4.5kg (8-10lb). Muscular, with strong legs set wide apart. Feet large and round. Paws well tufted.
Tail. Blunt ended, but well furnished with long fur, and plume-like. Wider at the base. No kinks allowed.
Head. Small in proportion to the body, set on a medium length powerful neck. Square muzzle. Firm chin, not undershot. High cheekbones. Nose is medium length and may have a slight nose break. Ears large and well tufted, wide at the base and tapering to a point; set high on the head.
Eyes. Slightly slanting, large and set wide apart.

MAINE COON COLOURS
Maine Coons are bred in all coat colours and patterns, and combinations of colours and patterns, such as tabby with white. In this case, there should be white on the bib, stomach and all four paws, and preferably on one-third of the body. Eye colour can be green, gold or copper, though white cats may also be blue-eyed or odd-eyed. There is no relationship between eye colour and coat colour or pattern.

The colour standards for show cats are the same as those given for Persians.

white. Noseleather and paw pads rose. Eyes brilliant orange or copper.

Smoke Tortoiseshell. The undercoat should be white, heavily tipped with black, red and cream in clearly defined patches on the back and flanks to give the appearance of a tortoiseshell cat, until the animal moves. Face and feet solid red, black and cream, with preference given to a facial blaze of red or cream. (Colours solid to the roots in the United Kingdom; white at the roots in the United States.) Ruff and ear tufts white. Noseleather and paw pads charcoal, rose, pink or a combination of these colours. Eyes brilliant copper.

TORTOISESHELL PERSIAN

Despite the fact that tortoiseshell shorthaired cats have been domesticated in Europe since the days of the Roman Empire, the longhaired Tortoiseshell was not recorded before the end of the nineteenth century.

Tortoiseshells first appeared at cat shows in the early 1900s, and became popular on both sides of the Atlantic, although because they are difficult to breed, they are still relatively rare. As a result, the demand for a Tortoiseshell kitten invariably exceeds the supply and they may be more expensive than other Persians

Grooming
Daily grooming with brush and comb throughout the year is essential to keep the coat in good condition. Grooming powder should not be used as it will deaden the colour.

Breeding
As this is a female-only variety, and the rare male seems invariably sterile, like-to-like mating is not possible and breeding is difficult and unpredictable. Mating Tortoiseshells to various self-coloured males — Black, Blue, Red or Cream — or to Bicolours cannot be relied upon to produce a single Tortoiseshell kitten! It is more by luck that one appears as an occasional kitten in a litter. Tabby sires should not be used as they would produce unwanted bars and markings.

mated to a very ns ot

head and ears and the fur should be particularly long on the ruff and tail. White hairs and tabby markings are faults. Noseleather and paw pads pink or black. Eyes copper or deep orange.

BLUE-CREAM PERSIAN

The Blue-cream is a female-only variety, genetically a dilute form of the Tortoiseshell, and a most attractive and popular cat. Although relatively slow to gain championship status, achieving official recognition in the United Kingdom only in 1930, they had appeared in litters resulting from Blue and Cream matings ever since pedigree cat breeding began, and were first shown in the United States as Blue Tortoiseshells in the early 1900s.

It is now generally recognized that they are very valuable as breeding stock for Blues, Creams and Blue-creams. The crossing of two longhaired varieties has given stamina to both Blues and Creams and the Blue-creams themselves are a very healthy and robust variety of good Persian type.

The British and American standards are quite different. The former calls for evenly intermingled blue and cream throughout the coat, but the latter requires well-broken patches of blue and cream.

Grooming
Daily grooming with brush and comb is essential. A bath may be necessary before a show, and a little grooming powder to fluff the coat into show condition.

Breeding
If a Blue-cream is mated to a Cream sire, the resulting kittens will be everything except Blue females. If a Blue-cream is mated to a Blue sire, the resulting kittens will be everything except cream females. Similarly, a Blue female mated to a Cream male will produce Blue-cream female and Blue male kittens, whereas a Blue male mated to a Cream female will produce Blue-cream female and Cream male kittens.

Kittens
The kittens are very pretty and colourful, and there may be Blues, Creams and Blue-creams in any litter. Those with the palest coats will probably develop into the best adults from a competition point of view. Often a very fine Blue-cream will look much like pale blue in the first few weeks, so breeding Blue-creams can be quite exciting.

TORTOISESHELL -AND-WHITE PERSIAN (Calico)

The Tortoiseshell-and-white (Calico) Persian is another female-only variety, with a delightfully patched coat of black, red and cream with white. Beautiful cats, they are always in demand.

Although shorthaired Tortoiseshell-and-white cats have been known in Europe for centuries, the origin of the longhaired variety is obscure. Like the Tortoiseshell, it is said to have no distinct history, and probably arose by chance in litters of solid-coloured Persians with mixed colour backgrounds.

The colour is sex-linked genetically to produce females only, and when the rare male occurs, it is invariably sterile. Cats with this coat pattern were known in the past as 'chintz' cats, because of the bright, bold colour patches.

On the show bench, the pedigree variety is relatively new, attaining recognition only in the 1950s. More recently, the dilute variety, Blue Tortoiseshell-and-white (Dilute Calico), has also attained recognition in Europe and the United States. Such cats often appear in the same litter as Tortoiseshell-and-whites, and have patched coats of blue and cream with white.

In the United Kingdom, the standard requires the colour patches to be interspersed with white, but in the United States, the preference is for white to be concentrated on the underparts. One American association describes the cat as a Tortoiseshell that has been dropped into a pail of milk, the milk having splashed up onto the face and neck.

Grooming
This cat's coat is said not to mat as much as most Persian varieties, but a daily brushing and combing is still advisable. If it is being prepared for a show, a little Fuller's earth can be rubbed into the lighter parts of the coat and then thoroughly brushed out.

Breeding
Like Tortoiseshells, Tortoiseshell-and-whites are also renowned for producing kittens in a lovely assort-

ment of colours, but it appears that more Tortoiseshell-and-white kittens are born when sired by Red-and-white or Black-and-white Bicoloured cats. Those producing the best patched coats are males with too much white in their own coats, according to the Bicolour standard. Tabbies should not be used as they might introduce bars and markings, which are rather undesirable.

Kittens
The kittens often have patches of dull blue, dark cream or drab white when young, but these usually turn into jet black, bright red and pure white patches in the adult. Blue Tortoiseshell-and-white kittens, which often appear in the same litter, are generally paler in colour. In both cases, however, it is difficult to assess the quality of the coat colouring when the kittens are young.

SHOW SUMMARY
Tortoiseshell-and-white (Calico). The cat should be strikingly patched with black, red and cream, interspersed with white. The patches should be equally distributed, bright and clear, without white hairs (brindling) or tabby markings, and should be evenly spread over the body with white on the legs, feet, chest and face. Too much white is a fault. The American standard requires white to be concentrated on the underparts. A cream or white blaze from the top of the head to the nose is desirable, especially when it sharply divides the black side of the face from the red side. Noseleather and paw pads pink, black or a combination of the two. Eyes brilliant copper.

Blue Tortoiseshell-and-white (Dilute Calico). Coat should be patched with blue and cream. Patches should be evenly distributed over the body, clear and unbrindled, with white on the legs, feet, chest and face, and concentrated on the underparts (US). A cream or white blaze on the face is desirable. Noseleather and paw pads pink. Eyes brilliant copper or orange.

Below: A fine example of a Blue Tortoiseshell-and-white Persian.

Shaded Cameo Persian

Shaded Silver Persian

Persian
(Longhair)

Masked Silver Persian. A Chinchilla with a pure white undercoat and top coat tipped lightly with black on the back, flanks and tail, but with darker, heavier tipping on the face and paws. Noseleather brick red. Paw pads black or deep brown. Eyes green or blue-green.

Chinchilla Golden. The undercoat should be a rich, warm cream. The coat on the back, flanks, head and tail is lightly tipped with seal brown to give a sparkling golden appearance. The legs may be very lightly tipped. The chin, ear tufts, stomach and chest should be cream. The lips, nose and eyes should be outlined with seal brown. Noseleather deep rose. Paw pads seal brown. Eyes green or blue-green.

Shell Cameo. (Red Chinchilla). The undercoat should be pure white with the coat on the back, flanks, legs and tail lightly tipped with red (and/or cream in United Kingdom) to give an enchanting sparkling pink tinsel effect. The chin, ear tufts, stomach and chest are pure white. Tabby markings are a fault. Noseleather and paw pads rose. Eyes brilliant copper, outlined in rose.

Shell Tortoiseshell. (Tortoiseshell Cameo, Tortie-cream Cameo). Females only. The undercoat should be pure white, lightly tipped with red, black and cream in well-defined patches, and well broken on the face. The chin, ear tufts, stomach and chest are white. A blaze of red or cream tipping on the face is desirable. Noseleather and paw pads black, pink or a combination of the two. Eyes brilliant copper.

Blue-cream Particolour Cameo. Females only. The undercoat should be pure white. The coat on the back, flanks, legs and tail is lightly tipped with blue and cream, softly intermingled, to give the effect of a mantle of mother of pearl. Noseleather and paw pads blue, pink or a combination of the two. Eyes deep copper.

Cameo Tabby. Undercoat should be off-white, lightly tipped with red in either classic or mackerel tabby coat pattern. Noseleather and paw pads rose. Eyes brilliant copper.

SHADED PERSIAN

Similar to the Chinchillas and Shell Cameos, the Shaded Persians also have pale (usually white) undercoats, but approximately a quarter of the hair length is tipped with a contrasting colour to give the effect of a coloured mantle over the body.

Shaded kittens appear in the same litters as Chinchillas and Cameos, and the information given about breeding also applies to the Shaded Persians (see page 22). In the early days of pedigree cat breeding, when Chinchillas were darker than they are today, it was difficult to distinguish between the two types. It is only recently that interest in the shaded cats has been revived and a standard introduced for them. They are very much loved in the United States and Australia and are now bred in several colours, although the original variety was Silver. There is no reason why, with well-regulated outcrossing to other coloured Persians, they should not be bred in any coat colour or pattern.

Grooming
Daily grooming is essential. Show preparation requires the same treatment as for Chinchillas and Shell Cameos.

SHOW SUMMARY
Shaded Silver. The undercoat should be pure white, the top coat tipped in black to give the effect of a black mantle overlying the undercoat, on the back, flanks, face, legs and tail. Generally darker than the Chinchilla. Noseleather and paw pads brick red. Eyes green or blue-green, rimmed with black.

Shaded Cameo. (Red Shaded). The undercoat should be pure white, with the top coat tipped in red to give the effect of a red mantle overlying the undercoat, on the back, flanks, face, legs and tail. Generally darker than the Shell Cameo. Noseleather and paw pads rose. Eyes brilliant copper, rimmed with rose.

Shaded Golden. The undercoat should be a rich, warm cream, with the top coat tipped in seal brown to give the effect of a golden overcoat. Generally darker than the Chinchilla Golden. Noseleather deep rose. Paw pads seal brown. Eyes green or blue-green, rimmed in seal brown.

Shaded Tortoiseshell. The undercoat should be pure white, with the top coat tipped in black, red and cream in well-defined patches of the tortoiseshell pattern. Generally much darker than the Shell Tortoiseshell. A blaze of red or cream on the face is desirable. Noseleather and paw pads black, pink, or a combination of the two. Eyes brilliant copper.

Pewter. The undercoat should be white, with the top coat tipped in black, giving the effect of a black mantle overlying the undercoat. Generally darker than the Chinchilla but similar to the Shaded Silver. Lips, nose and eyes outlined in black. Noseleather brick red. Paw pads black. Eyes orange or copper, with no green tinge.

SMOKE PERSIAN

Like the Chinchillas and Shaded Persians, the Smokes are also characterized by their white undercoats and contrasting tipped top coats. But these hairs are tipped for at least half their length with colour and at first glance, Smoke Persians may look like solid-coloured cats until they move,

Above: A Black Smoke Persian with the pale undercoat showing through.

when the beautiful pale undercoat shows through. The ruff and ear tufts are generally of the paler colour, making these cats among the most striking of the Persians.

Smoke-coloured cats have been recorded in the United Kingdom since the 1860s, and appeared originally as the result of chance matings of Chinchilla, Black, Blue, and White Persians. Very good Smokes were shown in England in the first 20 years of this century, but then, oddly, their popularity declined, until interest was revived again in the 1960s. Now several colours are being bred, but so far not all are recognized for competition in all countries.

Grooming
More than most varieties, Smoke Persians require frequent and expert grooming to look their best. In fact, it may take many weeks of dedication before the contrasting coat is ready to be shown to perfection.

Apart from a bath a week before the show to remove grease, the undercoat must be well brushed up to show through the dark top coat. This is a job that requires patience and skill; too much brushing may pull out the undercoat. Strong sunlight tends to bleach the coat, so Smokes are best shown during the winter months.

Breeding
Outcrosses to improve type can be made to Black, Blue or Tortoiseshell Persians, giving Black, Blue or Tortoiseshell Smokes; this will preserve the copper eyes. Silver Tabbies should not be used, because they would reintroduce the green eye and tabby markings, neither of which is desirable, although there was a time in the United Kingdom when green eyes were permitted. Another good cross is to a Chinchilla, to improve the undercoat, though again this may introduce the green eye colour.

In order to produce all-Smoke kittens, the parents must have a Smoke in their backgrounds; but Black is dominant over Smoke, and therefore Black-to-Smoke matings will produce all-Black kittens. Even Smoke-to-Smoke matings may produce some all-Black kittens. Unfortunately mating Smokes with Smokes repeatedly results in loss of Persian type.

Kittens
Smokes are difficult to distinguish at birth from their solid-coloured counterparts, except that Smoke kittens sometimes have white around the eyes and a paler stomach. It may take some months to distinguish which will be Smokes, and the full coat colour and pattern is sometimes not seen until the adult coat is grown at about two years of age. Kittens whose undercoats get paler quickest usually become the best adult Smokes. The undercoat begins to show through at about three weeks, and by six to eight weeks old the cats have a mottled appearance. At six months they are ready to be shown. Kittens with unsatisfactory coats can be sold as pets and will make affectionate, even-tempered companions.

SHOW SUMMARY
Black Smoke. The undercoat should be white, heavily tipped on the back and flanks with black to give the effect of a solid coloured cat, until the animal moves. The coat shades to silver on the lower flanks. The face and feet are black, with no markings (colour solid to the roots in the United Kingdom; white at the roots in the United States). The ruff and ear tufts are silver. Noseleather and paw pads black. Eyes brilliant copper or orange.

Blue Smoke. The undercoat should be white, heavily tipped with blue on the back and flanks to give the appearance of a solid blue cat, until the animal moves. The face and feet are blue, without markings (colour solid to the roots in the United Kingdom; white at the roots in the United States). The ruff and ear tufts are silver. Noseleather and paw pads blue. Eyes brilliant orange or copper.

Cameo Smoke. (Red Smoke). The undercoat should be white, heavily tipped with red on the back and flanks to give the appearance of a solid red cat, until the animal moves. The face and feet are red, without markings (colour solid to the roots in the United Kingdom; white at the roots in the United States). The ruff and ear tufts are

Cameo Tabby Persian
(Shown in moult)

Shell Cameo Persian

Persian
(Longhair)

Chinchilla Persian

Brown Tabby-and-white
Norwegian Forest Cat

Norwegian
Forest Cat

Maine Coon

Blue-and-white
Bicolour Maine Coon

ANGORA
(Turkish Angora)

Good points
- *Very beautiful*
- *Graceful*
- *Intelligent*
- *Loyal*
- *Friendly*
- *Quiet*
- *Adaptable*

Take heed
- *Needs some daily grooming*
- *Moults in spring and summer*

The Angora makes a charming, dainty companion and is very attractive in appearance, with its long lithe body and plumed tail. It is not a talkative cat but is loyal, affectionate and adaptable; it would be happy living in either town or country, but would prefer to be given the run of the home. Alert, lively and intelligent, it loves to play games and to show off to an audience.

Angoras are bred in most colours and patterns, although white is probably the most popular. Some of the blue-eyed and odd-eyed whites may be deaf, and it is advisable to make sure before purchase that your chosen kitten is not deaf, unless you feel competent to take full care of such an animal and protect it against the inevitable dangers.

At present the Angora is still a rather rare breed, and may be expensive to buy. However, it is possible to purchase a non-show class kitten more reasonably.

Grooming
Although the Angora is easier to groom than a Persian, it nevertheless needs and will enjoy a daily grooming session. Use a medium-toothed comb with a handle to remove dead hairs. Grooming is particularly important in spring and early summer when much of the coat is shed.

Origin and history
The Angora is thought to be the oldest longhaired breed in Europe and came originally from Ankara in Turkey, where it is known to exist today, both as a free roaming domestic cat and in the local zoo.

Angoras arrived in the United Kingdom via France at the end of the sixteenth century, and so were known for a time as French cats. In the early days they were unfortunately mated indiscriminately with other longhaired cats (the original Persians), and in the process the Persian type was dominant and the Angora type was lost until quite recently, except of course in Turkey. Apparently the early Persians had long, thick coats, lacking the silkiness of the Angora coat, and it is thought that Angoras may have been used to improve the Persian coat.

Recently the breed has been revived in the Eastern United States, where cats have been imported direct from the Ankara Zoo. These cats are white, but other colours have been bred and

Above: A graceful Blue-eyed White Angora. Unfortunately, some Blue-eyed Whites are born deaf; check before buying or you may encounter problems as the kitten matures.

many are now recognized for showing on both sides of the Atlantic, although numbers in the United Kingdom are still small.

Breeding
Angora litters usually contain four to five kittens, though six or seven is not uncommon. Although many colours occur naturally within the breed, white is so dominant that it nearly always appears in the coat, and it is difficult to produce show quality Angoras in other colours.

Deafness is particularly common among blue-eyed and odd-eyed white Angoras, and unless you are prepared to take on considerable responsibility, it is best not to use a deaf cat for breeding.

Kittens
Angora kittens are charming, fluffy and playful. White kittens born with a smudge of black hairs on the top of their heads are likely to have good hearing in at least one ear. The kittens mature slowly, and the long, silky coat is not fully developed until two years of age.

SHOW SUMMARY
The Angora is a medium-sized cat, solidly built, but graceful and lithe, with a long, flowing coat.
Coat. Medium length silky hair; slightly wavy, especially on the stomach. No thick woolly undercoat. The hair is long on the underparts and ruff, and shorter along the back and on the face.
Body. Medium in size, long, graceful and lithe. Fine but strong-boned. Long but sturdy legs; hind legs slightly longer than forelegs. Feet small, oval to round and dainty; toes well tufted.
Tail. Long and tapering, wider at the base and well plumed. When moving, the tail is carried horizontally over the body, sometimes almost touching the head.
Head. Medium sized, wide, gently pointed wedge. Nose straight without a stop. Neck long and slim.

Ears set high on head, large and pointed, broad based and tufted.
Eyes. Large, round to oval in shape and slightly slanted.

ANGORA COLOURS
Chalky white is the favourite colour, but all other longhaired coat colours are accepted. Particularly liked are Black, Blue, Chocolate and Lilac in self and tabby patterns, Red, Tortoiseshell, Cinnamon and Bicolours. (Chocolate and Lilac are not accepted in the United States.) Eyes are amber in all colours, but Brown and Silver Tabbies may have green or hazel eyes, and Whites may be blue- or odd-eyed (one blue, one amber). Balinese have the same body shape as Angoras.

TURKISH
(Turkish Van cat)

Good points
- *Distinctive appearance*
- *Elegant*
- *Intelligent*
- *Hardy*
- *Lively*
- *Likes playing with water and can swim*

Take heed
- *Needs some daily grooming*
- *Moults in spring and summer*

The Turkish cat makes an exotically different pet, with its beautiful chalk-white coat and striking auburn face and tail. Its main claim to originality is that it enjoys swimming and playing with water. In colder climates, care must be taken to ensure that the cat does not catch cold, although in its native Turkey the winters are very severe, and Turkish cats are generally strong and hardy.

This is still a rare breed, so you must expect to pay quite a lot and to have to wait for a kitten, as demand will probably exceed the supply. It is worth the wait, however, as the Turkish cat is lively and affectionate and makes a charming, intelligent companion. A neutered male would make an excellent pet and may be obtained more reasonably because not as

many studs will be kept for breeding as female kittens.

Grooming
The Turkish is an easy cat to groom, but a light daily combing is recommended to remove dead hairs, particularly when the cat is moulting in spring and summer. Occasionally a little non-toxic grooming powder may be dusted into the coat to keep away greasy marks, which would otherwise mar the lovely chalk-white appearance. Unlike many other cats, the Turkish will enjoy a bath, but keep the animal warm afterwards to prevent it catching a chill.

Origin and history
Turkish cats are thought to have originated as a result of natural selection due to interbreeding within a geographically isolated area, the Van region of Turkey, where they have been domesticated for centuries. They were first introduced into the United Kingdom in the 1950s, when a pair was brought from Turkey by an English breeder. The line was gradually established, with more cats being imported from Turkey, and is now becoming popular in Europe.

At present the breed is not recognized for competition in the United States, although some are bred and kept as pets.

Breeding
Turkish cats breed true, the kittens always resembling their parents, and the breed is being kept pure by not outcrossing to any other breed or colour variety. The average litter contains four kittens.

Kittens
The kittens are born pure chalk white—not pink, like most all-white animals—with the auburn markings already quite clearly visible. Their eyes open very early, at four or five days, and are blue, gradually changing to pale amber.

SHOW SUMMARY
The Turkish is a medium-sized cat, sturdy and strong in build, with a long, silky coat. Males are rather larger and more muscular than females.
Coat. Very silky, long, straight fur, without a thick woolly undercoat.
Body. Long but sturdy, with medium-length legs. Feet small and round, with tufted toes.
Tail. Medium in length and full.
Head. Short and wedge-shaped. Medium-length neck. Nose long, not snub. Ears large, upright, close together, shell pink inside and well tufted.
Eyes. Round, pink-rimmed.

TURKISH COLOUR
Chalk white with auburn markings on the face, around and below the ears, with a white blaze continuing up between the ears. Nose, cheeks and chin are white. The tail is ringed in two shades of auburn, and the tail markings are particularly obvious in kittens. Small auburn markings are allowed elsewhere on the body. Noseleather and paw pads pale pink. Eyes pale amber.

Angora
(Outline beneath fur)

Amber-eyed White Angora

Turkish

Turkish

Turkish
kitten

CYMRIC

(Longhaired Manx)

Good points
- *Intelligent*
- *Quiet*
- *Loyal*
- *Affectionate*
- *Strong*
- *Gentle*
- *Good mouser*
- *Good with children and dogs*

Take heed
- *Needs daily grooming*

The Cymric's unique appearance distinguishes it from other cats: it has no tail, but it differs from the Manx in that it also has long hair. The Cymric has the same temperament and personality as the Manx, being loyal and affectionate, intelligent and gentle, courageous and strong. It makes an excellent family pet, being good with children and dogs, and is amusing as well as sensitive. Like the Manx it would make an excellent mouser for offices or hotels, especially since there is no tail to get caught in doors! A fast runner and a good hunter, the Cymric needs plenty of space to roam.

Grooming
Although the Cymric has long hair, the fur does not mat easily, and the cat is therefore easy to groom. A good comb-through daily is all that is required to remove dead hairs. Their eyes and ears should be examined regularly for dirt or ear mites.

Origin and history
The Manx is an old-established breed, particularly common on the Isle of Man, but also known elsewhere. However, it seems that longhaired kittens first appeared in Manx litters in Canada in the 1960s. At no time in recorded pedigree cat breeding history was the Manx knowingly outcrossed to a longhaired cat, but it is reasonable to assume that a recessive gene for long hair must have been present for many generations. Consequently, the Cymric is one of the newer breeds in the show ring, and is confined at present to North America.

Breeding
Mating two Cymrics produces 100 percent Cymric kittens, but tailless cats have a lethal factor when like is mated to like too often; therefore for the best results tailed or stumpy tailed cats should be mated to tail-less cats. The show animal must, however, be completely tail-less, with a hollow where the root of the tail should be. Many of the tailed or stumpy tailed kittens that are born in the same litters make excellent pets, and are just as intelligent and affectionate.

Kittens
Cymric kittens are courageous and venturesome and very playful, even though denied the built-in toy that other breeds have in the nest, that inviting feature—mother's tail.

SHOW SUMMARY
The principal feature in the show Cymric is a complete absence of tail. The whole cat should have a round, rabbity look, with a short back and long hind legs.
Coat. Medium to long and double. The undercoat is thick and cottony. The top coat is silky and glossy.
Body. A solid, rounded cat, with a short back, rounded rump, very deep flanks and muscular thighs. The forelegs are set well apart and are short and heavily boned. The hind legs are longer than the forelegs. The back is arched from the shoulder to the rump. The feet are neat and round.
Tail. Absent, with a decided hollow at the end of the spine. A residual tail is a fault.
Head. Large and round, with prominent cheekbones. Short, thick neck, and strong chin. Nose of medium length with a gentle nose break. The whisker pads are rounded and there is a decided whisker break. Ears are large, wide at the base, tapering to slightly pointed tips, set on top of the head, and with ear tufts at the ends.
Eyes. Large, round and expressive; set at an angle to the nose, outer corners being slightly higher than inner corners.

CYMRIC COLOURS
All coat colours and patterns and combinations of coat colours and patterns, such as white with tabby, are permitted. However, Chocolate, Lilac and the Himalayan pattern are not accepted, nor these colours with white. For colour standards, see Persians.

SOMALI

Good points
- *Easy to groom*
- *Almost voiceless*
- *Amusing and entertaining*
- *Affectionate*
- *Gentle*
- *Even-tempered*
- *Good with children*
- *Easy to care for*

Take heed
- *Does not like to be caged*

The Somali is a longhaired Abyssinian, similar in temperament and colouring, but a little less boisterous. The Somali makes an interesting pet, as it is playful and lively, yet very quiet to have around, being almost voiceless. Gentle and well-mannered, it makes an excellent family pet, and is almost always good tempered.

However, like the Abyssinian, a Somali would be happiest if given plenty of freedom and space to run around; it may fret if caged.

Grooming
Although fairly long, the Somali coat does not mat and therefore daily grooming is not essential, though a run-through with a medium-toothed comb is advisable to remove dead hairs, and will probably be appreciated by the cat.

Origin and history
Longhaired kittens began to appear in Abyssinian litters in Canada and the United States, and even in Europe, during the 1960s, and were thought to be a natural mutation. However, most of their ancestry can be traced back to Abyssinians in the United Kingdom that were experimentally mated to longhaired cats. Consequently, it is now thought that the gene for long hair was introduced by breeders. The subsequent export of British- and American-bred Abyssinians all over the world has spread the longhaired factor abroad, and so attractive is it that some Abyssinian breeders in Australia are now concentrating on breeding the Somali instead of the Abyssinian.

The first breed club was formed in 1972, and by 1978 the breed was officially recognized by all the various American and Canadian governing bodies.

Breeding
Mating two Somalis will produce all-Somali kittens, but they may also appear in Abyssinian litters where both parents carry the gene for long hair. Somalis can also be mated to Abyssinians to improve type.

Kittens
Somali litters rarely contain more than three or four kittens and the ratio of males to females is high. They are slightly larger than Abyssinian kittens, and are slower to develop their full adult coats.

SHOW SUMMARY
The Somali is a medium-sized, lithe-bodied cat, firm and muscular, with a long coat and distinctive colouring.
Coat. Full, dense, silky and fine-textured. A ruff around the neck and breeches are desirable. The coat is longer on the stomach and shorter over the shoulders. The full beauty of the coat may take as long as two years from birth to develop.
Body. Medium in length, lithe, graceful and muscular. Rib cage rounded. Back slightly arched.

Below: A Red Somali in contemplative mood. These beautiful cats—really Abyssinians with long hair—are gentle and very easy to care for.

Legs long and slim. Paws small and oval, with tufted toes.
Tail. Full brush; thick at the base and gently tapering.
Head. Rounded short wedge, all lines gently curving. Wide between the ears, which are large and alert, pointed, wide at the base, set well apart towards the back of the head, and furnished with long ear tufts. Chin rounded, firm and full. No whisker break. Slight nose break.
Eyes. Almond-shaped, large, brilliant and expressive.

SOMALI COLOURS
At present the Somali is recognized in two colours—Ruddy and Red—although, with Abyssinians being bred in different colours, more colours are likely to appear in due course.

Ruddy. Coat colour orange-brown, each hair ticked (banded) with black. The first band should start next to the skin, and double or treble banding is preferred. On the back there is darker shading that forms a line along the spine and continues along the tail, which ends in a black tip. The ears should be tipped with black or dark brown. The face is characteristically marked with a short, dark vertical line above each eye, and another line continues from the upper eyelid towards the ear. The eyes are dark-rimmed and surrounded by a pale area. The underside, insides of the legs and chest should be an even ruddy colour, without ticking or other markings. The toe tufts on all four feet are black or dark brown, with black between the toes extending up the back of the hind legs. White or off-white is allowed only on the upper throat, lips and nostrils. Noseleather brick red. Paw pads black or brown. Eyes gold or green, deeper colours preferred.

Red. Body colour warm, glowing red ticked with chocolate brown. Deeper shades of red preferred. The ears and tail should be tipped with chocolate brown. The underside, insides of the legs and chest are reddish brown without ticking or other markings. The toe tufts are chocolate brown, the colour extending slightly beyond the paws. Noseleather rosy pink. Paw pads pink. Eyes gold or green, deeper colours preferred.

*Blue Tortoiseshell-and-white
(Dilute Calico) Cymric*

Cymric

Red Somali kitten

Ruddy Somali

Somali

41

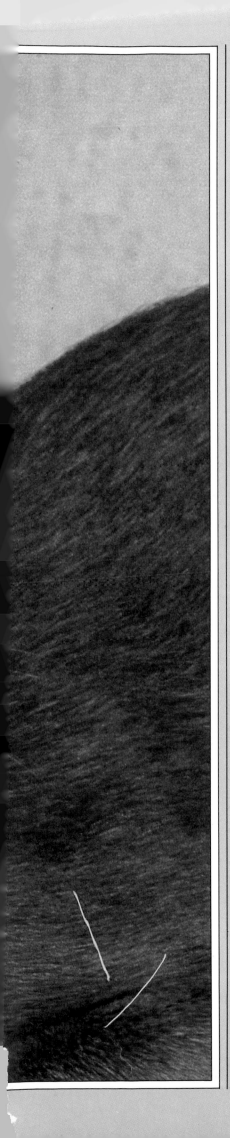

SHORTHAIRED CATS

Cat lovers who do not have a lot of time to look after a pet would do well to choose a shorthaired cat. There are many to choose from, from the plush-coated British Shorthairs to the very smooth-lying coats of the 'Foreign' type cats, such as the very popular Siamese and Burmese. For those who like something different, the curly-coated Rex cats might be a good choice. In the USA and Canada, you might even sport a Wirehaired cat or even a completely hairless one, if you find them attractive. For lovers of the unusual, the Scottish Fold, with its curious 'buttoned down ears', may appeal. The tail-less Manx and the charming Japanese Bobtail also have a distinct fascination. The newly developed Snowshoe, a Siamese with white feet and muzzle, may take your eye. Or you may prefer the lithe elegance of one of the pure Oriental Shorthairs. The affectionate Tonkinese, a hybrid between the Siamese and Burmese, may be your choice or perhaps you may favour the sleek Bombay, with its glossy black coat and bright new penny copper eyes. The quiet Russian Blue and Korat may suit your own temperament or you may find the independent nature of the Abyssinian more in keeping with your lifestyle. Look through the pages of this section and you are sure to find a shorthaired breed that will suit you perfectly.

*Left: The inquisitive gaze of a
Blue Oriental (Foreign) Shorthair.*

BRITISH SHORTHAIR

Good points
- *Strong and sturdy*
- *Healthy*
- *Good mouser*
- *Affectionate*
- *Good with children and dogs*
- *Quiet*
- *Easy to groom*

Take heed
- *No drawbacks known*

Because the British Shorthair is a natural breed that has not been altered to suit a breeder's whims, it is healthy and sound in mind and body. Not susceptible to illnesses and even-tempered, it will make an excellent pet for children and old people. The most popular colour is probably the Blue, followed by the Silver Tabby and the spotted varieties. Basically, this is a strong, sturdy shorthaired cat; it is active, graceful, intelligent and curious.

British Shorthairs are less expensive than most other breeds. It may be possible to obtain, for nothing, a cat that resembles this breed, but one is never sure that the kitten comes from sturdy, reliable stock. With a pedigree kitten from a reliable breeder, it should be possible to have a healthy, trouble-free pet that could be with the family for 20 years, barring accidents.

Grooming
Daily grooming is advisable to remove dead hairs, together with lots of hand stroking, which the cat will love. However, a weekly combing is sufficient to keep a British Shorthair looking neat and trim, and therefore anyone who leads a very busy life would find a shorthaired cat to be the best choice.

Origin and history
Records of pedigree cats have been kept for less than 100 years, but it is well known from history books, literature of the day and art forms that these cats have been around for centuries. They were some of the first to be shown at the end of the nineteenth century, when shows first started in the United Kingdom, and they are generally regarded as being native to the British Isles, although some of the strains may have been imported by the Romans. All the earliest known cats were shorthaired, even on the show bench. Longhaired cats have been known in Europe only since the sixteenth century. Once cat shows started, however, the longhaired cats superseded the shorthaired cats numerically on the show bench.

British shorthaired cats were imported into North America by the early English immigrants, who took them to their new home as pets and mousers. These cats mated with other shorthaired cats brought to America from other parts of the world, and gave rise to the American Shorthair breed.

Both the British and American Shorthairs are therefore breeds recognized by the American associations.

Shorthaired cats are bred in Europe and closely resemble the British Shorthair. Often breeding stock is imported from the United Kingdom and the standards set for the breed and its colour varieties are very similar to those in Britain. Only the Chartreuse in France is said to differ because of its distinct history, but in recent years, the British Blue and the Chartreuse have become almost indistinguishable.

SHOW SUMMARY
The British Shorthair is a medium to large cat; strong and sturdy on short legs and with a short, thick coat. Males are larger than females.
Coat. Short, resilient and dense, without being double or woolly.
Body. Hard and muscular, medium to large, with a full, broad chest built on strong, short legs and with a level back. The straight forelegs are the same length as the hindlegs. The paws are neat, well rounded and firm.
Tail. Short, thick at the base, tapering to a round tip.
Head. Broad and rounded, the face round on a short neck. The nose is straight, broad and short, without a stop. The ears are set apart so that the inner ear and eye corners are perpendicular to each other; the ears are small and rounded.
Eyes. Large, round and level. They should be wide awake and full of expression. There should be the width of an eye between the eyes.

BRITISH SHORTHAIR COLOURS
Seventeen colours are recognized in the United Kingdom, but every colour known to cats is possible and will probably appear in time.

BRITISH BLACK

Black cats have a long and chequered past. In the Middle Ages they were often persecuted for being the familiars of witches, and generally regarded with sus-

Above: The highly prized Orange-eyed White British Shorthair.

picion. At other times in history, as now, they were considered lucky, at least in the United Kingdom. They are certainly very striking and often have very healthy-looking, glossy coats. The current show standard calls for deep copper eyes; whereas many black non-pedigree cats have lovely coats but decidedly green eyes.

Grooming
Preparing a shorthaired Black for showing requires very little trouble, but the coat must be combed daily. A little bay rum used to clean the coat for a few days before the show is an advantage, and will enhance the shine. The coat may become bleached in strong sunlight, so black cats are best shown in the winter months.

Breeding
Black cats can be obtained by mating two Blacks, or they can appear in Tortoiseshell litters. Blacks themselves are very valuable in producing Tortoiseshells and Tortoiseshell-and-whites (Calicos) and in Bicolour breeding. Type can be improved by mating Blacks to Blues, or even to Black Persians, provided that the longhaired kittens resulting from the mating are not used again for breeding, but are neutered and sold as pets.

Kittens
Black kittens may look rusty coloured when very young, but the reddish tinge disappears as the cat approaches adulthood. The important thing to look for is a coat that is a solid black down to the roots. There should be no white hairs, and the eyes should be pure copper with no tinge of green when changing from baby blue.

SHOW SUMMARY
The dense coat should be glossy and an even jet black throughout from root to tip, with no white hairs. Noseleather and paw pads black. Eyes brilliant copper or orange with no green tinge.

BRITISH WHITE

There are three types of pedigree shorthaired White cat: those with blue eyes; those with orange eyes; and those with one of each colour (odd-eyed). Non-pedigree white cats usually have green eyes.

White cats have always been loved for their pure looks and were particularly prized in Japan where they were regarded as symbols of purity and perfection. There have been white cats ever since there have been cats, but despite their obvious popularity, they have always been rather rare.

Grooming
A white cat, even if it looks after itself well, will need daily grooming to remove dead hairs, and it will need more careful attention if destined for a show career. It may be necessary to shampoo the coat a week before the show, being careful to keep the animal warm after the bath. When it is dry, baby powder can be shaken into the coat and then brushed out again. A show White must have an immaculate coat, with no yellow tinge or grey areas. All signs of powder must be removed before show day, and the whole coat smoothed with a silk handkerchief.

Breeding
Blue-eyed White cats are often deaf, which may contribute to their rarity, as deaf cats are not used frequently for breeding. Orange-eyed Whites solved the deafness problem, but in the process of their development, Odd-eyed White cats also appeared: such animals may have perfect hearing or may be deaf on the blue-eyed side. If a deaf queen is used for breeding, she will require more supervision than a normal cat because she cannot hear the cries of her kittens. She should be placed on a hard surface covered with newspaper for warmth, so she can feel her kittens and the vibrations of cries.

The average White litter contains three or four kittens, and all the kittens are born with blue eyes. Those destined to have orange eyes begin to change colour at about two weeks. The odd eyes are readily distinguished, as there is a difference in the depth of the blue colour from the start. Whites can be mated to Whites or to solid Blacks, Reds, Creams and Blues, to produce Bicolours; or to Tortoiseshells to produce Tortoiseshell-and-whites (Calicos).

Kittens
It is said that even a single black hair in the coat of a blue-eyed kitten will mean that the cat will have good hearing, at least in one ear. White kittens of any eye colour are always sought after and seem to take a pride in their appearance.

SHOW SUMMARY
The coat colour should be pure white with no yellow tinge. Noseleather and paw pads pink. Eyes gold, orange or copper; very deep sapphire blue; or one gold or copper, one deep blue.

British
Shorthair

Odd-eyed White
British Shorthair

Black British Shorthair

BRITISH BLUE

The British Blue, with its light blue, plush coat, is the most popular of all the British shorthaired varieties in the United Kingdom. Blues are said to prefer a quiet life and are renowned for their quiet, well-balanced temperaments.

Although shown in reasonable numbers at the first cat shows, during the Second World War there were very few studs available. After the War outcrosses to other breeds were made, which unfortunately resulted in loss of type. Further outcrosses were made to longhaired Blues that did improve type, however, although they produced coats that were too long. Selective breeding during the 1950s saw the re-establishment of the shorthaired Blues, and now kittens are much in demand.

Grooming
For Blue Shorthairs, this will entail a daily combing to remove dead hairs and lots of hand stroking, which all cats enjoy. It should not be necessary to shampoo a Blue, but a little bay rum rubbed into the coat the day before the show will remove any greasiness, which otherwise might mar the colour.

Breeding
It is advisable to outcross to longhaired Blues or shorthaired Blacks occasionally to maintain good type and colour. Some of the resulting kittens will have undesirable features such as over-long fur; these are not suitable for the show bench, but, of course, make excellent and charming pets. Litters usually contain three or four kittens. Blues are particularly useful for producing Blue-creams, when mated to Creams.

Kittens
Blue kittens are especially pretty. They are usually born with faint tabby markings, but these disappear within the first few months as the coat grows.

SHOW SUMMARY
The coat colour should be a light to medium blue, sound from root to tip with no white hairs or tabby markings. Noseleather and paw pads blue. Eyes brilliant copper or orange in colour.

CHARTREUSE
(Chartreux)

The Chartreuse is a shorthaired blue cat similar to the British Blue, although some maintain that it is different. The breed was said to have developed in France in the Carthusian monastery of the monks who made the liqueur Chartreuse. Apparently the monks originally brought the cats from South Africa.

Wherever it came from, the Chartreuse has a long history in France and some claim to fame. The French author Colette (1873-1954), who was a great lover of cats and kept many Persians throughout her life, nevertheless

Above: The Chartreuse, a French breed resembling the British Blue.

chose a Chartreuse as her last companion, and it was with her when she died. The French poet Joachim du Bellay (1522-60) is reputed to have been very fond of a blue-grey cat, which could have been a Chartreuse.

In its early days, the Chartreuse was a larger, more massive cat with a grey-blue coat, but recently, selective breeding has brought the type much closer to the British Blue and now most governing bodies in Europe accept the same standard for both cats. (See British Blue).

BRITISH CREAM

The British Cream Shorthair is a very attractive variety, but comparatively rare. The coat should be a pale, even cream with no tabby markings, and in practice this is very difficult to achieve.

Pedigree Cream Shorthairs have never been very numerous. This is partly due to the fact that in the early days of pedigree cat breeding no one knew for sure how to produce these cats to order. They appeared from time to time in Tortoiseshell litters and were usually regarded as 'sports' or freaks. They were not recognized for competition until the late 1920s.

Grooming
Preparing a Cream Shorthair for showing may require a shampoo a few days previously, as any grease or dirt in the coat will mar the colour. It also needs daily combing to remove dead hairs, and lots of hand stroking. No hand cream!

Breeding
To breed good Cream Shorthairs is not easy because, like red, of which cream is a dilute genetically, the colour is sex-linked to produce more males than females. However, they can be produced from Tortoiseshells and from Blue-creams. The Blue-cream with Blue or Cream sires produce the best Creams, and it seems that these matings are of benefit to both Blues and Creams, making the varieties of especially good type.

Kittens
Cream female kittens are obtained by mating a Blue-cream to a Cream sire; Cream males are obtained by mating a Blue-cream to a Blue sire. Creams are very attractive as kittens, although few possess the desired pale coat; many have tabby markings or are too dark to be shown. Nevertheless they make delightful pets and will not be difficult to find homes for.

SHOW SUMMARY
The coat should be a light even cream all over without white hairs or markings of any kind. Noseleather and paw pads pink. Eyes brilliant copper or orange.

BRITISH BICOLOUR SHORTHAIR

Two-coloured cats have been common for centuries and were seen at the earliest cat shows, although they did not achieve official recognition as a variety until relatively recently, when they were found to be essential in the breeding of Tortoiseshell-and-whites and dilute Calicos.

The Bicolour is particularly attractive when the standard is met, although the symmetrical distribution of the colour patches and white is, in practice, very hard to achieve. This may account for the comparative scarcity of this variety on the showbench. Bicolours may be Black-and-white (Magpie), Blue-and-white, Red-and-white or more rarely, Cream-and-white.

Grooming
Bicolours are easy to groom and just need a daily combing and hand stroking. The paler colours may require a shampoo a few days before a show. Powder should not be used on the black parts or it may detract from the colour.

Breeding
Bicoloured cats appear in mixed litters of Self-coloured and Tortoiseshell-and-white kittens and result from matings between Self-coloured males and Tortoiseshell-and-white females, between Bicolour males and Tortoiseshell-and-white females and between two Bicolours or a Self-coloured and a White cat.

Bicoloured queens make excellent mothers and have kittens of various colours, according to the sire involved and both parents' genetic backgrounds.

Kittens
Bicolour kittens are very colourful; they mature early and are independent, intelligent, healthy and hardy.

SHOW SUMMARY
The show Bicolour must have a certain percentage of white and colour on the body. The patches must be distinct from the white, never intermingled. The coat pattern should be similar to that of a Dutch rabbit, with symmetrical patches of colour (either black, blue, red or cream) evenly distributed on the head, body and tail, with white predominantly on the feet, legs, face, chest and underparts. Not more than two-thirds should be coloured, and not more than a half should be white. A white facial blaze is desirable, and the markings should be as symmetrical as possible on both sides of the body. Tabby markings and white hairs in the colour patches are faults. Noseleather and paw pads according to the 'main' colour or pink. Eyes brilliant copper or orange.

BRITISH TIPPED SHORTHAIR

These cats are the shorthaired equivalents of the longhaired Chinchillas, Cameos, Shaded Silvers and Shaded Cameos, and have a similar though more recent history.

They are one of the most striking varieties with their white undercoats tipped lightly with a contrasting colour. As yet, the different colours do not have separate classes at the shows, unlike the Persian equivalents, but as these cats are sure to gain in popularity, their numbers are certain to increase. The tipping can be of any colour.

Grooming
These cats need daily combing and hand stroking like other Shorthairs. Before a show they would benefit from powdering the undercoat or from a shampoo if very dirty.

Breeding
Various breeders have reported the most unexpected crosses that have produced British Shorthair Tipped kittens, such as Siamese to Chinchilla, but the most usual is Silver Tabby Shorthair to Chinchilla and thereafter back to Chinchilla Shorthairs. With the Chocolate and Lilac Tipped the matings now would be Chocolate and Lilac Shorthairs to shorthaired Chinchillas, but they were probably developed from Kashmirs (Longhaired Chocolate and Lilacs) to British Shorthairs.

Kittens
Because of the outcrossing to longhairs in the ancestry, the kittens have rather longer coats at birth but this disappears with the adult coat. They are charming and jolly.

SHOW SUMMARY
The undercoat should be as white as possible. The top coat should be tipped on the back, flanks, head, ears, legs and tail, with a contrasting colour to give a sparkling effect. The chin, stomach, chest and underside of the tail should be white. Tabby markings are faults. Noseleather and paw pads in keeping with the colour tipping. Eyes green in black-tipped cats; rims of eyes, nose and lips outlined in black. Eyes orange in other colours, or copper; eye rims and lips deep rose.

Red-and-white
Bicolour British Shorthair

British
Shorthair

Blue British Shorthair

British Tipped
Shorthair (Chinchilla)

Cream
British Shorthair

47

BRITISH SMOKE SHORTHAIR

These cats are the shorthaired equivalents of the Persian Smokes and have a similar breeding history. The hair for the most part is one colour, but near the roots is white or silver. Consequently, the coat appears a solid colour until the fur is parted or the cat moves.

Grooming

Daily combing and hand grooming is all that a normal shorthaired cat will require. Show cats will also need powdering to remove grease or, if they are very dirty, a shampoo a few days before a show. All powder must be brushed out.

Breeding

In order to obtain these lovely cats, it is necessary to mate Silver Tabby Shorthairs to solid coloured Shorthairs of the required colour. Thereafter Smokes are mated to Smoke and occasionally to solid Blue Shorthairs for type.

Kittens

Smoke kittens at birth look like solid coloured kittens; the lovely smoke effect is seen only as the adult coat develops.

SHOW SUMMARY

Black Smoke. Undercoat pale silvery white. The top coat heavily tipped almost to the roots with black. Long white hairs or tabby markings are faults. Noseleather black. Paw pads black or dark brown. Eyes deep yellow to copper.

Blue Smoke. Undercoat pale silvery white. Top coat heavily tipped almost to the roots with blue. No white hairs. Noseleather and paw pads blue. Eyes yellow to orange.

BRITISH TORTOISESHELL SHORTHAIR

Cats with the tortoiseshell pattern, that is, with a patched coat of black, red or cream, have been known for centuries and have appeared on the show bench ever since cats were first exhibited. In the British Shorthair, the patches show up very distinctly and are most attractive and colourful. Tortoiseshell cats are generally very sweet-natured, affectionate and gentle, with a charm all their own. They are a female-only variety, although the occasional male has occurred and one is even recorded as having sired a litter; at present, however, it is not known what factor makes 99.9 percent of tortoiseshell cats female.

Grooming

Apart from a daily combing, no special attention is necessary. Bay rum, rubbed into the coat before a show, will enhance the colours, and hand stroking will add sheen.

Breeding

Because this is a female-only variety, to produce Tortoiseshell kittens a Tortoiseshell female must be mated to a Self-coloured male of one of the required colours—black, red or cream. Even then, there is no guarantee that there will be Torties in the resultant litters. Much more research will have to be done before breeders can produce Tortoiseshell kittens unfailingly. Bicolours are not usually used as sires, as this will often give rise to Tortoiseshell-and-white (Calico) kittens as the offspring.

Kittens

Tortoiseshell kittens appear in litters with Black, Red and Cream kittens. The Tortoiseshell or Tortoiseshell-and-white kittens are always the first to be sold as they are so rare. The kittens are pretty and playful and develop early. They are usually strong, healthy and resistant to diseases and illnesses, and are not accident-prone. The markings on a kitten may not be very bright, and may be blue, pale red and dirty cream when it is very young, but when the adult coat begins to grow the blue turns to jet black, and the red and cream become clear.

SHOW SUMMARY

The coat should be evenly patched with black, red and cream, without intermingling of the colours, or any white hairs. Colour patches should be evenly distributed on the legs and face, and a facial blaze of red or cream is desirable. Noseleather and paw pads pink, black or a combination of the two. Eyes brilliant copper or orange.

BRITISH BLUE-CREAM SHORTHAIR

A dilute form of the Tortoiseshell, the Blue-cream is also a female-only variety. A relative newcomer to the show scene, this variety was not officially recognized in the United Kingdom until 1956, although Blue-cream kittens had appeared in litters of Blue and Cream matings and in Tortoiseshell litters (when both parents carried a gene for blue) for many years. The two palest shades of blue and cream are preferred, with no touch of red.

Grooming

Preparation for a show is relatively easy for the Blue-creams. They should be combed daily to remove dead hairs, and the coat cleaned with a little bay rum a few days before the show. Lots of hand grooming will gloss the coat.

Breeding

Blue-creams can be produced by mating a Blue with a Cream shorthair, or from Tortoiseshells. When a Blue-cream female is mated to a Cream sire, it is not possible to get Blue female kittens, but kittens of all other colours and both sexes are possible; but when mated to a Blue sire, there will be no Cream female kittens, but all other possibilities. No Blue-cream males have grown to adulthood or are known to have sired any kittens. If any appeared, it is thought that they would be sterile.

Kittens

It is not immediately apparent, when the kittens are born, which is to be a Blue-cream, and some of the best Blue-creams may look more like pale Blues at first.

SHOW SUMMARY

Coat colour should be blue and cream softly intermingled over the body, without a facial blaze. Tabby markings and white hairs or patches are faults. Noseleather blue. Paw pads blue and/or pink. Eyes copper or orange.

BRITISH TORTOISESHELL -AND-WHITE SHORTHAIR

(British Calico Shorthair)

The tortoiseshell-and-white coat pattern, like the tortoiseshell, has been well known for centuries amongst alley cats, particularly in countries such as Spain, and it is always highly prized for its brilliant colouring. Again, this is a female-only variety, and the occasional male is invariably sterile. Hardy and robust, they make excellent mousers. They were formerly known as Chintz or Spanish Cats.

Below: An orange-eyed Tortoise-shell-and-white British Shorthair

Grooming

A daily comb is advisable. Bay rum rubbed into the coloured patches before a show will enhance their brilliance.

Breeding

It was realized only after the Second World War that the best sires for this variety are the Bicolours, particularly those from a Tortie-and-white mother. Black-and-white or Red-and-white males are the most likely sires to produce Tortie-and-white kittens when mated with a Tortie-and-white.

Kittens

The kittens are exceptionally well balanced in temperament, happy and healthy. They develop early but the coat patches may not be very bright at first, only developing their full glory as the adult coat develops at about nine months.

SHOW SUMMARY

The coat should be boldly patched with black, cream and red with white, the patches equally balanced; white must not predominate. The tricolour patchings should cover the top of the head, ears and cheeks, back, tail and part of the flanks. Patches to be clear and well defined. A white facial blaze is desirable. Noseleather and paw-pads pink, black or a combination of the two. Eyes brilliant copper or orange.

BLUE TORTOISESHELL-AND-WHITE

(Dilute Calico)

There is a dilute form of the Calico or Tortoiseshell-and-white cat where blue replaces the black and cream replaces the red in the coat. Paw pads and noseleather are slate blue or pink or a combination of the two. Eyes gold.

Tortoiseshell-and-white
British Shorthair

British
Shorthair

Tortoiseshell
British Shorthair

Blue-cream British Shorthair

49

BRITISH TABBY SHORTHAIR

The shorthaired Tabbies occur in brown, red and silver and in several coat patterns, notably the classic, mackerel and spotted. In some countries, blue and cream tabbies are also recognized.

The name 'tabby' is said to have come originally from the similarity of the cats' coat pattern to tabby or plain woven watered silk or taffeta. This type of weaving produces a striped or ridged effect on the cloth, and was known as tabbisilk in England. The word itself derives from Attabiya, a district of Baghdad where this material was made. They were also known as Cyprus Cats.

The tabby pattern is very common among domestic cats, and non-pedigree shorthaired cats are usually varieties of Brown Tabbies or 'ginger toms'. Judging from the markings of many wild felines, the original domestic tabby was probably a striped or spotted cat, and many of the cats depicted on Egyptian scrolls have spotted coats. Spotted tabbies were shown at the first cat shows, but at the beginning of this century seemed to have disappeared from the show bench, presumably because the classic tabby pattern had preference in the hearts of the breeders of the time. Fortunately, they began to make a come-back in 1965, and are now bred in the five colours, although at present only Brown, Silver and Red are recognized for competition in the United Kingdom.

It appears that the classic or blotched pattern, the most common tabby pattern in pedigree cats, is a mutation from the striped form, which first appeared in Europe among domestic and feral cats, and was already common by the middle of the seventeenth century.

Of the tabby colours, the Silver Classic Tabby is now, and seems always to have been, the most popular variety. Since the Second World War, breeding lines have been greatly improved as a result of crossing with excellent Silver Tabbies from France, and the British ones now have good type and markings.

Brown Tabbies are not common on the show bench, possibly because it is difficult to breed a cat to the required colour standard.

The fact that the name 'Red Tabby' is so often associated with the marmalade or ginger alley cat, may have contributed to the relative lack of popularity of this variety. This is a pity, as the pedigree Red Tabby in no way resembles the 'ginger tom', and is very striking with its rich red coat.

Blue and Cream Tabby Shorthairs are awaiting recognition for competition in the United Kingdom at present; Blue Tabbies are becoming popular in Europe.

Grooming

Like all shorthaired cats, Tabbies will benefit from a daily combing to remove all the dead hairs. A little bay rum, rubbed into the coat a few days before a show, imparts the rich gloss to the coat required to show the markings off at their best. Plenty of hand stroking — with clean hands of course — will enhance the sheen and please the cat at the same time!

Breeding

Mating two Tabbies of the required colour together will give several generations of good type but then breeders sometimes mate to other self-coloured short or longhairs to improve type. Usually this will be to Blues but can also be to the solid colour in the coat pattern. Brown Tabby to a Black, Red Tabby to a Tortoiseshell, Silver Tabby to a Chinchilla, Blue Tabby to a Blue, and Cream Tabby to a Cream British Shorthair or Persian (Longhair) in each case.

Kittens

Tabby kittens are born with obvious markings and usually the best marked kittens at birth become the best marked adults. However, soon after birth, the markings may fade and may then take up to six months to develop fully. Imperfectly marked kittens with white hairs or patches or incorrect coat pattern will not be suitable for showing.

SHOW SUMMARY

Classic Tabby pattern. All markings should be clearly defined from the ground colour. The characteristic head marking is a letter 'M' resembling frown marks on the forehead. Unbroken lines run from the outer corners of the eyes towards the back of the head and there should be other pencillings on the cheeks. Lines extend back from the top of the head to the shoulder markings, which are shaped like a butterfly. Three unbroken lines run parallel to each other down the spine from the shoulder markings to the base of the tail. A large blotch on each flank is circled by one or more unbroken rings; these markings should be symmetrical on either side of the body. There should be several unbroken necklaces on the neck and upper chest, and a double row of 'buttons' running from chest to stomach. The legs should be evenly barred with narrow bracelets and the tail should be evenly ringed.

Mackerel Tabby pattern. The head is marked with the characteristic 'M', and there is an unbroken line running from the outer corner of the eyes towards the back of the head. There are other fine pencillings on the cheeks. A narrow unbroken line runs from the back of the head to the base of the tail. The rest of the body is marked with narrow unbroken lines running vertically down from the spine line. These lines should be as narrow and numerous as possible, and ideally clearly defined from the ground colour. There should be several unbroken necklaces on the neck and upper chest, and a double row of 'buttons' on the chest and stomach. The legs should be evenly barred with narrow bracelets and the tail evenly ringed.

Spotted Tabby pattern. All markings should be dense and clearly defined from the ground colour. The head should be marked with the characteristic 'M'. There is an unbroken line running from the outer corner of the eyes towards the back of the head, and there are other fine pencillings on the cheeks. Ideally, all the stripes in the tabby coat are broken up into spots, which may be round, oval or rosette-shaped and should be as numerous and as distinct from the ground colour as possible. A dorsal stripe runs the length of the back, but it should be broken up into spots. There should be a double row of spots on the chest and stomach, and spots or broken rings on the legs and tail.

Brown Tabby. The ground colour should be a rich sable brown or coppery brown. The markings in classic, mackerel or spotted tabby patterns are dense jet black. The hind legs from paw to heel should be black. Noseleather brick red. Paw pads black. Eyes orange, hazel or deep yellow.

Red Tabby. The ground colour should be a rich red. The markings, lips, chin and sides of the feet dark red. Noseleather brick red. Paw pads deep red. Eyes deep brilliant copper.

Silver Tabby. The ground colour should be a clear silver with no white hairs and no tinge of brown on the nose. The chin and lips should be silver. The markings in classic, mackerel and spotted patterns should be dense jet black. Noseleather brick red or black. Paw pads black. Eyes green or hazel (UK); brilliant gold, orange or hazel (US), according to different associations.

Blue Tabby. The ground colour should be pale bluish-white. The markings in classic, mackerel and spotted patterns should be dark slate-blue. Noseleather rose pink. Paw pads rose. Eyes brilliant gold.

Cream Tabby. The ground colour should be pale cream. The markings in classic, mackerel and spotted patterns dark cream, but not too hot. Noseleather and paw pads pink. Eyes brilliant gold.

Below: A Blue Classic Tabby British Shorthair kitten — full of curiosity.

British Shorthair

*Silver Spotted Tabby
British Shorthair*

*Silver Classic Tabby
British Shorthair kitten*

*Brown Mackerel Tabby
British Shorthair*

*Red Classic Tabby
British Shorthair*

AMERICAN SHORTHAIR

Good points
- Attractive
- Dignified
- Hardy
- Companionable
- Well balanced
- Good hunter
- Easy to groom

Take heed
- Likes to roam free

This hardy cat with its tough background makes an excellent pet, not easily affected by ailments or disease. The American Shorthair is independent and likes to roam free, so may be more suited to out-of-town living than to apartment life. In the house, it will continue to 'hunt', chasing and pouncing on whatever moves with velvet paws.

It enjoys excursions in the open air and is typically active and curious. Being a robust natural breed, it makes a trouble-free pet with an affectionate, companionable nature. It also makes an excellent working mouser.

Grooming
The coat of the American Shorthair is very easily maintained. However, it should be combed regularly to avoid a fur ball forming in the stomach. Regular attention should also be paid to the eyes and ears to make sure they are clean and free from ear mites.

Origin and history
These cats are reputed to have come to the United States with the original settlers from Europe, who brought them on their ships, not only as companions but as working rodent officers. Every ship had its cat or cats to protect the ship's stores, and many would have left ship in the New World and been missing when it sailed again. These cats mated freely without restriction or regard for pedigree or for any colour discrimination. After years of separation from the parent European stock, they developed characteristics of their own. Although they are still quite similar to the British Shorthair, American Shorthairs are larger, with less rounded heads and with longer noses. Years of free-ranging ancestry have also made this a hardy, fearless, intelligent breed. It was somewhat neglected as a pedigree variety until American breeders decided to breed it selectively to maintain all that is natural and lovely in their native domestic cats.

Breeding
American Shorthairs make good breeders and sensible mothers. They have endless patience.

Kittens
The kittens are confident, courageous and not prone to disease.

SHOW SUMMARY
The American Shorthair is a strong, well built cat, looking natural rather than contrived. It has the body of an athlete, built for an active outdoor life.

Coat. Thick, short, even and hard in texture. Not as plush as that of the British Shorthair and heavier and thicker in winter.

Body. Large to medium in size, lean and hard, athletic and powerful. Well developed chest and shoulders. Legs sturdy and medium in length, built for jumping and hunting. Paws full, rounded, with heavy pads. Excessive cobbiness or ranginess are faults.

Tail. Medium in length, wide at the base, tapering slightly to a blunt tip. No kinks.

Head. Large and full-cheeked. Face bright and alert: medium long, thick, muscular neck, carrying an oval face, only slightly longer than its width. Square muzzle, firm chin. Nose medium long and uniform width. In contour a gentle curve from forehead to nose tip. Ears set wide apart, not unduly wide at the base, with slightly rounded tips.

Eyes. Large, round and wide awake. Very slightly higher on the outer edge; set wide apart.

AMERICAN SHORTHAIR COLOURS

White. Pure white. Noseleather, paw pads pink. Eyes deep blue or brilliant gold; or one deep blue and one gold in Odd-eyed Whites.

Black. Dense coal black, sound throughout coat with no rusty tinge. Noseleather black. Paw pads black or brown. Eyes brilliant gold.

Blue. One level tone of blue throughout, lighter shades preferred. Noseleather and paw pads blue. Eyes brilliant gold.

Red. Deep, rich clear red without shading or tabby markings. Lips and chin red. Noseleather and paw pads brick red. Eyes brilliant gold.

Cream. One level shade of buff-cream, without markings. Lighter shades preferred. Noseleather and paw pads pink. Eyes brilliant gold.

Bicolour. White with unbrindled patches of black, or blue, or red, or cream. Noseleather and paw pads in keeping with solid colour or pink. Eyes brilliant gold.

Chinchilla. Undercoat pure white. Coat on back, flanks, head and tail sufficiently tipped with black to give a characteristic sparkling silver appearance. Rims of eyes, lips and nose outlined with black. Some tipping allowed on the legs. Chin, ear tufts, stomach and chest pure white. Noseleather brick red. Paw pads black. Eyes green or blue-green.

Shaded Silver. Undercoat white with a mantle of black tipping shading down from the sides, face and tail, from dark on the ridge to white on the chin, chest, stomach and under the tail. Legs to be the same tone as the face. General effect should be much darker than the Chinchilla. Rims of eyes, lips and nose outlined with black. Noseleather brick red. Paw pads black. Eyes green or blue-green.

Shell Cameo. Undercoat white. Coat on the back, flanks, head and tail to be sufficiently tipped with red to give the characteristic sparkling appearance. Face and legs may be slightly shaded with tipping. Chin, ear tufts, stomach and chest white. Rims of eyes rose. Noseleather and paw pads rose. Eyes brilliant gold.

Shaded Cameo (Red Shaded). Undercoat white with a mantle of red tipping shading down the sides, face and tail, from dark on the ridge to white on the chin, chest, stomach and under the tail. Legs to be same tone as the face. General effect to be much redder than Shell Cameo.

Black Smoke. Undercoat white, deeply tipped with black. Cat in repose appears black. Points and mask black with narrow band of white at the base of the hairs, which may be seen only when the fur is parted. Noseleather and paw pads black. Eyes brilliant gold.

Blue Smoke. Undercoat white, deeply tipped with blue. Cat in repose appears blue. Noseleather, paw pads blue. Eyes brilliant gold.

Cameo Smoke (Red Smoke). Undercoat white, deeply tipped with red. Cat in repose appears red. Noseleather, paw pads rose. Eyes brilliant gold.

Tortoiseshell Smoke. Undercoat white, deeply tipped with black, with clearly defined patches of red and cream tipped hairs in the tortoiseshell pattern. Cat in repose appears tortoiseshell. A facial blaze of red or cream tipping is desirable. Noseleather and paw pads brick red and /or black. Eyes brilliant gold.

Tortoiseshell. Black with unbrindled patches of red and cream, clearly defined and well broken on body, legs and tail. A facial blaze of red or cream desirable. Noseleather and paw pads brick red and/or black. Eyes brilliant gold.

Calico (Tortie-and-white). White with unbrindled patches of black and red. White predominant on the underparts. Noseleather and paw pads pink. Eyes brilliant gold.

Dilute Calico. White with unbrindled patches of blue and cream. White predominant on the underparts. Noseleather and paw pads pink. Eyes brilliant gold.

Blue-cream. Blue with patches of solid cream, clearly defined and well broken on body, legs and tail. Noseleather and paw pads blue and/or pink. Eyes brilliant gold.

Van Colours. Mostly white with colour on head, legs and tail. Noseleather and paw pads in keeping with the coloured patches or pink. Eyes should be brilliant gold colour.

Van Bicolour. Black, blue, red or cream patches on head, legs, and tail, white elsewhere.

Van Calico. Patches of black and red on head, legs and tail, white elsewhere.

Van Blue-cream. Patches of blue and cream on head, legs and tail.

Classic Tabby pattern. Markings dense and clearly defined from ground colour. Legs evenly barred. Tail evenly ringed. Several unbroken necklaces on neck and upper chest. Frown marks form letter 'M' on forehead. An unbroken line runs back from outer corner of eye. Swirls on cheeks. Vertical lines over back of head extend to shoulder markings that resemble a butterfly. Three parallel lines run down the spine from the butterfly to the tail, the three stripes well separated by the ground colour. Large solid blotch on each side should be encircled by one or more unbroken rings. Side markings symmetrical. Double row of 'buttons' on chest and stomach.

Mackerel Tabby pattern. Markings dense and clearly defined, and all narrow pencillings. Legs and tail evenly barred. Distinct necklaces on neck and upper chest. Forehead carries characteristic 'M'. Unbroken lines run backwards from the eyes. Lines run down the head to meet the shoulders. Spine lines run together to form a narrow saddle. Narrow pencillings run around the body.

Brown Tabby. Ground colour coppery brown. Markings dense black. Lips and chin and rings around eyes paler. Backs of legs black from paw to heel. Noseleather brick red. Paw pads black or brown. Eyes brilliant gold.

Red Tabby. Ground colour red. Markings deep rich red. Lips and chin red. Noseleather and paw pads brick red. Eyes brilliant gold.

Silver Tabby. Ground colour, lips and chin pale, clear silver. Markings dense black. Noseleather brick red. Paw pads black. Eyes green or hazel.

Blue Tabby. Ground colour, lips and chin pale bluish-ivory. Markings very deep blue. Noseleather and paw pads rose. Eyes brilliant gold.

Cream Tabby. Ground colour, lips and chin very pale cream. Markings buff-cream, sufficiently darker than ground colour to afford a good contrast, but not dark. Noseleather and paw pads rose. Eyes brilliant gold.

Cameo Tabby. Ground colour, lips and chin off white. Markings red. Noseleather and paw pads rose. Eyes brilliant gold.

Patched Tabby (Torbie). An established Silver, Brown or Blue classic or mackerel Tabby with patches of red and/or cream.

Shaded Silver American Shorthair

Silver Classic Tabby
American Shorthair

American
Shorthair

Blue-cream
American Shorthair

53

EXOTIC SHORTHAIR

Good points
- *Intelligent*
- *Quiet*
- *Even-tempered*
- *Playful but not destructive*
- *Responsive*
- *Sweet and loving*
- *Good with other animals and children*

Take heed
- *No known drawbacks*

If you like the docile nature of the Persian but do not have the time to groom a longhaired cat, this may be the breed for you. The Exotic Shorthair is really a hybrid breed, produced by crossing a Persian with an American Shorthair, and resulting in a 'Persian with short hair'. In looks it resembles a Persian, with its short, snub nose and wide cheeks, cobby body and short tail, yet it has a much more manageable coat. The Exotic also combines the best characteristics of both breeds, having a quiet, gentle nature and an even-tempered, sweet disposition, yet being alert, playful and responsive. It is not as destructive about the house as some of the more energetic breeds, and therefore makes an ideal pet, ever willing to please its owner.

Grooming
The Exotic Shorthair is easy to groom but the coat must be combed daily to remove dead hairs, so that too many are not swallowed and a hair ball formed in the stomach. The coat is short, but plush, so a medium-toothed comb would be best, with the occasional use of a rubber spiked brush for massage.

Origin and history
The Exotic Shorthair was deliberately developed to satisfy the desire of some breeders to have a Persian type cat with a short coat. The results have been good. At first, Persians were mated to both American Shorthairs and Burmese, but now the cross is restricted to American Shorthairs. From 1966, these hybrids became known as Exotic Shorthairs at American shows. Earlier American Shorthairs that approximated to the Exotic in type were allowed to be re-registered as Exotics, and to keep any wins they had already gained as American Shorthairs.

Being healthy, affectionate and easy to care for, they are becoming more and more popular, and are a joy to handle in the show ring.

Breeding
To be registered as Exotic Shorthair, a cat must have one parent Persian and the other American Shorthair or both Exotic Shorthair; all colours and patterns are allowed. The queens are robust and have healthy kittens, not prone to disease or weakness.

Kittens
Exotic kittens are playful but not too boisterous, and they love other animals and people. They respond well to gentle handling and lots of affection.

SHOW SUMMARY
In type the Exotic Shorthair should conform to the standard set for a Persian, but have a short, plush coat.
Coat. Medium in length, dense, soft, glossy and resilient. Not close-lying, but standing out from body.
Body. Medium to large in size, cobby and low on the legs. Deep in the chest, massive across the shoulders and rump, with a short, rounded middle. Back level. Legs short, thick and sturdy. Forelegs straight. Paws large, round and firm.
Tail. Short, thick, straight and carried low. Rounded at the tip. No kinks.
Head. Wide, round and massive, with a sweet expression. A round face on a short, thick neck. Short, broad snub nose with a nose break. Cheeks full and chin well developed. Ears small, set wide apart and low on the head, fitting into the curve of the head. The ears have rounded tips and tilt forward on the head. They are not unduly open at the base.
Eyes. Large, round, full and brilliant; set wide apart.

EXOTIC SHORTHAIR COLOURS
All colours and patterns within the American Shorthair and Persian are allowed including white, with blue, orange or odd eyes; black; blue; red; cream; chinchilla; shaded silver; chinchilla golden; shaded golden; shell cameo; shaded cameo; shell tortoiseshell; shaded tortoiseshell; black smoke; blue smoke; cameo smoke; smoke tortoiseshell; classic and mackerel tabby in silver, red, brown, blue, cream and cameo; patched tabby in brown, blue, and silver; tortoiseshell; calico; dilute calico; blue-cream; bicolour; van-bicolour; van-calico; van blue-cream and white.

Below: A Blue-cream Exotic Shorthair, a Persian type of cat but with a short, more manageable coat.

SCOTTISH FOLD

Good points
- *Great personality*
- *Gentle and sweet*
- *Sensible*
- *Loves people, including strangers*
- *Good with other animals and children*

Take heed
- *Cannot be shown in the United Kingdom*

A Scottish Fold is certainly distinctive in appearance as it wears its ears like a hat! But beauty is in the eye of the beholder and this breed has attracted criticism in some countries. The ear formation is a deformity and for this reason the Scottish Fold is not recognized for competition in the United Kingdom. However, the cat has its devotees, and is charming, sensible and good with other pets, children and strangers. It makes a good pet, does not seem to suffer any ill effects from its folded ears, and has plenty of personality.

In the United States the Scottish Fold has been bred specifically to preserve the distinctive ears, whereas in the United Kingdom the reverse is true and such features have been bred out.

Grooming
No special attention to the ears is necessary, except that they have to be kept clean. A weekly check of the teeth and a daily brush and comb will suffice to keep the coat looking neat and tidy.

Origin and history
The Scottish Fold appeared as a natural mutation from the British Shorthair in Scotland in a litter of farm cats in 1961. The first was a white cat, but the folded ear is not restricted to colour, and folds can have any coat colour or pattern. The *Universal Magazine of Knowledge and Pleasure,* published in China in 1796, refers to a cat with folded ears. They were also known in China in 1938, which shows that the gene responsible for producing folded ears has been present in the domestic cat population for at least 150 years.

Above: An Orange-eyed White Scottish Fold, popular in the USA.

Breeding
Folds mated to shorthaired domestics produce litters that contain 50 percent of kittens with normal (pricked) ears and 50 percent whose ears are folded downwards and forwards. Breeders recommend that Folds are mated only to normal-eared cats; Fold-to-Fold matings give rise to skeletal deformities. (cf Manx).

Kittens
The ears of Scottish Fold kittens may be only slightly folded, the definite forward folding not becoming fully apparent until they are about nine months old.

SHOW SUMMARY
The Scottish Fold is a cat of domestic shorthair type but with distinctive ears that are folded forwards and downwards.
Coat. Thick, short, dense and soft; resilient.
Body. Medium sized, short, rounded and cobby. The same width across the shoulders and rump. Full, broad chest. Powerful and compact build. Medium length legs with neat, round paws.
Tail. Medium in length, thick at the base. Kinks, broad, thick or short tails are faults.
Head. Massive and round. Well-rounded whisker pads. Short, thick neck; cheeks full, chin rounded, jaw broad. Ears wide apart and distinguished by a definite fold line, the front of the ear completely covering the ear opening. Small neat ears are preferred, rounded at the tips. Nose should be short and broad, with a gentle nose break.
Eyes. Large, round, set wide apart.

SCOTTISH FOLD COLOURS
Almost all colours and coat patterns are recognized, including: solid white, black, blue, red, cream; chinchilla, shaded silver, shell cameo, shaded cameo, black smoke, blue smoke, cameo smoke; tortoiseshell, calico, dilute calico, blue-cream; bicolour; classic and mackerel tabby patterns in silver, brown, blue, cream and cameo tabby. Eye colour should be in keeping with the coat colour.

*Blue Classic Tabby
Scottish Fold Kitten*

Scottish Fold

*Tortoiseshell-and-white
(Calico) Scottish Fold*

Exotic Shorthair

Shaded Cameo Exotic Shorthair

MANX

Good points
- *Unique appearance*
- *Intelligent and courageous*
- *Good with children and dogs*
- *Affectionate*
- *Good mouser*

Take heed
- *Does not like to be ignored*
- *Needs daily grooming*

The Manx, or 'rumpy' as it is sometimes called, is unique in appearance. It has no tail and because the hind legs are longer than the forelegs and the back is short, it has a rabbity look and gait, and a rounded rump. The Manx is similar to the Domestic Shorthair, but has a decided hollow where the tail should be; this does not affect its balance, however, and the powerful hind legs are capable of strong, high springs. It can also run very fast. It makes a good mouser and is able to catch its own supper in the local streams (don't count on it and not feed the cat!).

The Manx makes a loyal and affectionate pet, as it is curious, intelligent and amusing, and likes to be part of the family. It may resent being left out of things or being on its own. It would make an ideal office cat because it cannot get its tail caught in doors!

Grooming
With its short, thick undercoat and soft medium length top coat, the Manx will benefit from a daily grooming session with a medium-soft brush and a medium-toothed comb to remove the dead hairs and to keep the coat shining and healthy. The ears, eyes and teeth should have regular attention too.

Origin and history
Tail-less cats have been known for centuries. Charles Darwin reported seeing them frequently in Malaysia. They also occur in Russia and China. It is possible that they were brought to the Isle of Man by ships from the Far East. However they arrived, once there they were geographically isolated, and because there were few other domestic cats on the island, the tail-lessness was perpetuated, and the gene for tail-lessness spread among the island's cats. There is a book, written 200 years ago and now in the Manx Museum at Douglas, Isle of Man, which refers to the tail-less cats of the island. They were considered lucky and appeared on jewellery, in paintings and on coins.

A state cattery on the island is now breeding Manx cats with some success, and holidaymakers can buy them to take home as souvenirs; they are also being exported. The cats were first exported from the United Kingdom to the United States in the 1930s, and they have a considerable following. It is said that King Edward VIII owned a Manx cat when he was Prince of Wales. Supreme Adult Exhibit at the British Supreme Cat Show 1979

was a magnificent Black Manx male Grand Champion.

Breeding
Manx cats are difficult to breed because like to like tail-less does not necessarily produce tail-less kittens. In fact, tailed, tail-less and stumpy-tailed kittens may result, and continuous like-to-like Manx matings result in a lethal factor coming into play, with the majority of kittens dying either before or just after birth. The tail-less gene seems to be connected with other skeletal defects, and results in other vertebrae being fused together, giving deformed kittens with spina bifida. Frequent outcrossings to normal-tailed Shorthairs (UK) or to tailed Manx (US and UK) must be made.

Manx litters may contain the completely tail-less Manx or 'rumpy'; a 'riser', which has a very small number of vertebrae, usually immobile; a 'stubby', which has a short tail, often knobbly or kinked; and a 'longy', with a medium length tail. The show Manx must have a complete absence of tail, and, in fact, a hollow where the tail would have been. But many of the others make excellent pets and can be used for breeding with rumpies.

Kittens
Many kittens of other breeds seem to regard mother's tail as a built-in toy, but Manx kittens still seem to find plenty to play with.

SHOW SUMMARY
The principal feature of a show-standard Manx cat is the complete absence of any tail, and there should be a hollow in the rump where the tail would have been. It should also have the rounded, rabbity look of a short-backed cat, with hind legs longer than forelegs and a deep flank.
Coat. Short, glossy double coat. The undercoat is thick and cottony, the top coat longer, but not too long; soft and open.
Body. A solid cat with rounded rump, strong hindquarters, deep flanks, and a short back. The hind legs are longer than the forelegs, with muscular thighs. The back arches from shoulder to rump. The feet are neat and round.
Tail. Entirely missing, with a hollow where the tail would have been. A residual tail is a fault.
Head. Large and round with prominent cheeks. Short, thick neck and a strong chin. Nose medium long, with a gentle nose dip (USA) or no nose break (UK). There are rounded whisker pads and a definite whisker break. Ears large, wide at base, tapering to slightly pointed tips (UK), rounded tips (USA). Set on top of head.
Eyes. Large, round and expressive. Set at an angle to the nose; outer corners higher than inner corners.
Colour. All colours and coat patterns, or a combination of colours and coat patterns, are permitted, except (in the United States) the chocolate, lavender and Himalayan colours and patterns or these colours with white. Colour in

a Manx is a very secondary consideration after tail-lessness, shortness of back, depth of flank, and rounded rump. Eye colour should be in keeping with the coat colour. White Manx may be blue-eyed, orange-eyed, or odd-eyed (one blue, one orange).

JAPANESE BOBTAIL
(Mi-Ke cat)

Good points
- *Distinctive appearance*
- *Relatively non-shedding coat*
- *Intelligent and friendly*
- *Easy to groom*

Take heed
- *No drawbacks known*

As its name suggests, the rare Japanese Bobtail is native to Japan, where it is called the Mi-Ke (mee kay) cat. Its most distinctive feature is the short bobbed tail. It is intelligent, loyal and friendly, is said to love swimming and can retrieve like a dog. It is vocal without being noisy and has a large vocabulary of chirps and meows.

Characteristically, the Bobtail will stand with one front paw uplifted in welcome, and in fact the store windows and counters in Japan often display china models of this cat with its paw lifted to welcome shoppers and passers-by. Such cats are called Maneki-neko or welcoming cats. This cat is said to mix well with other cats but to seek out members of its own breed.

Grooming
The Japanese Bobtail is very easy to maintain in perfectly groomed condition as it has a non-shedding coat and there is no thick undercoat to get tangled up. A light brushing and combing with a medium-toothed comb and pure bristle brush will suffice.

Origin and history
The Japanese Bobtail is a natural breed, native to the Far East, notably to Japan, China and Korea. Such cats have appeared in Japanese prints and paintings for centuries and even decorate a temple in Tokyo, called the Gotokuji. The cats shown are numerous and all have one paw lifted in greeting. They were first imported into the United States in 1968 but are still a rare breed.

Breeding
The Bobtail gene is recessive, and therefore a Bobtail mated to an ordinary-tailed Domestic Shorthair produces only tailed kittens. Bobtail-to-Bobtail mating, however, produces 100 per cent bobtailed kittens. No outcrossing to other breeds is necessary or permitted. Bicoloured males are the best to produce the red, black and predominantly white females.

Kittens
Japanese Bobtail kittens are lively; usually four in a litter. There

is no lethal factor with Bobtails; they are usually very healthy.

SHOW SUMMARY
The Japanese Bobtail is a medium-sized cat, slender and shapely, with a distinctive bobbed tail and a decidedly Japanese set to the eyes.
Coats. Very soft and silky, single and not prone to shedding. Medium in length but shorter on the face, ears and paws. Longer and thicker on the tail than elsewhere, camouflaging the tail conformation.
Body. Medium in size, long and slender, but sturdy and well muscled. Not fragile or dainty, like some of the other Orientals, but not cobby either. Same width across the shoulders as the rump. Legs long and slender but not fragile or dainty. Hind legs longer than forelegs. Hind legs bent in stance when relaxed. One foreleg often raised. Paws oval.
Tail. The tail vertebrae are set at angles to each other and the furthest extension of the tail bone from the body should be approximately 5-7.5cm (2-3in), even though, if it could be straightened out to its full length, the tail might be 10-12.5cm (4-5in) long. The tail is normally carried upright when the cat is relaxed. The hair on the tail grows outwards in all directions producing a fluffy pom-pom effect, which camouflages the underlying bone structure.
Head. Forms an equilateral triangle, curving gently at the sides of the face. The high cheekbones give way to a distinct whisker break. The muzzle is broad and rounded, neither square nor pointed. The long nose dips gently at, or slightly below, eye level.
Eyes. Large and oval, slanted and wide apart, with an alert expression.
Colour. The preferred colour is the tricolour: black, red and white, with patches large and distinct and with white predominating. However, this is a female-only variety. Males are preferred that will give rise to this female colouring in the kittens. The only colours not allowed are the Himalayan pattern and the unpatterned agouti (Abyssinian). The more brilliant and bizarre the colours the better. White (pure glistening white), black (jet black free from rust), red (deep-rich and glowing), black-and-white, red-and-white, Mi-Ke (tricolour: black, red and white, or tortoiseshell-and-white), tortoiseshell (black, red and cream). Other Japanese Bobtail colours (known as OJBC on the show bench) include any other colour or pattern or combination thereof, with or without any other solid colour. Other solid colours include blue or cream. Patterned self colours: red, black, blue, cream, silver or brown. Other bicolours: blue-and-white and cream-and-white. Patterned bicolours: red, black, blue, cream, silver or brown combined with white. Patterned tortoiseshell. Blue-cream. Patterned blue-cream. Dilute tricolours: blue, cream and white. Patterned dilute tricolours. Patterned Mi-Ke (Tricolour).

Red Tabby-and-white Manx

Manx

Black Manx kitten

Mi-Ke (Tricolour)
Japanese Bobtail
and kitten

SIAMESE

Good points
- *Svelte and elegant*
- *Intelligent*
- *Smart and resourceful*
- *Companionable*
- *Good with children*
- *Takes readily to harness and lead*
- *Extrovert personality*

Take heed
- *Very demanding*
- *Very active*
- *Dislikes being left alone*
- *Dislikes being caged*
- *Likes to talk!*
- *Needs warmth*
- *Should be inoculated early in life*

Judging by the number appearing at shows, the Siamese is one of the most popular breeds. It is loving and lovable, enchanting and delightful, but also exasperating, demanding and very talkative. Some Siamese seem to talk, or rather shout, all day long, and a Siamese queen when calling may be particularly trying. Prospective owners should make sure that everyone in the family is going to enjoy this boisterous temperament before deciding on the Siamese.

A Siamese will enjoy walks on harness and lead, but unlike a dog, it will rarely walk to heel! With its very extrovert personality it loves performing tricks and playing games, but dislikes being ignored and is wary and jealous of strangers and other animals.

With its terrific personality and affectionate nature, the Siamese has a tremendous following and becomes more and more popular as a pet every year.

Grooming
Easy to groom, all a Siamese needs is a twice-weekly brushing and a combing with a fine- or medium-toothed comb to remove the dead hairs. A polish with a chamois leather together with lots of hand stroking will give a shine to the coat. If greasy, give the coat a bran bath before a show (See page 112.)

Health care
Siamese may be more prone than other cats to feline illnesses, and when ill need a great deal of attention and affection or they give up and die. To guard against illness, they should be inoculated as early as possible, between 8 and 12 weeks of age.

Spectacle marks around the eyes or white hairs in the points are signs of ill health or distress.

Origin and history
Siamese cats are believed to have existed in Siam (Thailand) for 200 years before they finally made their way to Europe and then America in the nineteenth century. They are certainly of Eastern origin, although their exact early history has unfortunately been lost. Two of the first to come to England were thought to have been a gift to the British Consul from the King of Siam, and they were shown at the Crystal Palace, London, in 1885. The first Siamese had round faces and darker coats than those seen today, tail kinks and eye squints also being permitted at the early shows. Such 'faults' have now been bred out, and the modern Siamese does not look much like its earlier counterpart.

Breeding
Siamese are prolific breeders, having two litters a year and an average of five to six kittens in a litter, although 11 and 13 have been recorded. Siamese make good mothers as a rule though those that are highly strung are unlikely to care for their kittens when the time comes. It is there-fore best not to use very nervous or bad-tempered cats for breeding.

Kittens
Siamese kittens develop early. They have individual personalities very soon after birth and are precocious and self-assured. When born they are all-white, the point colour developing only gradually. In the seal and blue points, a blob of colour appears on the nose after about 10 days, but it may be three months before the chocolate and lilac points become apparent. In all colours the points are often not fully developed until a year old.

Kittens should not be taken from their mothers until they are at least 12 weeks old. They need to be with their mothers to finish their education, and if left with them for at least part of the day until this age, they always seem to be more balanced as adults.

SHOW SUMMARY
The Siamese is a medium-sized cat, long, slim, lithe and muscular, with the characteristic Himalayan coat pattern of pale body colour and darker contrasting points.
Coat. Short, fine and close-lying with a natural sheen.
Body. Medium in size, dainty, long and svelte; fine boned but strong and muscular. Not fat or flabby. Hind legs slightly longer than forelegs. Paws small, neat, oval.
Tail. Whip-like, long, thin and tapering to a point. No kinks.
Head. Long, narrow, tapering wedge with flat width between the ears. Profile straight although there may be a slight change of angle above the nose. No decided nose break. Strong chin, jaws not undershot and no whisker break. Ears very large and pointed, open at the base.
Eyes. Almond-shaped, medium in size and slanted towards the nose. There should be the width of an eye between the eyes. No squints.

SIAMESE COLOURS
The first recorded Siamese cat was a Seal-point. The Blue-, Chocolate- and Lilac-points followed later. All appeared naturally within the breed, and are dilutions of the Seal-point, genetically. At present, these are the only colours recognized as Siamese in the United States (cf. page 60.)

Coat pattern. Body should be an even pale colour, with the main contrasting colour confined to the points (mask, ears, legs and tail). The mask should cover the whole face, but not the top of the head, and be connected to the ears by tracings (except in kittens). Apparently, paler coats are easier to achieve in warmer climates, and all Siamese coats darken with age.

Seal-point. Body colour an even warm cream, slightly darker on the back, lighter on the stomach and chest. Points deep seal brown. Noseleather and paw pads seal brown. Eyes deep vivid blue.

Chocolate-point. Body colour ivory all over. Points warm milk-chocolate colour. Noseleather and paw pads cinnamon pink. Eyes deep vivid blue.

Blue-point. Body colour glacial, bluish-white, shading to a warmer white on the chest and stomach. Points slate blue. Noseleather and paws pads slate blue. Eyes deep vivid blue.

Lilac-point. Body colour magnolia (UK) or glacial white (USA) all over. Points frosty grey with a pinkish tone (lilac). Noseleather and paw pads lavender-pink. Eyes deep vivid blue.

Below: Seal-point Siamese kittens in alert mood. Vivacious as kittens, Siamese make extrovert adults.

Red Tabby-and-white Manx

Manx

Black Manx kitten

Mi-Ke (Tricolour)
Japanese Bobtail
and kitten

Japanese Bobtail

SIAMESE

Good points
- *Svelte and elegant*
- *Intelligent*
- *Smart and resourceful*
- *Companionable*
- *Good with children*
- *Takes readily to harness and lead*
- *Extrovert personality*

Take heed
- *Very demanding*
- *Very active*
- *Dislikes being left alone*
- *Dislikes being caged*
- *Likes to talk!*
- *Needs warmth*
- *Should be inoculated early in life*

Judging by the number appearing at shows, the Siamese is one of the most popular breeds. It is loving and lovable, enchanting and delightful, but also exasperating, demanding and very talkative. Some Siamese seem to talk, or rather shout, all day long, and a Siamese queen when calling may be particularly trying. Prospective owners should make sure that everyone in the family is going to enjoy this boisterous temperament before deciding on the Siamese.

A Siamese will enjoy walks on harness and lead, but unlike a dog, it will rarely walk to heel! With its very extrovert personality it loves performing tricks and playing games, but dislikes being ignored and is wary and jealous of strangers and other animals.

With its terrific personality and affectionate nature, the Siamese has a tremendous following and becomes more and more popular as a pet every year.

Grooming
Easy to groom, all a Siamese needs is a twice-weekly brushing and a combing with a fine- or medium-toothed comb to remove the dead hairs. A polish with a chamois leather together with lots of hand stroking will give a shine to the coat. If greasy, give the coat a bran bath before a show (See page 112.)

Health care
Siamese may be more prone than other cats to feline illnesses, and when ill need a great deal of attention and affection or they give up and die. To guard against illness, they should be inoculated as early as possible, between 8 and 12 weeks of age.

Spectacle marks around the eyes or white hairs in the points are signs of ill health or distress.

Origin and history
Siamese cats are believed to have existed in Siam (Thailand) for 200 years before they finally made their way to Europe and then America in the nineteenth century. They are certainly of Eastern origin, although their exact early history has unfortunately been lost. Two of the first to come to England were thought to have been a gift to the British Consul from the King of Siam, and they were shown at the Crystal Palace, London, in 1885. The first Siamese had round faces and darker coats than those seen today, tail kinks and eye squints also being permitted at the early shows. Such 'faults' have now been bred out, and the modern Siamese does not look much like its earlier counterpart.

Breeding
Siamese are prolific breeders, having two litters a year and an average of five to six kittens in a litter, although 11 and 13 have been recorded. Siamese make good mothers as a rule though those that are highly strung are unlikely to care for their kittens when the time comes. It is therefore best not to use very nervous or bad-tempered cats for breeding.

Kittens
Siamese kittens develop early. They have individual personalities very soon after birth and are precocious and self-assured. When born they are all-white, the point colour developing only gradually. In the seal and blue points, a blob of colour appears on the nose after about 10 days, but it may be three months before the chocolate and lilac points become apparent. In all colours the points are often not fully developed until a year old.

Kittens should not be taken from their mothers until they are at least 12 weeks old. They need to be with their mothers to finish their education, and if left with them for at least part of the day until this age, they always seem to be more balanced as adults.

SHOW SUMMARY
The Siamese is a medium-sized cat, long, slim, lithe and muscular, with the characteristic Himalayan coat pattern of pale body colour and darker contrasting points.
Coat. Short, fine and close-lying with a natural sheen.
Body. Medium in size, dainty, long and svelte; fine boned but strong and muscular. Not fat or flabby. Hind legs slightly longer than forelegs. Paws small, neat, oval.
Tail. Whip-like, long, thin and tapering to a point. No kinks.
Head. Long, narrow, tapering wedge with flat width between the ears. Profile straight although there may be a slight change of angle above the nose. No decided nose break. Strong chin, jaws not undershot and no whisker break. Ears very large and pointed, open at the base.
Eyes. Almond-shaped, medium in size and slanted towards the nose. There should be the width of an eye between the eyes. No squints.

SIAMESE COLOURS
The first recorded Siamese cat was a Seal-point. The Blue-, Chocolate- and Lilac-points followed later. All appeared naturally within the breed, and are dilutions of the Seal-point, genetically. At present, these are the only colours recognized as Siamese in the United States (cf. page 60.)

Coat pattern. Body should be an even pale colour, with the main contrasting colour confined to the points (mask, ears, legs and tail). The mask should cover the whole face, but not the top of the head, and be connected to the ears by tracings (except in kittens). Apparently, paler coats are easier to achieve in warmer climates, and all Siamese coats darken with age.

Seal-point. Body colour an even warm cream, slightly darker on the back, lighter on the stomach and chest. Points deep seal brown. Noseleather and paw pads seal brown. Eyes deep vivid blue.

Chocolate-point. Body colour ivory all over. Points warm milk-chocolate colour. Noseleather and paw pads cinnamon pink. Eyes deep vivid blue.

Blue-point. Body colour glacial, bluish-white, shading to a warmer white on the chest and stomach. Points slate blue. Noseleather and paws pads slate blue. Eyes deep vivid blue.

Lilac-point. Body colour magnolia (UK) or glacial white (USA) all over. Points frosty grey with a pinkish tone (lilac). Noseleather and paw pads lavender-pink. Eyes deep vivid blue.

Below: Seal-point Siamese kittens in alert mood. Vivacious as kittens, Siamese make extrovert adults.

*Blue Classic Tabby
Scottish Fold Kitten*

Scottish Fold

*Tortoiseshell-and-white
(Calico) Scottish Fold*

Exotic Shorthair

Shaded Cameo Exotic Shorthair

MANX

Good points
- *Unique appearance*
- *Intelligent and courageous*
- *Good with children and dogs*
- *Affectionate*
- *Good mouser*

Take heed
- *Does not like to be ignored*
- *Needs daily grooming*

The Manx, or 'rumpy' as it is sometimes called, is unique in appearance. It has no tail and because the hind legs are longer than the forelegs and the back is short, it has a rabbity look and gait, and a rounded rump. The Manx is similar to the Domestic Shorthair, but has a decided hollow where the tail should be; this does not affect its balance, however, and the powerful hind legs are capable of strong, high springs. It can also run very fast. It makes a good mouser and is able to catch its own supper in the local streams (don't count on it and not feed the cat!).

The Manx makes a loyal and affectionate pet, as it is curious, intelligent and amusing, and likes to be part of the family. It may resent being left out of things or being on its own. It would make an ideal office cat because it cannot get its tail caught in doors!

Grooming
With its short, thick undercoat and soft medium length top coat, the Manx will benefit from a daily grooming session with a medium-soft brush and a medium-toothed comb to remove the dead hairs and to keep the coat shining and healthy. The ears, eyes and teeth should have regular attention too.

Origin and history
Tail-less cats have been known for centuries. Charles Darwin reported seeing them frequently in Malaysia. They also occur in Russia and China. It is possible that they were brought to the Isle of Man by ships from the Far East. However they arrived, once there they were geographically isolated, and because there were few other domestic cats on the island, the tail-lessness was perpetuated, and the gene for tail-lessness spread among the island's cats. There is a book, written 200 years ago and now in the Manx Museum at Douglas, Isle of Man, which refers to the tail-less cats of the island. They were considered lucky and appeared on jewellery, in paintings and on coins.

A state cattery on the island is now breeding Manx cats with some success, and holidaymakers can buy them to take home as souvenirs; they are also being exported. The cats were first exported from the United Kingdom to the United States in the 1930s, and they have a considerable following. It is said that King Edward VIII owned a Manx cat when he was Prince of Wales. Supreme Adult Exhibit at the British Supreme Cat Show 1979

was a magnificent Black Manx male Grand Champion.

Breeding
Manx cats are difficult to breed because like to like tail-less does not necessarily produce tail-less kittens. In fact, tailed, tail-less and stumpy-tailed kittens may result, and continuous like-to-like Manx matings result in a lethal factor coming into play, with the majority of kittens dying either before or just after birth. The tail-less gene seems to be connected with other skeletal defects, and results in other vertebrae being fused together, giving deformed kittens with spina bifida. Frequent outcrossings to normal-tailed Shorthairs (UK) or to tailed Manx (US and UK) must be made.

Manx litters may contain the completely tail-less Manx or 'rumpy'; a 'riser', which has a very small number of vertebrae, usually immobile; a 'stubby', which has a short tail, often knobbly or kinked; and a 'longy', with a medium length tail. The show Manx must have a complete absence of tail, and, in fact, a hollow where the tail would have been. But many of the others make excellent pets and can be used for breeding with rumpies.

Kittens
Many kittens of other breeds seem to regard mother's tail as a built-in toy, but Manx kittens still seem to find plenty to play with.

SHOW SUMMARY
The principal feature of a show-standard Manx cat is the complete absence of any tail, and there should be a hollow in the rump where the tail would have been. It should also have the rounded, rabbity look of a short-backed cat, with hind legs longer than forelegs and a deep flank.
Coat. Short, glossy double coat. The undercoat is thick and cottony, the top coat longer, but not too long; soft and open.
Body. A solid cat with rounded rump, strong hindquarters, deep flanks, and a short back. The hind legs are longer than the forelegs, with muscular thighs. The back arches from shoulder to rump. The feet are neat and round.
Tail. Entirely missing, with a hollow where the tail would have been. A residual tail is a fault.
Head. Large and round with prominent cheeks. Short, thick neck and a strong chin. Nose medium long, with a gentle nose dip (USA) or no nose break (UK). There are rounded whisker pads and a definite whisker break. Ears large, wide at base, tapering to slightly pointed tips (UK), rounded tips (USA). Set on top of head.
Eyes. Large, round and expressive. Set at an angle to the nose; outer corners higher than inner corners.
Colour. All colours and coat patterns, or a combination of colours and coat patterns, are permitted, except (in the United States) the chocolate, lavender and Himalayan colours and patterns or these colours with white. Colour in

a Manx is a very secondary consideration after tail-lessness, shortness of back, depth of flank, and rounded rump. Eye colour should be in keeping with the coat colour. White Manx may be blue-eyed, orange-eyed, or odd-eyed (one blue, one orange).

JAPANESE BOBTAIL
(Mi-Ke cat)

Good points
- *Distinctive appearance*
- *Relatively non-shedding coat*
- *Intelligent and friendly*
- *Easy to groom*

Take heed
- *No drawbacks known*

As its name suggests, the rare Japanese Bobtail is native to Japan, where it is called the Mi-Ke (mee kay) cat. Its most distinctive feature is the short bobbed tail. It is intelligent, loyal and friendly, is said to love swimming and can retrieve like a dog. It is vocal without being noisy and has a large vocabulary of chirps and meows.

Characteristically, the Bobtail will stand with one front paw uplifted in welcome, and in fact the store windows and counters in Japan often display china models of this cat with its paw lifted to welcome shoppers and passers-by. Such cats are called Maneki-neko or welcoming cats. This cat is said to mix well with other cats but to seek out members of its own breed.

Grooming
The Japanese Bobtail is very easy to maintain in perfectly groomed condition as it has a non-shedding coat and there is no thick undercoat to get tangled up. A light brushing and combing with a medium-toothed comb and pure bristle brush will suffice.

Origin and history
The Japanese Bobtail is a natural breed, native to the Far East, notably to Japan, China and Korea. Such cats have appeared in Japanese prints and paintings for centuries and even decorate a temple in Tokyo, called the Gotokuji. The cats shown are numerous and all have one paw lifted in greeting. They were first imported into the United States in 1968 but are still a rare breed.

Breeding
The Bobtail gene is recessive, and therefore a Bobtail mated to an ordinary-tailed Domestic Shorthair produces only tailed kittens. Bobtail-to-Bobtail mating, however, produces 100 per cent bobtailed kittens. No outcrossing to other breeds is necessary or permitted. Bicoloured males are the best to produce the red, black and predominantly white females.

Kittens
Japanese Bobtail kittens are lively; usually four in a litter. There

is no lethal factor with Bobtails; they are usually very healthy.

SHOW SUMMARY
The Japanese Bobtail is a medium-sized cat, slender and shapely, with a distinctive bobbed tail and a decidedly Japanese set to the eyes.
Coats. Very soft and silky, single and not prone to shedding. Medium in length but shorter on the face, ears and paws. Longer and thicker on the tail than elsewhere, camouflaging the tail conformation.
Body. Medium in size, long and slender, but sturdy and well muscled. Not fragile or dainty, like some of the other Orientals, but not cobby either. Same width across the shoulders as the rump. Legs long and slender but not fragile or dainty. Hind legs longer than forelegs. Hind legs bent in stance when relaxed. One foreleg often raised. Paws oval.
Tail. The tail vertebrae are set at angles to each other and the furthest extension of the tail bone from the body should be approximately 5-7.5cm (2-3in), even though, if it could be straightened out to its full length, the tail might be 10-12.5cm (4-5in) long. The tail is normally carried upright when the cat is relaxed. The hair on the tail grows outwards in all directions producing a fluffy pom-pom effect, which camouflages the underlying bone structure.
Head. Forms an equilateral triangle, curving gently at the sides of the face. The high cheekbones give way to a distinct whisker break. The muzzle is broad and rounded, neither square nor pointed. The long nose dips gently at, or slightly below, eye level.
Eyes. Large and oval, slanted and wide apart, with an alert expression.
Colour. The preferred colour is the tricolour: black, red and white, with patches large and distinct and with white predominating. However, this is a female-only variety. Males are preferred that will give rise to this female colouring in the kittens. The only colours not allowed are the Himalayan pattern and the unpatterned agouti (Abyssinian). The more brilliant and bizarre the colours the better. White (pure glistening white), black (jet black free from rust), red (deep-rich and glowing), black-and-white, red-and-white, Mi-Ke (tricolour: black, red and white, or tortoiseshell-and-white), tortoiseshell (black, red and cream). Other Japanese Bobtail colours (known as OJBC on the show bench) include any other colour or pattern or combination thereof, with or without any other solid colour. Other solid colours include blue or cream. Patterned self colours: red, black, blue, cream, silver or brown. Other bicolours: blue-and-white and cream-and-white. Patterned bicolours: red, black, blue, cream, silver or brown combined with white. Patterned tortoiseshell. Blue-cream. Patterned blue-cream. Dilute tricolours: blue, cream and white. Patterned dilute tricolours. Patterned Mi-Ke (Tricolour).

Siamese

Seal-point Siamese

Lilac-point
Siamese kitten

Chocolate-point Siamese

Blue-point
Siamese kitten

COLOURPOINT SHORTHAIR

Basically this is a Siamese cat with point colours others than seal, chocolate, blue or lilac. Other colours have been obtained by outcrossing of Siamese to short-haired cats (British and American Shorthairs) of the required colours in order to introduce these colours into the points of the Siamese.

Although regarded as Siamese in most countries, and having the same temperament and type, because of the crossbreeding involved in their production, they are classified as Colorpoint Short-hairs in the United States. The colours recognized include red, cream and tortoiseshell points, and tabby (lynx) points in all recognized point colours.

SHOW SUMMARY

Coat pattern. Body should be an even pale colour, with the main contrasting colour confined to the points (mask, ears, legs and tail). The mask should cover the whole face, but not the top of the head, and be connected to the ears by tracings (except in kittens).

Red-point. Body clear white with any shading in the same tone as the points. Points bright apricot to deep red, deeper shades preferred, without barring. Nose-leather and paw pads flesh or coral pink. Eyes deep vivid blue.

Cream-point. Body clear white with any shading in the same tone as the points. Points pale buff-cream to light pinkish cream without barring. Noseleather and paw pads flesh to coral. Eyes deep vivid blue.

Seal Tortie-point. Body pale fawn to cream, shading to lighter colour on the stomach and chest. Points seal brown, uniformly mottled with red and cream. A blaze is desirable. Noseleather seal brown or flesh pink where there is a blaze. Paw pads seal brown or flesh pink. Eyes deep vivid blue.

Chocolate Tortie-point. Body ivory. Points warm milk-chocolate uni-formly mottled with red and/or cream; a blaze is desirable. Nose-leather and paw pads cinnamon or flesh pink. Eyes deep vivid blue.

Blue-cream-point. Body bluish

white to platinum grey, cold in tone shading to lighter colour on the stomach and chest. Points deep blue-grey uniformly mottled with cream; a blaze is desirable. Nose-leather and paw pads slate or flesh pink. Eyes deep vivid blue.

Lilac-cream-point. Body glacial white. Points frosty grey with pinkish tone, uniformly mottled with pale cream; a facial blaze is desirable. Noseleather and paw pads lavender-pink or flesh pink. Eyes deep vivid blue.

Seal Tabby-point. Body cream or pale fawn, shading to lighter colour on the stomach and chest. Body shading may take the form of ghost striping. Points seal brown bars, distinct and separated by lighter background colour. Ears seal brown with paler thumbprint in the centre. Noseleather seal brown or pink edged in seal brown. Paw pads seal brown. Eyes deep vivid blue.

Chocolate Tabby-point. Body ivory, body shading may take the form of ghost striping. Points warm milk-chocolate bars, distinct and separated by lighter background colour. Ears warm milk-chocolate with paler thumbprint in centre. Noseleather cinnamon-pink or pink edged in cinnamon. Paw pads cinnamon. Eyes deep vivid blue.

Blue Tabby-point. Body bluish white to platinum grey, cold in tone, shading to lighter colour on the stomach and chest. Body shading may take the form of ghost striping. Points deep blue-grey bars, distinct and separated by lighter background colour; ears deep blue-grey with paler thumbprint in centre. Noseleather slate or pink edged in slate. Paw pads slate. Eyes deep vivid blue.

Lilac Tabby-point. Body glacial white, body shading may take the form of ghost striping. Points frosty grey with pinkish tone bars distinct and separated by lighter back-ground colour. Ears frosty grey with pinkish tone. Paler thumbprint in centre. Noseleather lavender-pink or pink edged in lavender. Paw pads lavender-pink. Eyes deep vivid blue.

Below: A fine example of a Seal Tortie-point Colourpoint Shorthair.

Red Tabby-point. Body white, body shading may take the form of ghost striping. Points deep red bars, distinct and separated by lighter background colour. Ears deep red, paler thumbprint in centre. Noseleather and paw pads flesh or coral. Eyes deep vivid blue.

Cream Tabby-point. Body white, shading to palest cream on the back. Points deeper buff-cream bars on white background. Ears cream with paler thumbprint in centre. Noseleather and paw pads pink. Eyes deep vivid blue.

Torbie-point. Colours and point markings as for Tabby-points, with patches of red and/or cream, irregularly distributed over the tabby pattern on the points. Red and/or cream mottling on the ears and tail permissible. Noseleather and paw pads as appropriate to the basic point colour or mottled with pink. Eyes deep vivid blue.

SNOWSHOE

Good points
● *Striking appearance*
● *Good natured*
● *Easy to groom*
● *Good with children*

Take heed
● *Vocal*

The Snowshoe is a hybrid breed produced by mating Siamese with bicolour American Shorthairs, and it therefore has the characteristics of both. It is not usually as noisy as a Siamese, but is not as quiet as most shorthaired cats. It is calm but alert and makes an ideal pet, although it should not be left alone for long periods.

Because of its origin, the Snow-shoe has a modified Oriental body type, usually larger and heavier than a Siamese with less extreme features. It has a rounder head and a distinct nose break, which distin-guishes it from other Siamese-derived breeds.

Grooming
Being shorthaired, the Snowshoe needs the minimum of grooming with a brush or comb to remove dead hairs. Plus hand stroking.

Origin and history
The Snowshoe is one of the newer breeds and rather like a short-haired Birman in appearance, having the Himalayan coat pattern with white feet but, unlike the Birman, it has a white muzzle, too.

There are many unregistered Snowshoes about as a result of Siamese queens mating with local bicoloured alley cats! However, the variety was considered to be so attractive that its devotees are selectively breeding these cats in the United States and a show standard is being developed.

At present only Seal-and-white and Blue-and-white are being bred, although there is no reason why the other Siamese point colours should not be available in the Snowshoe in due course.

Breeding
Any solid colour Himalayan pat-terned cat without white that results from the breeding of Snowshoe with Snowshoe or Snowshoe with Siamese can be used for breeding, although it would not be eligible for competition. In this way it is hoped to build up foundation stock.

Kittens
Snowshoe kittens are lively and healthy and respond to affection. There may be three to seven in a litter. Many kittens that do not have the correct markings will be available from early matings at a reasonable price and will make excellent pets, although they cannot be shown.

SHOW SUMMARY
The Snowshoe is a modified Oriental-type shorthaired cat with white and coloured points.
Coat. Medium coarse in texture, short, glossy and close lying.
Body. Medium to large, well muscled and powerful. Long back; heavy build; males larger than females. Sleek, dainty, Oriental type is a fault. Legs long and solid with well rounded paws.
Tail. Medium in length, thick at the base, tapering slightly to the tip. Whip or very long tail is a fault.
Head. Triangular wedge of medium width and length. Obvious nose break. Round or long Siamese-like head is a fault. Neck medium in length, not thin. Ears large, alert and pointed, broad at the base. Small or over-large ears are faults.
Eyes. Large and almond-shaped, slanted upwards from nose to ear.

SNOWSHOE COLOURS
Coat pattern. The mask, ears, legs and tail should be clearly defined from the body colour, and of the same depth of colour. The mask covers the whole face and is con-nected to the ears by tracings. Slightly darker shading of the body colour is allowed across the shoulders, back and top of the hips. Chest and stomach are paler. Forefeet should be white, symmetrical with the white ending in an even line around the ankle. Hind feet should be white, with symmetrical white marking extending up the leg to the heel. Muzzle should be white; the nose may be white or of the point colour. There should be no other white hairs or patches.

Seal-point. Body colour an even fawn, warm in tone, shading gradually to a lighter tone on the stomach and chest. Points, except feet and muzzle, deep seal brown. Noseleather pink if nose is white or black if nose is seal. Paw pads pink or seal or a combination of the two. Eyes deep vivid blue.

Blue-point. Body colour an even bluish white, shading gradually to a lighter colour on the chest and stomach. Points, except feet and muzzle, a deep greyish blue. Nose-leather pink if nose is white, or slate grey if nose is blue. Paw pads pink and/or grey. Eyes vivid blue.

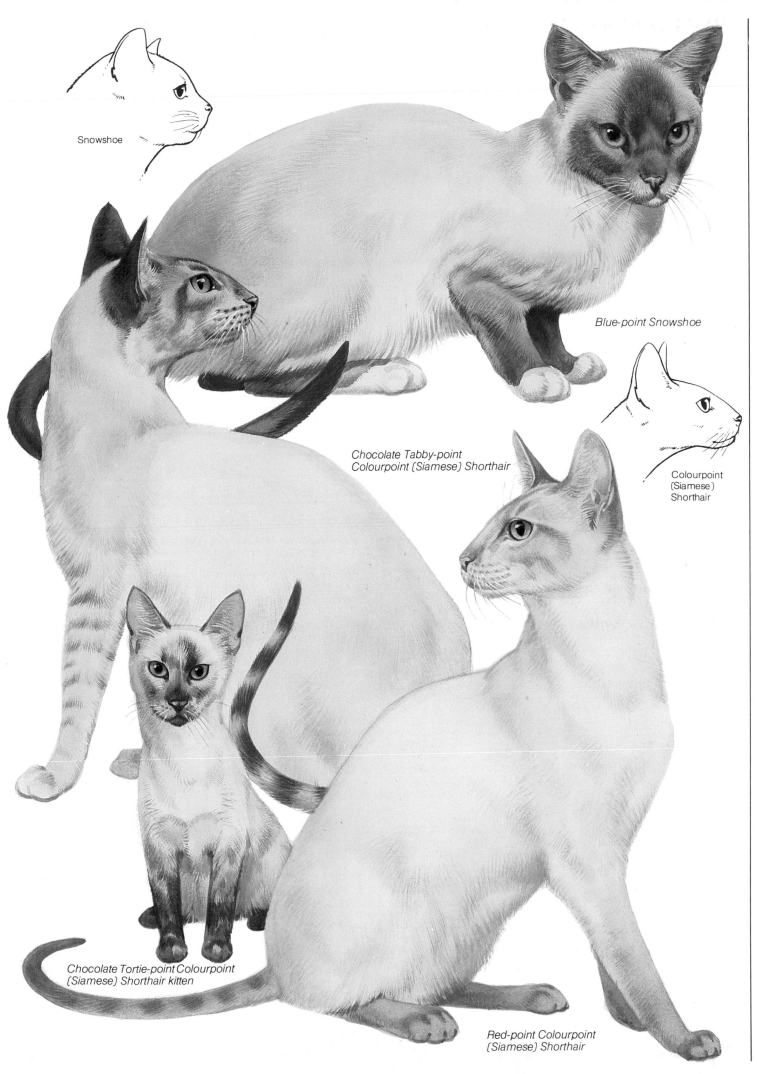

Snowshoe

Blue-point Snowshoe

Chocolate Tabby-point
Colourpoint (Siamese) Shorthair

Colourpoint
(Siamese)
Shorthair

Chocolate Tortie-point Colourpoint
(Siamese) Shorthair kitten

Red-point Colourpoint
(Siamese) Shorthair

HAVANA BROWN

Good points
- *Attractive*
- *Agile*
- *Intelligent*
- *Active*
- *Hardy*
- *Playful*
- *Affectionate*

Take heed
- *Needs human companionship*

The American Havana Brown is a very active and highly intelligent cat. It loves people and needs human companionship and affection. It loves to play and hunt and partake in lots of other activities with the family. It is gentle by nature and makes a hardy, attractive pet.

Grooming
The medium length hair is easy to groom. A daily comb using a fine-toothed comb and a polish with a chamois leather before a show is all that is required.

Origin and history
Named Havana after its similarity in coat colour to the tobacco of a Havana cigar, the American Havana Brown has developed differently from the British (European) Havana (Self-brown Oriental Shorthair) although both had the same origins. Both were developed from a Seal-point Siamese mated to a domestic shorthair, but whereas the British Havanas were thereafter bred back to Siamese to preserve the oriental type, the American Havanas were not allowed to mate back to Siamese. Thus a less oriental, more rounded type has developed in the United States. In fact, the American Oriental self-brown is almost the equivalent of the British Havana.

Breeding
Havana queens call loudly, clearly and frequently. They usually have four to six kittens in a litter and make good mothers. (American breeders no longer mate Havanas back to Siamese; they do not wish to perpetuate the Oriental type.)

Kittens
The kittens are very playful and agile. They are born the same colour as their parents, but their coats are a rather dull brown, and do not have the gloss of the adults. The white hairs found frequently in the kitten coat disappear when the adult coat is grown.

SHOW SUMMARY
The overall impression of the Havana Brown is of a medium-sized cat, of rich, solid colour, with firm muscle tone.
Coat. Medium in length, smooth and lustrous.
Body. Medium-sized, well muscled; medium length neck. Medium length legs; oval paws.
Tail. Medium length, tapering to a point; no kinks.

Head. Slightly longer than wide. Distinct nose break and whisker break. Chin strong. Ears large and tilted forward, with rounded tips.
Eyes. Oval; no squints.
Colour. Rich solid mahogany brown all over, solid from tip to root with no tabby markings and no white patches. Noseleather and paw pads rosy pink. Eyes pale to mid green.

ORIENTAL SHORTHAIR

Good points
- *Attractive*
- *Affectionate*
- *Active and intelligent*
- *Good with children and dogs*
- *Easy to groom*

Take heed
- *Great escapologist*
- *Needs a lot of exercise*
- *Needs companionship*
- *Needs warmth*
- *Must be inoculated early in life*

This long-legged, sleek, svelte cat is the tomboy of the feline world. Always into everything, with its boundless energy, it will take an intelligent interest in all the family's activities and loves being taken for walks with the dogs, on or off a harness and lead. But, unlike a dog, it cannot be relied upon to obey every command or to walk to heel, particularly if something more interesting takes its attention! Because the Oriental Shorthair is energetic and has an inquisitive nature, it may be inclined to stray from home. Consequently, in towns it may be necessary to impose some restriction on its freedom for its own safety. A wired-in run, as large as you can afford, leading from a room in the house if possible, is ideal for use during the day, but it must have a range of shelves at different heights.

Since this cat may become morose if left alone for long periods, it is a good idea to have more than one, or another domestic pet for companionship. With its need for company met, the Oriental Shorthair makes the most charming and affectionate pet.

Grooming
A daily comb to remove dead hairs and a rub with a chamois leather or silk cloth is all that is required, plus plenty of hand stroking to burnish the coat. The ears and teeth should be checked regularly.

Health care
Since the Oriental Shorthair is more susceptible than some breeds to feline illnesses, it is advisable to have the kittens inoculated before they are two months old.

Origin and history
The original Oriental Shorthaired cats came from arranged matings between Siamese (for type) and other shorthaired cats (for colour). Later, Siamese were mated to longhaired Chinchillas to produce Oriental cats with tipped coats and this unusual mating combination opened up the field for all kinds of possibilities in the colour range, including new solid colours (caramel, apricot and beige), tipped tabbies, torbies (patched tabbies) and shaded, tipped and smoke tortoiseshells.

In the United Kingdom, the self or solid coloured cats are known as Foreign Shorthairs, although this name is gradually being replaced by Oriental. The tabby and other varieties are already known as Oriental Shorthairs, and in the United States, all cats of this type are known as Oriental Shorthairs. These foreign breeds had their first all foreign show in the United Kingdom in July 1979.

Breeding
Oriental queens are very prolific and can have two litters per year, often of five or six kittens each.

Kittens
The kittens are born the same colour as the adults from birth (unlike the Siamese from which they were originally derived, and whose kittens are paler at birth).

SHOW SUMMARY
Oriental Shorthairs are Siamese in type with long, svelte, lithe and muscular bodies, and long, thin tapering tails.
Coat. Short, fine, glossy and close lying.
Body. Medium-sized, long, svelte and muscular. Fine boned. Shoulders and hindquarters same width. Legs long and slim; hind legs longer than forelegs. Paws small, dainty and oval.
Tail. Long and tapering to a point, thin at the base. No kinks.
Head. Long wedge with no whisker break and no nose break. Flat skull; fine muzzle; strong chin. Neck long and slender. Ears large and pointed, wide at the base.
Eyes. Clear, almond shaped, medium in size, slanted towards the nose. No squints.

ORIENTAL SHORTHAIR COLOURS
Scientific breeding programmes have produced an exceptionally varied selection of colours and patterns within this breed.

ORIENTAL SELF BROWN
(Havana UK, Chestnut-brown Foreign)

The first all-brown shorthaired cat was exhibited in England in 1894 and called the Swiss Mountain Cat. It was believed to be a cross between a black Domestic Shorthair and a Seal-point Siamese that had resulted from an accidental mating, and the line was not perpetuated. The type, now known in the United Kingdom as Havana, was first bred in the 1950s and was the result of a planned mating between a Chocolate-point Siamese and a Domestic Shorthair of Oriental type. The name has been subject to much alteration: originally called Havana because of the likeness of the colour to Havana tobacco, the variety was actually first registered as Chestnut-brown Foreign. Exported to the United States, these cats then became Havana Browns, and in 1970 the British and European governing bodies also re-adopted the name Havana. This has caused some confusion, because the variety developed quite differently on either side of the Atlantic. In the United Kingdom and Europe the Oriental type was encouraged and the cats were outcrossed to Siamese. The American Havana Brown is a cat of less extreme type, and outcrossing to Siamese is not permitted.

SHOW SUMMARY
Coat should be a rich warm chestnut brown, the same colour from root to tip. Tabby or other markings, white hairs or patches are faults. Noseleather brown. Paw pads pinkish brown. Eyes green.

ORIENTAL LILAC
(Oriental Lavender; Foreign Lilac)

These cats were developed in the United Kingdom in the 1960s, during the Havana breeding programme. Mating two Self-browns (Havanas) will give rise to Lilac kittens if the parents were produced from a cross between a Russian Blue and a Seal-point Siamese. Soon, however, there will be sufficient Lilac studs for outcrosses to be unnecessary.

SHOW SUMMARY
The Oriental Lilac should have a pinkish grey coat, with a frosty grey tone: neither too blue nor too fawn. White hairs or patches, or tabby markings are faults. Noseleather, paw pads lavender. Eyes rich green.

ORIENTAL CINNAMON

Originally developed from a Seal-point Siamese carrying factors for chocolate mated to a red Abyssinian. It is a lighter colour

Above: An Oriental (Foreign) Cinnamon, a striking new variety.

Havana Brown (UK)
and Oriental Shorthair

Lilac Oriental (Foreign) Shorthair

Havana
Brown (US)

Havana Brown (UK)
Oriental Shorthair

Havana Brown (US)

than the Havana, but similar, and is becoming popular in the United States and Europe.

SHOW SUMMARY
Coat colour should be a warm milk chocolate brown throughout, sound from root to tip. No white hairs or tabby markings. Eyes green.

ORIENTAL WHITE (Foreign White)

One of the most striking varieties, Oriental White cats look like porcelain with their smooth white coats and china blue eyes. They were developed in the 1960s and 1970s by mating white Domestic Shorthairs to Siamese. As the white coat is dominant genetically to other coat colours, it obscured the Himalayan (point restricted) coat pattern. Later, the Oriental Whites were outcrossed again to Siamese to improve the eye colour. In the early stages, green-, yellow- and odd-eyed kittens were born. Now blue is the preferred eye colour and selectively bred, Blue-eyed White Oriental Shorthairs are not deaf.

SHOW SUMMARY
Coat should be pure white throughout with no black hairs. Noseleather pale pink. Paw pads dark pink. Eyes brilliant sapphire or china blue (UK); green or blue (USA); odd eyes not allowed on the show bench.

ORIENTAL EBONY (Foreign Black)

A dramatic combination of a long, svelte, jet black cat with emerald green eyes and an alert, intelligent expression.

Interest in the Black Oriental Shorthair began in the 1970s, although previously many had been bred either experimentally or accidentally, but had been sold as pets, as there was no official show standard for them.

They were originally obtained from mating Self-browns (Havanas) to Seal-point Siamese, but today as there are sufficient Oriental Black studs available, back crossing to Siamese is no longer necessary.

SHOW SUMMARY
Coat should be raven black all over from root to tip. A rusty tinge to the fur is considered a fault. Noseleather black. Paw pads black or brown. Eyes emerald green.

ORIENTAL BLUE (Foreign Blue)

Oriental-type blue cats have appeared from time to time in Siamese breeding programmes, but little notice was taken of them because of the other rather similar 'foreign' blue cats already estab-lished (Russian Blue and Blue Burmese). However, they appear naturally in litters of Self-browns (Havanas) and Lilacs, and they are now beginning to appear on the show bench.

SHOW SUMMARY
Coat should be a light to medium blue all over, sound from root to tip. A lighter shade of blue is preferred in the United States. White hairs or patches, especially on the chin and stomach, are faults. Noseleather and paw pads blue. Eyes green.

ORIENTAL RED (Foreign Red)

These cats were developed from the Red-point Siamese breeding programme, at a time when Red Tabby British Shorthairs were being mated to Siamese to introduce the red colour into the Oriental type. They were a natural product of these matings, but today are obtained by mating Oriental Blacks to Red-point Siamese. Oriental Reds are difficult to breed without tabby markings, so it is best to use breeding stock without any tabby ancestry, or markings may persist into adulthood. It would now be possible to use Red Burmese as Burmese breeders have succeeded in eradicating the markings in the coat of the Red Burmese. However, only British-type Burmese should be used as the American Burmese is rather more cobby.

SHOW SUMMARY
Coat should be a rich, deep, clear and brilliant red without shading or markings. Lips and chin red. Noseleather and paw pads brick red. Eyes copper to green; green preferred.

ORIENTAL CREAM (Foreign Cream)

The Oriental Creams were a by-product of the breeding programme used to produce Oriental Blue and Lilac Tortoise-shells. In these programmes, Domestic (British) Shorthaired Tortoiseshells were mated to Siamese and all the solid colours appeared in the mixture. The Cream is genetically a dilute of the Red, and with the Oriental type, makes a very elegant cat.

SHOW SUMMARY
Coat should be buff-cream all over without markings, and an even colour from root to tip. Noseleather and paw pads pink. Eyes copper to green; green preferred.

OTHER SELF(SOLID) COLOURS

In order to produce the Shaded Oriental Shorthairs, a Chocolate-point Siamese male was mated to a Chinchilla Persian female. Their offspring were mated to Red-point Siamese to introduce all the other colours simultaneously. In the process, other self-coloured cats were produced, including Oriental (Foreign) Caramel, a cafe au lait colour; Oriental (Foreign) Apricot, a Red bred from a Caramel; and Oriental (Foreign) Beige, a Cream bred from a Caramel. All have pale green eyes. These are, however, still experimental colours and cannot be produced reliably.

ORIENTAL TIPPED

A revolution occurred with the Orientals when the Siamese was mated to a Chinchilla Persian in the hope of producing Oriental-type cats with tipped coats. The resulting kittens were originally mated back to Siamese for type, but now Oriental tipped coats are mated only to Oriental tipped in order to preserve the coat pattern.

The tipping is similar to that of the British Shorthair Tipped, and such cats look very striking with their sparkling coats. Tipping of any colour is possible and any colour is allowed in the United Kingdom, including silver, cameo, cameo tabby, blue, chestnut, lilac, and tortoiseshell in brown, blue, chestnut and lilac.

SHOW SUMMARY
Undercoat should be pure white. Top coat very lightly tipped on the back, flanks, head and tail with a contrasting colour to give a sparkling sheen to the coat. Chest and underparts should be white. Noseleather and paws pads appropriate to the tipping colour(s). Eyes according to tipping colour but green preferred.

ORIENTAL SHADED

The Shaded Oriental Shorthairs were also developed from the Siamese × Chinchilla Persian mating. Their offspring were mated back to Siamese, Oriental Blacks or British Havanas. Thereafter, selective breeding took place to preserve the amount of tipping required. Any colour tipping is possible, and all colours are allowed in the United Kingdom, including silver, cameo, cameo tabby, blue, chestnut, lilac, and tortoiseshell in brown, blue, chestnut and lilac. Also being bred are caramel shaded silvers!

SHOW SUMMARY
Undercoat should be pure white sufficiently tipped on the back, flanks, head and tail with a contrasting colour or colours, to give the effect of a mantle overlying the white undercoat. Noseleather and paws pads according to tipping colour(s). Colour of eyes according to tipping colours but green preferred.

ORIENTAL SMOKE

Another by-product of the Siamese × Chinchilla Persian mating, the first Oriental Smoke was produced by mating a Shaded Silver to a Red-point Siamese. Today the best Oriental Smokes are mated back to Siamese, Oriental Blacks and British Havanas to preserve type. The tipping is heavy, giving the appearance of a solid coloured cat except when the fur is parted to reveal a narrow band of white hair.

Like the Tipped and Shaded Oriental Shorthairs, any colour Smoke is possible and most are now allowed for competition. These include black (ebony), blue, cameo (in red and cream), chocolate (chestnut), lilac (lavender); and tortoiseshell in brown, blue, chocolate and lilac.

SHOW SUMMARY
Undercoat should be pure white. The top coat should be very heavily tipped with a contrasting colour or colours so that the cat in repose appears of that colour(s). Noseleather, paw pads in keeping with tipping colour(s). Eyes green.

ORIENTAL PARTICOLOUR (Oriental Torties)

The Oriental Particolours are all female-only varieties derived from the Red and Cream Oriental Short-hairs. Originally they were produced from the mating of Oriental Blacks with Red-point Siamese or Havana with Red-point Siamese, but today Oriental Torties are mated to Siamese or other solid coloured Oriental Shorthairs.

SHOW SUMMARY
Brown Tortie. Coat should be black with unbrindled patches of red and cream, clearly defined and well broken on body, head, legs and tail. A facial blaze of red or cream is desirable. Noseleather, paw pads black and/or pink. Eyes copper to green, green preferred.

Blue Tortie (Blue-cream). Coat should be blue with patches of solid cream, clearly defined and well broken on body, head, legs and tail. Noseleather and paw pads blue and/or pink. Eyes copper to green, but green preferred.

Chestnut Tortie. Coat should be chestnut brown with unbrindled patches of red and cream, clearly defined and well broken on body, head, legs and tail. A facial blaze of red or cream is desirable. Noseleather and paw pads dark and/or light pink. Eyes copper to green, but green preferred.

Lilac-cream (Lavender-cream). Coat should be lilac grey with patches of solid cream, clearly defined and well broken on body, head, legs and tail. Noseleather and paw pads pink. Eyes copper to green, but green preferred.

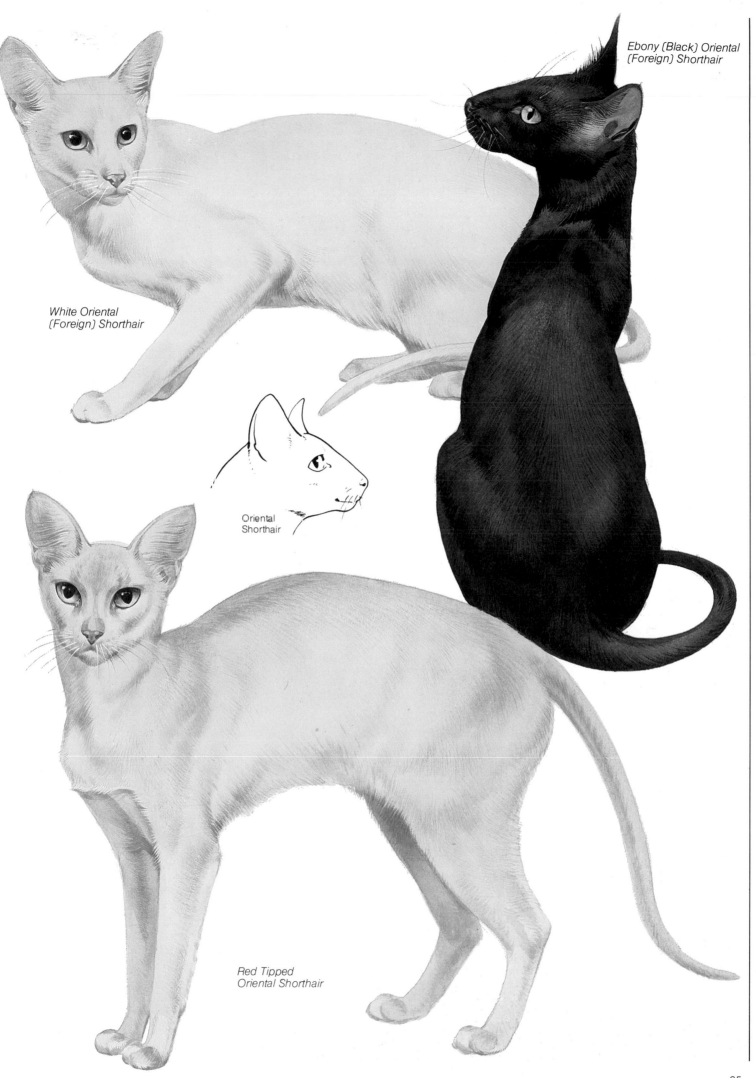

Ebony (Black) Oriental
(Foreign) Shorthair

White Oriental
(Foreign) Shorthair

Oriental
Shorthair

Red Tipped
Oriental Shorthair

65

ORIENTAL TORBIE

Oriental Torbies (patched tabbies) appeared during the breeding programme used to obtain the Oriental Tipped, and resulted from matings between Shaded Silver Orientals and Red-point Siamese.

SHOW SUMMARY

An established brown (ebony), with patches of red, silver or chocolate (chestnut) tabby with patches of red; or a blue or lilac (lavender) tabby with patches of cream. Noseleather and paw pads patched with appropriate solid colours. Green eyes preferred.

ORIENTAL TABBY

Tabby Oriental Shorthairs were produced during the breeding programme for Tabby- (Lynx-) point Siamese, using mongrel tabbies and Siamese, and later, British Havanas mated to Tabby-point Siamese.

All colours and tabby patterns have been developed. In the United Kingdom the Spotted Tabbies were formerly called Egyptian Maus, but the name Oriental Spotted Tabby has now been adopted to save confusion with the American-bred Egyptian Mau, which is not Siamese-derived.

SHOW SUMMARY

Classic Tabby pattern. All markings dense and clearly defined. Frown lines on the forehead form the characteristic letter 'M'. Unbroken lines run from the outer corners of the eyes towards the back of the head. Other pencil-thin lines on the face form swirls on the cheeks. Lines extend from the top of the head to the shoulder markings, which are shaped in a butterfly pattern. Three unbroken lines run parallel to each other down the spine from the shoulder markings to the base of the tail. A large blotch on each flank is circled by one or more unbroken rings; these markings should be symmetrical on either side of the body. There should be several unbroken necklaces on the neck and upper chest, and a double row of 'buttons' running from chest to stomach. Both legs and tail should be evenly ringed.

Mackerel Tabby pattern. Head is marked with the characteristic 'M'. An unbroken line runs from the outer corner of the eyes towards the back of the head. There are other fine pencil markings on the cheeks. A narrow unbroken line runs from the back of the head to the base of the tail. The rest of the body is marked with numerous narrow unbroken lines running vertically down from the spine line. There should be several unbroken necklaces on the neck and upper chest and a double row of 'buttons' on the chest and stomach. The legs should be evenly barred with narrow bracelets and the tail should be evenly ringed.

Spotted Tabby pattern (see also Egyptian Mau). Head markings as Classic Tabby. Body markings broken up into spots, which should be as numerous as possible, and may be round, oval or rosette-shaped. Dorsal stripe along the spine should be broken up into spots. There should be a double row of spots on the chest and stomach, and spots or broken rings on the legs and tail.

Ticked Tabby pattern. Body hairs to be ticked with various shades of marking colour and ground colour. Body when viewed from above to be free from noticeable spots, stripes or blotches except for darker dorsal shading. Lighter underside may show tabby markings. Face, legs and tail must show distinct tabby striping. There must be at least one distinct necklace on neck or upper chest.

Brown Tabby (Ebony Tabby). Ground colour brilliant coppery brown. Markings dense black. Eyes rimmed with black. Noseleather black or brick red rimmed with black. Paw pads black or brown. Green eyes preferred.

Blue Tabby. Ground colour pale bluish ivory. Markings deep blue. May have warm fawn highlights over the coat. Eyes rimmed with blue. Noseleather blue or rose rimmed with blue. Paw pads rose. Green eyes preferred.

Chocolate Tabby (Chestnut Tabby). Ground colour warm fawn. Markings rich chestnut brown. Eyes rimmed with chestnut. Noseleather chestnut or pink rimmed with chestnut. Paw pads chestnut or cinnamon-pink. Green eyes preferred.

Lilac Tabby (Lavender Tabby). Ground colour pale lavender (pinkish grey). Markings deep lilac-grey. Eyes rimmed with lilac. Noseleather faded lilac or pink rimmed with lilac-grey. Paw pads lavender-pink. Green eyes preferred.

Red Tabby. Ground colour reddish apricot. Markings deep rich red. Eyes rimmed with pink or red. Noseleather brick red or pink rimmed with red. Green eyes preferred (USA); all shades from copper to green allowed (UK).

Cream Tabby. Ground colour very pale cream. Markings deep cream. Eyes rimmed with pink or cream. Noseleather pink or pink rimmed with cream. Paw pads pink. Green eyes preferred (USA); all shades from copper to green allowed in the United Kingdom breed standard.

Silver Tabby. Ground colour clear silver. Markings dense black. Eyes rimmed with black. Noseleather black or brick red rimmed with black. Paw pads black. Green eyes.

Cameo Tabby. Ground colour off white. Markings red. Noseleather and paw pads rose. Green eyes.

OCICAT

Another Siamese-derived spotted breed has been produced recently in the United States originally by crossing a Chocolate-point Siamese male with a half-Siamese, half-Abyssinian female. At present, such cats are unknown outside the United States. Except for colour, they closely resemble the Oriental Spotted Tabbies.

SHOW SUMMARY

Dark Chestnut. Ground colour pale cream. Tabby spots and markings on the chest, legs and tail dark chestnut. Eyes gold.

Light Chestnut. Ground colour pale cream. Tabby spots and markings on the chest, legs and tail milk chocolate. Eyes gold.

EGYPTIAN MAU

Good points
- *Beautiful coat*
- *Agile*
- *Playful*
- *Friendly*
- *Quiet*
- *Easy to groom*
- *Good with children*

Take heed
- *It is best to restrict freedom, as it is a prey to cat thieves*

The Egyptian Mau is the only natural breed of spotted Oriental-type cat, and since it originated in Cairo it is thought to be a descendant of the cat revered and worshipped by the Ancient Egyptians. It is shy and loving and is said to have a good memory. It is strong and muscular, can easily be trained to perform tricks, and enjoys walking on a harness and lead. This is the best way to exercise an Egyptian Mau; if allowed out too much on its own, it may be stolen for its beautiful coat.

However, being a highly active cat it should not be too confined. The best solution if you cannot take the cat for walks yourself is to construct a wired-in pen in the garden, complete with roof and some means of access to the owner's house or a shelter to retreat from rain or too much sun. It adores people and should not be shut up on its own for long spells.

Grooming

As with all shorthaired cats, little grooming is required, although the Mau will benefit from and enjoy a daily brushing and combing to remove dead hairs, which it might otherwise swallow. Before a show, a little bay rum should be used. Do not use powder as this would mar the spots on the coat.

Origin and history

Thought to be the original domestic cats of Ancient Egypt, spotted cats or their descendants are depicted in early Egyptian art and symbolized in the gods Ra and Bast, both of whom were personified as cats. The name 'Mau' is simply the Egyptian word for cat.

The Egyptian Mau has been developed principally in the United States, and the similar spotted cats formerly called Egyptian Maus in the United Kingdom are now known as Oriental Spotted Shorthairs, as they are a Siamese-derived breed.

The first Egyptian Maus to be seen in Europe appeared at a cat show in Rome in the mid 1950s, and from there were taken to the United States in 1956. They were shown at the Empire Cat Show in 1957, attracting great interest.

Breeding

Since the Mau is a natural breed, outcrossing to other breeds is not permitted. With the original stock four colours have now been developed. The queens make excellent mothers; they are good tempered, quiet and devoted. The gestation period for Egyptian Maus is reputed to be 63-73 days!

Kittens

Egyptian Mau kittens are born with obvious spots, and are active and playful from the start. There are usually four to a litter.

SHOW SUMMARY

The Egyptian Mau is halfway in appearance between the svelte Oriental type and the cobby Domestic Shorthair. Egyptian Maus are alert, well balanced, muscular and colourful.

Coat. The fur is dense, resilient and lustrous. medium long, silky, fine.
Body. A modified Oriental type; medium in length, graceful and muscular, especially the males. Hind legs are longer than forelegs, and give the appearance that the cat is standing on tip-toe. The paws are small and dainty, round to oval.
Tail. Medium long, wide at the base, tapering slightly. A whip tail is considered a fault.
Head. A rounded wedge without flat planes. There is a slight rise from the bridge of the nose to the forehead, but no nose break. Ears large and wide apart, broad at the base, moderately pointed, with or without ear tufts. Small ears are considered a fault.
Eyes. Large, almond shaped. Small, round or Oriental eyes are considered a fault.

EGYPTIAN MAU COLOURS

Coat pattern. There should be a good contrast between the pale ground colour and the spots. Each hair carries two bands of colour and the pigmentation of spots and stripes can be seen both in the fur and in the skin.

The forehead is marked with the characteristic 'M', and other marks form lines between the ears that continue down the back of the neck, ideally breaking into elongated spots along the spine. As the spinal lines reach the hind-quarters, the spots merge to form a dorsal stripe which continues along to the tail tip. Two darker lines cross the cheeks; one starts at the outer eye corner and extends to below the ear, the second line starts at the centre of the cheek and curves upwards, almost meeting

Egyptian Mau

Egyptian
Mau Smoke

Silver Spotted Tabby
Oriental Shorthair

Chocolate (Chestnut)
Tabby Oriental Shorthair

Oriental Shorthair

the first. The upper chest has one or more necklaces, preferably broken in the centre. The shoulder markings may be stripes or spots. The front legs are heavily barred. Markings on the body should be spotted, the spots varying in size and shape; round, even spots are preferred. The spotting pattern on each side of the body need not be symmetrical, but spots should not run together in a broken, mackerel pattern. The hindquarters and upper hind legs should carry spots and stripes; bars on the thighs and back, spots on the lower leg. There should be 'vest button' spots on the chest and stomach.

Silver. Ground colour light silver, lighter on the undersides. Markings charcoal grey. Backs of ears greyish pink, tipped in black. Toes black, colour extending up the backs of the hind legs. Nose, lips and eyes rimmed in black. Noseleather brick red. Paw pads black. Eyes gooseberry green.

Bronze. Ground colour honey bronze, shading to pale creamy ivory on undersides. Markings dark brown. Backs of ears tawny pink edged with dark brown. Paws dark brown with dark colour extending up the backs of the hind legs. Nose, lips and eyes rimmed with black or dark brown. Bridge of the nose ochre coloured. Noseleather brick red. Paw pads black or dark brown. Eyes gooseberry green.

Smoke. Ground colour charcoal grey with silvery white undercoat. Markings jet black. Paws black, with black extending between the toes and up the backs of the hind legs. Nose, lips and eyes rimmed with black. Noseleather and paw pads black. Eyes gooseberry green.

Pewter. Ground colour pale fawn. Each hair on the back and flanks ticked (banded) with silver and beige, tipped with black, shading to pale cream on the undersides. Markings charcoal grey to dark brown. Nose, lips and eyes rimmed with charcoal to dark brown. Noseleather brick red. Paw pads charcoal to dark brown. Eyes gooseberry green.

BURMESE

Good points
- Great personality
- Good with children
- Highly intelligent
- Playful
- Elegant
- Easily trained
- Sweet natured

Take heed
- Very adventurous, may wander
- Not afraid of traffic, so needs some protection
- Needs some warmth
- Needs company

The Burmese makes an excellent pet. It has a sleek, shorthaired coat that is very easy to groom, is more

intelligent and more affectionate than many cats, but above all has a fantastic personality. It just loves people and is very good with children, but it does not like to be left alone. If you are out all day, then it is better to have two, so that they are company for each other. One cat is fun, but two cats are fun squared, especially Burmese!

The Burmese is tomboyish by nature, although many people consider the smooth shining coat and yellow eyes to be the height of elegance. This cat will always give a grand, bouncy welcome to the stranger, and time and affection devoted to this breed more than repays the owner in loyalty and affection. Beautifully behaved with the children, a Burmese loves to sleep in human beds if it gets the chance. There is usually little harm in this practice and both child and cat seem to appreciate the added warmth and friendship.

Grooming
The Burmese is one of the easiest cats to groom. A very fine-toothed comb used once or twice a week will remove dead hairs and be appreciated by the cat, as will plenty of hand stroking. For show cats, a bran bath a few days before the show will absorb any excess grease in the coat. However, the glossy Burmese coat is obtained only by keeping the cat in perfect condition; a healthy Brown Burmese should look like polished mahogany.

Origin and history
Although cats resembling the Burmese have been recorded in books from Thailand dating back to the 15th century, the breed as we know it today was developed in the United States in 1930, when a brown female cat of Oriental type, named Wong Mau, was imported to the West Coast from Burma. As there were no similar cats for her to mate with, she was mated to a Siamese. All the kittens born were therefore hybrids, but when they were mated back to their mother, brown kittens resembling the mother were produced. The personalities of these cats were so much admired, being as affectionate and as intelligent as the Siamese but less vocal and less destructive, that the breed soon became very popular.

The first Brown Burmese were imported into the United Kingdom in 1948, and this breed is now one of the most numerous on the show bench; indeed they now have their own all-Burmese shows. Of the other colours, the Blue was the first to appear in the United Kingdom (1955) and was such an unexpected event that the first kitten was registered as 'Sealcoat Blue Surprise'. Since then, with intensive breeding programmes, Lilac, Cream, Red, Chocolate and Tortie Burmese have been produced, all having the same lovable temperament.

In some American Associations the Blue, Chocolate (Champagne) and Lilac (Platinum) Burmese colours are considered a

separate breed known as the **Malayan,** as they were derived from other coloured shorthairs.

Breeding
The Burmese is more prolific than most cats. A queen usually has large litters—sometimes of up to 10 kittens, although four or five is the average number. Burmese make excellent mothers, bringing their kittens up very strictly with definite ideas on good manners.

Kittens
The kittens are exceptionally active and playful. They are born with much paler coats than the adults, and in the case of the Brown Burmese, mother and kittens look like plain and milk chocolate together. It is often difficult to assess the exact shade of the paler coated Burmese at birth, because the final coat colour takes some weeks to develop, as does the eye colour. Due to increasing demand, you may have to wait for one.

SHOW SUMMARY
The Burmese is a medium-sized cat of modified Oriental type with a muscular frame and heavier build than its looks would suggest. The British Burmese is slightly less rounded and cobby than the American Burmese, with longer and more slender legs.
Coat. Fine, sleek and glossy, short and close-lying.
Body. A medium-sized cat, hard and muscular; chest rounded and back straight; legs long and slender, hind legs slightly longer than forelegs; paws neat and oval (UK); round (USA).
Tail. Medium in length and tapering slightly to a rounded tip. Not whip-like or kinked.
Head. Slightly rounded on top between the ears, which are wide apart. The high, wide cheekbones taper to a medium-blunt wedge (UK); slight taper to a short, well developed muzzle (US). Chin firm; a jaw pinch is a fault. Ears rounded at the tips and open at the base, with a slight forward tilt in profile. The nose is medium in length with a distinct break in profile. Face should have a sweet expression.
Eyes. Oriental in shape along the top line and rounded underneath (UK); rounded (USA). Large and lustrous, set well apart.

BURMESE COLOURS
Brown was the first colour to be bred and recognized and is often considered the most attractive. Brown Burmese have been exported to many countries, from both the United Kingdom and the United States, and have immediately become popular everywhere. Although selective breeding in the United Kingdom has produced several colour varieties, in the United States only Sable (Brown), Blue, Champagne (Chocolate) and Platinum (Lilac) are recognized for competition.

Brown (Sable). Adult colour should be an even dark chocolate or sable brown, shading very slightly to a lighter tone on the

underparts. Noseleather and paw pads brown. Eyes deep yellow to gold, with no tinge of green.

Blue. Adult colour should be soft silver-grey, shading to a paler tone on the underparts. Ears, face and feet have a silver sheen. Noseleather dark grey. Paw pads grey. Eyes deep to golden yellow preferred, although a greenish tinge is acceptable.

Above: A handsome Blue Burmese kitten, always in demand as pets.

Chocolate (Champagne). Adult colour should be a warm milk chocolate all over, with slightly darker shading on the points permitted. Noseleather warm chocolate brown. Paw pads brick red to chocolate brown. Eyes deep to golden yellow.

Lilac (Platinum). Adults should be a delicate dove grey with a pinkish tinge. Ears and mask are slightly darker. Noseleather and paw pads lavender-pink. Eyes deep or golden yellow.

Red. Adults should be light tangerine in colour. Ears are slightly darker. Noseleather and paw pads pink. Eyes deep or golden yellow.

Cream. Adults should be a rich cream. Ears only slightly darker. Noseleather and paw pads pink. Eyes deep or golden yellow.

Brown Tortie. Adults should have brown and red patches without any barring. Noseleather and paw pads plain or blotched brown and pink. Eyes deep or golden yellow.

Blue Tortie. The adult coat should have patches of blue and cream without any barring. Noseleather and paw pads plain or blotched blue and pink. Eyes deep or golden yellow.

Chocolate Tortie. Adult coat should have chocolate and red blotches without barring. Noseleather and paw pads plain or blotched chocolate and pink. Eyes deep or golden yellow.

Lilac Tortie. Adult coat should have lilac and cream blotches without barring. Noseleather and paw pads plain or blotched lilac and pink. Eyes should be deep or golden yellow.

Brown Burmese
(US type)

Red Burmese

Burmese

Lilac Tortie
Burmese

TONKINESE
(Tonkanese)

Good points
- Friendly and affectionate
- Easy to groom
- Good with children
- Active and full of fun
- Loves people
- Takes happily to harness and lead

Take heed
- Gets lost easily, because it is curious and active
- Not afraid of traffic, sometimes to its cost

The Tonkinese is a hybrid breed, a cross between the Siamese and the Burmese, and—as would be expected—it has some characteristics of each (see pages 58 and 68). Because it loves people, it is apt to associate cars with people and lie down in front of them! Because of its curious nature, it goes for long walks and sometimes gets lost or risks meeting with a traffic accident. It should, therefore, have some restrictions to its freedom, although it would be cruel to confine it to a small and uninteresting room or cage. An ideal place for a Tonkinese to exercise during the day or during the owner's absence is a large, wired-in run with a roof, about 2m (6ft) high, and with lots of shelves at different heights. The cat will amuse itself for hours, running up and down and jumping from one shelf to the next, or just sit dozing in the sun at high level, keeping an eye on intruders into its garden. Some shelter should also be provided against the rain or too much sun.

Grooming
The Tonkinese is an easy cat to groom. All it needs is a fine-toothed comb, and perhaps a rubber spiked brush for massage. A bran bath just before a show will remove any excess grease from the coat, and a silk cloth or chamois leather will give it a polish. The ears should be inspected regularly for mites, and the outer ear only can be wiped out with a cotton wool bud when necessary.

Origin and history
This breed was developed in the 1960s and 1970s, mainly in the United States and Canada, although all over the world, no doubt, breeders with both Siamese and Burmese have experienced attractive cross-bred kittens and considered perpetuating them. The Tonkinese was finally accepted as a breed in the USA in 1975, although from the European view it is not strictly a breed at all.

Breeding
Tonkinese, or Tonks as they are affectionately known, are bred now only to Tonks in the USA, giving 50% Tonks, 25% Siamese and 25% Burmese. The first cross of Siamese to Burmese gives 100% Tonkinese. The non-Tonk kittens from these matings cannot be

Above: A Honey Mink Tonkinese, characteristically curious of the camera. Tonks make affectionate pets, but they like to wander.

shown because their pedigrees are not pure, but they make excellent pets.

Kittens
Tonkinese kittens are born paler in colour than their parents, the adult colour gradually developing.

SHOW SUMMARY
The Tonkinese is an Oriental-type cat, medium in size, lithe and well-muscled.
Coat. Soft and close-lying with a natural sheen.
Body. Medium-sized, well muscled, with long legs, the hind legs slightly longer than the forelegs. The slim legs terminate in small, dainty, oval paws.
Tail. Long and tapering from a thick base to a thin tip. No kinks.
Head. A modified wedge with a square muzzle. In profile there is a slight nose break. A medium long neck, but not as long as that of a Siamese. Ears medium in size, pricked forward and rounded.
Eyes. Almond-shaped, set wide apart.

TONKINESE COLOURS
Four colours are accepted. The adult coat should be a solid colour, shading to a slightly lighter tone on the underparts, and with clearly defined points.

Natural Mink. A warm brown with dark chocolate points. Noseleather, paw pads brown. Eyes blue-green.

Honey Mink. A warm, ruddy brown, with chocolate points. Noseleather and paw pads mid-brown. Eyes blue-green.

Champagne Mink. A soft, warm beige, with light brown points. Noseleather and paw pads cinnamon-pink. Eyes blue-green.

Blue Mink. A soft blue to blue-grey, with light blue to slate blue points. Noseleather and paw pads blue-grey. Eyes blue-green.

Platinum Mink. A soft silver body with metallic silver points. Noseleather lilac and paw pads pink. Eyes blue-green.

BOMBAY

Good points
- Striking appearance
- Delightful personality
- Even-tempered
- Reasonably quiet
- Mixes well with other cats, children and dogs
- Easy to groom

Take heed
- Does not like to be ignored

The Bombay has been described as a 'mini black panther' with a coat of patent leather and copper penny eyes. It has an ideal temperament and personality. It is hardy, affectionate and contented, and seems always to be purring.

The Bombay is very easy to groom because of its sleek coat, and so makes an ideal pet in many ways. However, it does not like to

be ignored, and therefore should not be left alone for hours at a time, deprived of human companionship. It is good with children and mixes well with other animals. It loves people and much activity, and it would be cruel to own only one if you have to be out all day.

Grooming
The close-lying coat needs combing daily with a very fine-toothed or flea comb to remove dead hairs; the show animal can be polished with a silk cloth or chamois leather. The cat might also enjoy a bran bath occasionally. Much hand stroking is appreciated, but please no hand-cream, which can spoil the whole effect! Ears and eyes should be examined regularly.

Origin and history
The Bombay is a man-made breed, produced by crossing Brown (Sable) Burmese with Black American Shorthairs, and the resultant cat has the black colour and hardiness of the American Shorthair and the sleek glossy coat, intelligence and affection of the Burmese.

Breeding
The Bombay, although developed as a hybrid, is found to breed true, and Bombay × Bombay produces 100 percent Bombay kittens. In the original crosses black was the dominant colour, and so even with the first cross, all the kittens could be registered as Bombay. Since then type, colour and eye colour have been maintained by careful, controlled breeding programmes. The queens make good sensible mothers, and they mature early from kittenhood.

Kittens
The kittens are lively, full of energy and very affectionate and trusting. They need companionship and should not be neglected. Kitten coats may be rusty coloured at first, maturing to pure black.

SHOW SUMMARY
More show points are given to the coat condition and colour in this breed than in any other, as the coat is considered to be more important even than the type.
Coat. Very short and close-lying with a patent leather sheen or satin finish. It most resembles the Burmese coat.
Body. Medium in size, and muscular, neither cobby nor rangy. Males larger than females. Females more dainty. Legs medium long.
Tail. Medium long, straight, no kinks.
Head. Rounded, without any flat planes. Face wide, with a good width between the eyes. Short, well-developed muzzle. Nose broad with a distinct nose break. Ears rounded, medium in size and alert. Broad at base, set wide apart on curve of head, tilted forward.
Eyes. Round, and set wide apart.
Colour. Black to the roots without white hairs or patches. Noseleather and paw pads black. Eyes new penny copper, deep and brilliant. Gold eyes sometimes accepted, but not green.

Tonkinese

Natural Mink
Tonkinese

Bombay

Champagne
Mink Tonkinese
kitten

Bombay

RUSSIAN BLUE
(Maltese)

Good points
- *Very sweet natured*
- *Unusually quiet*
- *Gentle and shy*
- *Companionable*
- *Easy to groom*
- *Takes well to living in an apartment*
- *May accept a harness and lead*

Take heed
- *It may be difficult for breeders to tell when the cat is calling because of its very small voice*

Whatever else is red in Russia, Russian cats are blue! The outstanding feature of the Russian Blue is its quiet sweetness. It is shy and gentle, and makes a loving, agreeable companion. It will become very attached to its owner, is willing to please, and seems to take easily to living in an apartment, in fact preferring an indoor life. Its blue plush coat is different from that of any other breed and somewhat seal-like in texture. The guard hairs are tipped with silver, which gives a silver sheen to the coat, enhancing the look of this lovely, docile cat.

The only disadvantage of this breed is that its voice is often so quiet that breeders may find it difficult to tell when a queen is calling; but because this cat is not prone to roam away from home, it is less likely to mismate with the local tom cats than many other breeds. If it is shut in somewhere this quietness may prevent the cat from being rescued.

Grooming
The Russian Blue is easy to groom, as the fur is very short and plush. It needs only an occasional brushing and a combing with a fine-toothed comb, and a polish with a chamois leather or an ungreasy hand. A show cat may be given a bran bath before the show to absorb any excess grease from the coat.

Origin and history
It is rumoured that the original cats came from Archangel in the USSR, brought to England by British sailors visiting the port. Before 1900, they were known as Archangel Blues, but also as Maltese and Spanish cats, and there seems to have been some confusion as to what was or was not a Russian Blue, although the fact that there are many of these cats in Scandinavia is supportive evidence of a Russian origin.

They were shown in the United Kingdom at the end of the nineteenth century, but as there were so few cats to mate them with, they were outcrossed to British Blues and Blue-point Siamese. This was nearly the death of the breed and had very undesirable results, particularly in the loss of the distinctive coat. After the Second World War every effort was made in the United Kingdom to reinstate this breed and now much better specimens are appearing.

Breeding
Russian Blues usually have one or two litters a year, with an average of four or five kittens to each. Finding appropriate breeding stock is still a problem, especially in the United States, where there are very few. Unfortunately it seems to be very difficult to breed a cat with both good type and a good coat.

Kittens
Russian Blue kittens are born with fluffy coats and may have faint tabby markings until the adult coat develops.

SHOW SUMMARY
The Russian Blue is a medium-to-large cat of Oriental type, lithe and graceful with a short, dense, plush coat.

Coat. Very short and dense. Very plushy, silky and soft, resembling sealskin.

Body. Long, lithe and graceful. Medium-strong bones. Long legs with small oval paws (UK); rounded (USA). Hind legs longer than forelegs.

Tail. Long and tapering, thicker at the base.

Head. Wedge-shaped, shorter than that of a Siamese, with a receding forehead. Straight nose and forehead with a change of angle above the nose. Flat, narrow skull. Prominent whisker pads. Strong chin. Neck long and slender but appearing shorter because covered with thick, short plush fur. Ears pointed, large and wide at the base, set vertical on the head. Almost transparent, and without ear tufts.

Eyes. Almond in shape and set wide apart, slanting to the nose.

Colour. A clear all-over blue, without shading or white hairs but with silver tipped guard hairs giving the whole coat a silvery sheen. A medium blue colour is preferred in the UK and a paler blue in the USA. Black Russians and White Russians are now being bred, particularly in New Zealand. Noseleather and paw pads slate blue. (Paw pads lavender-pink in the USA.) Eyes bright, vivid green.

KORAT

Good points
- *Pretty*
- *Quiet*
- *Sweet and gentle*
- *Intelligent*
- *Not destructive*
- *Good with other animals*

Take heed
- *Does not like loud or sudden noises*

The Korat has been described as having 'busy charm'. It loves to be petted, is smart, and likes energetic games. It dislikes sudden noises, however, and so would be best suited to a quiet, well-ordered household, rather than a mad house of boisterous children.

The Korat likes quiet, gentle people and gets very attached to its owner. It will get on well with other

Above: A charming Korat kitten with amber-tinged green eyes.

cats of different breeds, but prefers its own breed. It will also settle happily with a docile dog, provided it is introduced gently. The Korat is not too talkative, except when 'calling', and would make an ideal pet for someone wanting a sweet, loving, quiet companion.

However, it is still a rare breed, and you may have to wait for a kitten. At present there are more in the United States than elsewhere, but they are now being bred in the United Kingdom, Canada, South Africa, Australia and New Zealand, and are becoming popular.

Grooming
The Korat's single coat is very easy to keep in perfect condition. All it needs is a daily combing to remove dead hairs, so that the cat does not swallow them, and a polish with a chamois leather or silk cloth. It will enjoy lots of hand stroking, which will be good for the coat and make it shine.

Origin and history
The Korat is a natural breed, native to the Korat plateau in Thailand. Since 1959, several have been imported into the United States, and some began to arrive in the United Kingdom from America in 1972, although one specimen was apparently shown in England as early as 1896 at the National Cat Show; it was then thought to be a Blue Siamese but later was realized to be a Korat.

In the town of Korat these cats are known as Si-Sawat, which means 'good fortune'. In Thailand it is often called 'the cloud-coloured cat with eyes the colour of young rice'. One Thailand travel poster shows a girl in native Thai costume holding a Blue Korat cat. They are prized in their homeland, and a pair given to a bride means a fortunate, prosperous and happy marriage. The males are fearless fighters.

Korats have been known for hundreds of years in Thailand as is proved by a book of cat poems from the Ayudhya period (AD1350-1767), in which three cats are referred to: the Seal-point Siamese, a copper-coloured cat (probably Burmese) and the Korat.

They have now spread to all parts of the world where pedigree cats are bred and shown.

Breeding
When a kitten is sold, the new owner has to promise to neuter (alter) a kitten at the age of six months, or to mate it only to another Korat. This is to keep the breed as pure as it is, without contamination from other breeds. Korat queens make good mothers, very meticulous and clean, and the average Korat litter usually contains three or four kittens.

Kittens
The kittens are born the same colour as the adults, the beautiful silver grey coat present from the start. Kittens often have amber eyes, and the adult eye colour may take from two to four years to develop fully.

SHOW SUMMARY
The Korat is a medium-sized, strong and muscular cat. The males are more powerful than the females.

Coat. Single, short, glossy, fine and close lying. Extra short and fine on the back of the ears, nose and paws.

Body. Medium-sized, strong and muscular, semicobby with a rounded back and lying low on the legs. The forelegs are slightly shorter than the hind legs. Paws oval.

Tail. Medium long, tapering to a rounded tip.

Head. Heart-shaped head and face with a semipointed muzzle, a strong chin and jaw, and a large flat forehead. The nose is short with a downward curve above the tip of the nose. Gentle nose break. Ears alert with rounded tips, medium large, set high on head; open at the base; only slight interior furnishing.

Eyes. Prominent, over-large, luminous and set wide apart. Round when open, with slight slant when closed.

Colour. Silver-blue all over, tipped with silver to give a sheen, especially intense on backs of the ears, nose and paws. There should be no white hairs, spots or tabby markings. Noseleather dark blue or lavender. Paw pads dark blue or lavender with a pinkish tinge. Eyes brilliant green; amber tinge permitted in kittens.

Korat

Korat

Russian Blue
kitten

Russian Blue

Russian
Blue

73

ABYSSINIAN

Good points
- *Pretty*
- *Affectionate*
- *Playful*
- *Quiet*
- *Gentle*
- *Loving*
- *Good with children*
- *Easy to groom*

Take heed
- *Independent*
- *Very active*
- *Dislikes confinement*
- *Unsuitable for an apartment*

The Abyssinian is a highly intelligent cat, capable of showing a degree of obedience that is rare in cats. It is responsive to affection and likes to be part of the family. It can be easily trained to do tricks with its paws and to retrieve.

An Abyssinian looks like a little wild cat, and this appearance, coupled with its responsive personality, makes the cat particularly appealing to men. Men who think they do not like cats often succumb to the charm of an Abyssinian.

Because of its active nature, the Abyssinian prefers an outdoor life and dislikes being confined to a small area or caged in a cattery. It is best not to have an Abyssinian unless you live in the country or have a large garden.

Generally strong and healthy, feline leukaemia has taken its toll of the breed in the past, and it is best to obtain a leukaemia-free kitten. There is currently no cure for this virus disease.

Grooming
An Abyssinian is very easy to groom. It is advisable to brush daily to remove dead hairs, though once or twice a week will suffice. A shorthaired soft bristle brush or rubber brush is ideal and a very fine-toothed comb with a handle will remove loose hairs and double as a flea comb if necessary. For show cats, a little bay rum and a rub with a chamois leather will show off the coat to advantage. Daily hand stroking will gloss the coat, and be loved by the cat. The teeth and ears should also be checked regularly.

Origin and history
The early Abyssinian-like cats were known as hare or rabbit cats because of the similarity of their ticked coats, and they were also shown as Russian and Spanish cats at the early shows in the United Kingdom. Rabbit fur, however, has only a single band of colour (ticking) on each hair, whereas a good Abyssinian will have two or three bands of darker colour on each hair (double or treble ticking), with the pale colour next to the skin.

Because of its likeness to pictures of Ancient Egyptian cats, it has been claimed that the Abyssinian originates from the sacred cats of Egypt, but it is much more likely that breeders, impressed by this likeness, decided to perpetuate these features by judicious breeding. The Romans are known to have taken cats from Egypt and to have brought them to England, so the genes necessary to produce the 'Egyptian look' could have been introduced into Britain in this fashion. They would then be preserved within the British domestic cat population until someone wished to isolate them again by careful and selective breeding. All British Abyssinians are descended from other British cats, and all American Abyssinians can trace their origins to British imports after 1907.

Abyssinians were first recorded in Britain in 1882, and by 1970 all countries in the world had recognized the Abyssinian as a true breed. In 1979, which was the Golden Jubilee year of the UK Abyssinian Cat Club, the first all-Abyssinian cat show was held in Gloucester, England. Abyssinians are one of the most popular short-haired breeds in the United States, also. They are well represented in excellent competitive classes at the shows, and take many high honours, in both shorthair and all-breed championships.

Breeding
Abyssinians have never been numerous and usually have only three or four kittens to a litter, mostly males. Selective breeding and outcrossing to other breeds to obtain new colours will undoubtedly bring stamina to the breed. The queens are usually attentive mothers, interested in their offspring.

Kittens
Abyssinian kittens usually mature early and are fearless and playful. They arch their backs and purr loudly, demanding attention. It may take 18 months before the coats develop their full adult beauty.

SHOW SUMMARY
The Abyssinian is medium-sized, of modified Oriental type, firm, lithe and muscular with a distinctive ticked coat.
Coat. Short, fine and close-lying, lustrous and resilient.
Body. Medium-sized, slender and lithe, solid and muscular. Oriental in type, though not as extreme as a Siamese. Medium length, slim, fine-boned legs with small oval paws; characteristic stance as if on tip-toe.
Tail. Medium long, broad at the base and tapering. Not whip-like and no kinks.
Head. Medium broad, slightly rounded wedge on an elegant arched neck. Muzzle not sharply pointed. Ears wide apart, broad at the base, well cupped and tufted. Chin firm; slight nose break in profile.
Eyes. Set wide apart and expressive. Slightly slanted in setting, almond in shape.

ABYSSINIAN COLOURS
Originally only two colour varieties were recognized within this breed, the Ruddy and the Red (now Sorrel), and these are the only two colours accepted for competition in the United States at present.

A Blue Abyssinian also occurs naturally within the breed and was recognized in the United Kingdom in 1975. Now several other colours are appearing in the Assessment classes, including Lilac, Chocolate, Silver, Tortie, Red and Cream, although all these are the results of outcrossing to other shorthaired cats for colours.

Above: A Blue Abyssinian kitten, at five weeks already showing the assertive nature of the breed.

Ruddy (normal). Coat rich, rufous red, ticked with two or three bands of black or dark brown, with a paler orange-brown undercoat. Darker shading along the spine; tail tipped with black, and without rings. Black between the toes, with colour extending up the back of the hind legs. Tips and edges of ears black or dark brown. Nose-leather brick red. Paw pads black. Eyes green, yellow or hazel rimmed with black or dark brown, encircled by a paler area.

Sorrel (Red). Body colour a rich copper red, ticked with dark red or chocolate brown, with paler apricot undercoat. Darker spine and tail tip. Chocolate colour between the toes extends up the back of the hind legs. Noseleather and paw pads pink. Tips and edges of ears chocolate brown. White allowed only on lips and chin. Eyes green, yellow or hazel, the more brilliant and deep the colour the better. Pale eyes are a fault.

Blue. Body colour a soft warm blue-grey, ticked with a darker steel blue. Base hair is cream or oatmeal. Spine, tail tip and back of hind legs dark steel blue. Tips and edges of ears slate blue. Noseleather dark pink. Paw pads mauve-blue. Eyes green, yellow or hazel. Pale eyes are considered a fault.

SINGAPURA

Good points
- *Pretty*
- *Responsive*
- *Relatively quiet*
- *Loves people*
- *Can be trusted with babies*
- *Easy to groom*

Take heed
- *No drawbacks known*

The Singapura is known as the 'drain cat' of Singapore. In its native country, a large section of the community regards cats with suspicion, and consequently the native cats have to fend for themselves and are reserved and suspicious by nature. Foreigners living in the area have befriended some of them, and once they know no harm is intended, they become less shy and more trusting and responsive.

Several of these cats have been taken to the United States and are now becoming established as a new breed. With human care, the Singapura is an affectionate cat, though quiet and a little demure. It is generally smaller than other domestic cats, possibly because of its deprived ancestry.

In Singapore the cats are of many different colours and patterns, but those imported into the United States have ticked ivory and brown coats and golden eyes.

The breed is now receiving much publicity and there is a waiting list for kittens, both as pets and for breeding. As would be expected, Singapuras love to eat ocean fish!

Grooming
A Singapura needs very little grooming: just the normal daily comb through and, from time to time, attention to the ears and eyes.

Origin and history
The Singapura is a natural breed from Southeast Asia, where the majority of the native cats have ticked coats resembling those of Abyssinians, but are smaller and have different features. Generally roaming free and taking shelter in the drains of Singapore, these cats have been adopted by foreigners living on the island and have been given a standard for competition both in Singapore and in the United States. They were first shown in the United States in 1977, but being a new breed they are still extremely rare.

Breeding
As with many natural breeds, the queens make excellent and sensible mothers. Normally there are only three kittens in the litter, and unlike most Oriental-type Shorthairs, which are usually very precocious, both male and female may not mate for the first time until they are 15 to 18 months old.

Kittens
Singapura kittens mature slowly and often do not come out of the nesting box until five weeks old.

Singapura

Abyssinian

Singapura

Ruddy Abyssinian
kitten

Sorrel (Red)
Abyssinian

SHOW SUMMARY

The Singapura is a very small cat, but alert and healthy with noticeably large, cupped ears and large eyes.

Coat. Very fine, short, silky and close-lying. A little longer in kittens.
Body. Smaller than average: females 1.8kg (4lb) or less; males 2.7kg (6lb) or less. Medium long body, moderately stocky, dense and muscular. Back slightly arched, medium long legs and small tight paws. Body, legs and floor should form a square. Neck short and thick with high shoulder blades.
Tail. Medium long, tapering to a blunt tip. No kinks.
Head. Rounded, narrowing to a blunt, medium short muzzle with a definite whisker break. Full chin. In profile a slight break well down the bridge of the nose. Ears large, slightly pointed, wide open at the base and possessing a deep cup. Small ears are a show fault.
Eyes. Large, almond-shaped, wide open and slanted.
Colour. Each hair on the back and flanks and top of the head must have at least two bands of dark brown ticking separated by bands of lighter, warm, old-ivory ticking. The tip of each hair should be dark and the base light. A darker line along the spine is permitted, ending in a dark tail tip. Legs without barring preferred. Toes dark brown, the colour extending up the back of the hind legs. Muzzle, chin, chest and stomach should be a warm pale fawn. Ruddier tones are allowed on the ears and the bridge of the nose. White lockets or white hairs are faults. Eyes, nose and lips are rimmed in dark brown. Nose-leather red, paw pads dark brown. Eyes hazel, green or gold.

REX

Good points
- *Distinctive curly coat*
- *Intelligent*
- *Hardy and agile*
- *Quiet*
- *Great sense of fun*
- *Loves people*
- *Takes readily to cars or to a harness and lead*
- *Very easy to groom*

Take heed
- *Has a voracious appetite, but overfeeding will cause obesity*

Despite its short coat, the Rex does not appear to feel the cold. It does not need coddling and is quite hardy in even the coldest weather. It is a pretty, unusual-looking cat with a coat of curly hair and curly whiskers and eyebrows. Characteristically, the coat feels warm to the touch because the hair is so fine and short.

There are two types of Rex—the Cornish and the Devon—and although similar in many ways, the Devon Rex is particularly playful, and its pixie-like face betrays a devilish sense of mischief. It is also said to wag its tail like a dog when pleased. Intelligent and enterpris-ing, both Rexes make excellent pets for all the family.

One point to watch, however; the Rex has a tendency to over-eat and can easily ruin its streamlined figure. Overfeeding should be avoided as a fat Rex is particularly unattractive.

Grooming
Rexes are very easy to groom. All that is needed is a silk cloth or a chamois leather to polish the coat, and lots of hand grooming to remove any dead hairs. Before a show it is a good idea to give a bran bath to remove any grease in the coat, which might upset the flow of the waves and curls. If the coat is really dirty and requires a wet bath, it is advisable to do this a couple of weeks before a show, as the curl goes limp immediately after a bath.

Origin and history
The two strains of these curly-coated cats appeared as natural mutations in England, the United States, Germany and Canada almost simultaneously. The Cornish Rex is so called because it first appeared in Bodmin, Cornwall, in 1950, in an otherwise normal litter of farm cats. It was named after the Rex rabbit, which also has a curly coat. The curly kitten was mated back to its mother, and this produced more curly-coated kittens. Some of the offspring were imported into the United States, as were some from Germany. These, when mated together, appeared to be compatible, as they produced all curly-coated kittens. However, another strain of curly-coated cats appeared in a litter of kittens in Devon, England, in 1960, and these, when mated to the Cornish Rex, were obviously incompatible, as they produced all straight-coated kittens. Hence two separate varieties of Rex cat are recognized and should not be intermated, as they are genetically quite different.

The Rex was first recognized as a breed in 1967 and is now accepted in all countries of the world. Rex cats from England have been imported into Australia and New Zealand, and New Zealand breeders have introduced the Rex gene into Manx stock. Theoretic-ally, it is possible to rex the coat of any breed of cat, but a longhaired Rex is not being bred, as the coat tends to be lank and unattractive. The first all Rex cat show was held in Kentucky, November 1980.

Breeding
Mating two Cornish Rexes together and two Devon Rexes together produces 100 percent Rex-coated kittens. By mating a Rex to a Siamese, the Himalayan coat pattern is introduced and the very attractive Si-Rex is obtained. Rex queens kitten easily and make good mothers.

Kittens
Rex kittens are robust and healthy. They will certainly keep you busy, being highly active, precocious and mischievous.

CORNISH REX
SHOW SUMMARY
Although the original curly-coated kittens were British Shorthair type (as they were produced from British farm stock), a more stream-lined 'Foreign' type is now preferred on the show bench; the cat should be fine-boned and elegant with a longer wedge-shaped face and a long whip tail.

Above: A Dilute Calico Cornish Rex. The curly coat, which gives this agile breed its distinctive appearance, arose as a mutation.

Coat. Short, thin hair, but dense, plush and close-lying. No guard hairs. The hair should curl, wave or ripple, especially on the back and tail, but preferably all over, even on the paws. Whiskers and eyebrows should also be curly. Too short or shaggy a coat or hairless patches are faults.
Body. Hard, muscular, medium in size but slender, not cobby, standing high on long, straight legs. Back arched. Paws small, dainty and oval.
Tail. Long, thin and tapering.
Head. Modified Foreign type with medium length wedge, flat skull and straight profile with no nose break. Ears large, set high on the head, wide at the base, rounded at the tips, covered in fine short fur.
Eyes. Oval and medium in size.

DEVON REX
SHOW SUMMARY
The Devon Rex has a coarser coat than the Cornish Rex, but is similar in build, being muscular yet dainty, but different in face. A firm, medium-sized cat with a long tail and huge ears.

Coat. Very short, fine, wavy and soft, not shaggy, but coarser than that of the Cornish, due to the presence of minute guard hairs. Short curly whiskers and eyebrows, which tend to be brittle.
Body. Medium in size, slender, hard and muscular. Broad in the chest; carried high on long, slim legs. Hind legs generally longer than forelegs. Feet small and oval.
Tail. Long, fine and tapering, covered with short curly fur. No kinks.
Head. A rounded wedge with a flat top, set on a slender neck. Rounded cheeks with a whisker break, and a definite nose break in profile. Ears set low on the head, very large, with or without ear muffs and tufts; wide at the base, rounded at the tips, and covered in very fine soft fur.
Eyes. Wide-set, large, oval and slightly slanted.

REX COLOURS
Most colours and coat patterns are acceptable for competition, including the Himalayan coat pattern (Si-Rex). In the United Kingdom in the Cornish Rex any white markings should be sym-metrical (except in Tortoiseshell-and-white), and in the Devon Rex any white markings are unaccept-able (except in Tortoiseshell-and-white), as are Bicolours at present.

In the United States chocolate, lilac and Si-Rex are not accept-able at the present time, but most other colours and combinations of colours and patterns are currently recognized.

Eye colour should be in keeping with the coat colour or pale green, yellow or gold. White Rex may be gold-, blue- or odd-eyed (one gold, one blue); Si-Rex must be blue.

Below: A Cream Tabby Devon Rex. Note the brittle whiskers that have broken off at the ends.

Black Devon Rex
(UK eye colour)

Cornish Rex

Devon Rex

Devon Si-Rex kitten (UK)

Blue-cream
Cornish Rex (UK)

AMERICAN WIREHAIR

Good points
- *Interestingly different in appearance*
- *Sturdy and robust*
- *Sweet tempered*
- *Affectionate*
- *Adaptable*
- *Agile*
- *Intelligent*

Take heed
- *No drawbacks known*

The American Wirehair is an American shorthaired or domestic cat with a distinctive wiry coat that is hard and springy to the touch, and not unlike sheep's wool in texture. It is bred in all colours and is an interestingly different kind of cat to have as a pet. Not prone to illness, the Wirehair is a sturdy breed.

It will take a lively interest in its surroundings and is intelligent, active and agile. Being very sweet natured and affectionate, it makes an ideal family pet. However, as it is one of the more recent breeds on the cat scene it is relatively rare.

Grooming
Virtually no grooming is necessary. A gentle brushing with a soft brush once or twice a week will remove loose hairs. Plenty of hand stroking will help to keep the coat in good condition. It is essential to shampoo. This can be done just before a show; the hair springs quickly back into place.

Origin and history
The American Wirehair is a natural mutation that occurred in an otherwise normal Domestic Shorthair litter. The first to be recorded was at Verona, New York, in 1966, although it has also been recorded that kittens with identical coats were seen on London bomb sites after the Second World War. This strain now seems to have died out and may therefore have been sterile. Kittens from the American matings have now been exported to Canada and Germany.

Breeding
Wirehairs mated to normal-coated shorthaired cats will produce 50 percent wirehaired kittens. The gene is not linked to colour and all coat patterns are possible.

Kittens
Wirehair kittens are born with tight curly coats. They are healthy, playful and robust. An average litter contains four or five kittens.

SHOW SUMMARY
The overall impression of the American Wirehair is of a medium-sized cat, rounded and woolly rather like a lamb.
Coat. The distinctive feature of this cat is its unique coat, which is of medium length and tightly curled. All the hairs are crimped, even in the ears, and hooked at their ends. In some places, particularly on the head, the hair forms into ringlets

rather than waves. The whiskers are crimped or wavy and untidy.

The unique coat is formed by a change in the structure of the guard hairs (those of the top coat), which are normally smooth and tapering but have become crimped along the shaft, hooked at their ends and thinner than normal guard hairs. This gives rise to a woolly coat, which is thick, coarse, resilient and springy to the touch. The hair on the chin, chest and stomach is slightly less coarse.
Body. Medium to large, well-muscled, with shoulders the same width as haunches. Back level. Legs medium long; paws oval and compact.
Tail. Moderately full, tapering to a rounded tip.
Head. Round, with prominent cheekbones, well-developed muzzle and chin and a slight whisker break. Nose is concave in profile. Ears medium in size, set wide apart with rounded tips.
Eyes. Large, round, bright and clear, set well apart, at an angle.

AMERICAN WIREHAIR COLOURS
All colours and coat patterns are permissible and possible, and include solid white, black, blue, red and cream; chinchilla, shaded silver, shell cameo, cameo tabby, shaded cameo, black smoke, blue smoke, cameo smoke; tortoiseshell, calico, dilute calico, blue-cream; bicolour; classic and mackerel tabby patterns in silver, brown, red, blue and cream; and any other colour or pattern, or combination of colours and patterns with white, with the exception of the Himalayan pattern or chocolate and lilac (lavender). Eye colour appropriate to coat.

SPHYNX
(Moon Cat; Canadian Hairless)

Good points
- *Hardy, not susceptible to cold*
- *Affectionate*
- *Needs no brushing or combing*
- *Certainly attracts attention*

Take heed
- *Should be sponged regularly*

The hairless cat is an unusual animal and may not be to everyone's taste. The body feels hot and smooth to the touch, as there is little fur to act as a temperature barrier or to insulate the body warmth; however the Sphynx does not seem to feel the cold as might be expected.

Unlike other cats, the Sphynx sweats and leaves a dander on the skin which has to be sponged periodically.

It is an affectionate and good natured cat, quiet yet loyal. Its distinctive appearance certainly attracts attention at a show.

Grooming
No brushing or combing is required, but the dander that accumulates on the skin should be sponged away with warm water daily or as necessary.

Origin and history
Hairless kittens have appeared in litters of ordinary Domestic

Below: A Silver Tabby American Wirehair. The hard, springy fur appeared as a natural mutation. Distinctive and robust, this breed is still something of a rarity in the international cat world.

Shorthairs and other breeds in France, England (in connection with the Devon Rex) and Canada. It is the Canadians who, since 1966, have taken an interest in this breed and have developed a breeding programme to perpetuate it. This began in 1966 in Ontario, when a hairless male kitten was born to a Black-and-White Domestic Shorthair.

It is thought that the Aztecs had hairless cats, and some were recorded in Mexico at the end of the nineteenth century and known as Mexican Hairless. These are now thought to be extinct. Unlike the Sphynx they grew fine winter hair that moulted in the summer.

Breeding
Hairless cats breed true to type, but can also be produced from normal-coated cats carrying the gene for hairlessness. Outcrosses to Domestic Shorthairs are used from time to time to improve stamina, and do not seem to affect the Sphynx body type.

Kittens
Sphynx kittens are born with a fine covering of soft, short hair most of which is lost as they approach adulthood, when any hair is confined to the face, paws, tail tip and testicles in males. Kittens are usually bow-legged at first and have wrinkled and rather loose skins that appear to be too big for them.

SHOW SUMMARY
The Sphynx is a medium-sized cat, fine-boned but powerful, without hair on most of its body.
Coat. There is a short velvet pile covering the face and ears, that is longest and heaviest on the nose and sides of the mouth. The paws are also covered with fine hair up to the ankles, as is the end of the tail. There is a ridge of fine hair on the back and the testicles are covered in long, close-lying hair. Too much hair is a fault.
Body. Long, fine-boned and muscular. The skin is taut without wrinkles, except on the head. The legs are long and slim with small round paws; hind legs are slightly longer than forelegs.
Tail. Long, thin and hard. No kinks.
Head. Neither round nor wedge-shaped; flat between the eyes. The neck is fairly long and the chin square. The short nose is covered with velvet-like fur and there is a decided nose break. The ears are very large, wide at the base and rounded at the tips, sticking out from the head at the lobes.
Eyes. Deep set and slanted.

SPHYNX COLOURS
All colours and coat patterns are allowed (see American Wirehair), excluding the Himalayan pattern, chocolate, lilac (lavender), or any of these with white.

A pink locket at the neck is acceptable but white is allowed only around the nipples and navel. Particoloured patterns should be arranged symmetrically. Eyes gold, green or hazel, or in keeping with the coat colour.

American Wirehair

Black Smoke American Wirehair

Sphynx

Sphynx

A Seal-point Siamese and kitten in complete contentment

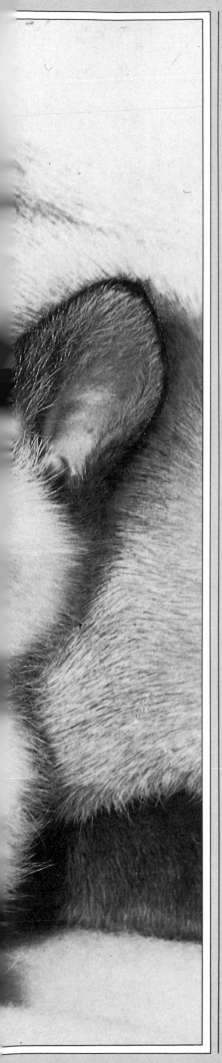

Part Two
PRACTICAL SECTION

*Essential information for everyone with a cat
or thinking of buying one.*

If your cat is to lead a healthy, happy life under your care, you must make certain decisions and face certain responsibilities, ideally before you acquire it, whether you buy it, receive it as a gift or have it wander into your home through an open door. A cat may be with you for 20 years, barring accidents. You must decide that you are prepared to love and care for it that long.

A small kitten will need extra care and attention; special food; a quiet place to sleep and get away from the children; a place to sharpen its claws other than on your furniture; and a litter tray in which to be clean. As it grows up, it will need constant attention to its coat, particularly if it is a longhair, and it will need your understanding of its nature, so that there is mutual respect between you and your cat.

Part Two of this book is the Practical Section, taking you through the various stages of buying, owning and caring for your cat. It starts with *Choosing a Cat*, which explains the necessity of considering all aspects of choice, from appearance through temperament to grooming requirements.

The New Kitten explains the first steps of owning a kitten, together with advice on the things it will need for eating, sleeping, play, cleanliness and exercise.

Understanding Your Cat contains much previously unpublished material on the psychology of cats and how you can build up relationships.

The three sections about *Feeding*,

Grooming and *Health Care* will enable you to maintain your cat in optimum health and happiness, arming you with information on food values, vitamins and table manners; how to give a wet or a dry shampoo; and how to nurse a sick cat, with sections on common ailments and parasites, and what to do about them.

For those of you who wish to consider it, the chapter on *Breeding and Rearing* will tell you all you need to know, and with the section on *History and Genetics* you will be armed with the necessary knowledge to breed champion cats of your chosen breed or even to create 'new' breeds and colours.

If you wish to show your cat you will find a wealth of information in *Showing Your Cat*, which explains everything from how to enter your first show to what to do on show day. You may even feel encouraged to help run a show or to become a judge.

Travelling often goes with showing and the chapter on *Travel and Boarding* outlines the type of carriers and methods of travel available to cat owners and how to cope with holidays, boarding catteries and quarantine.

The final chapter, *The Law and Your Cat*, informs you of your rights and responsibilities; the cat's rights; and what licences may be required before you can start up a boarding cattery or open a pet shop.

The entire section should help you to make everyday life enjoyable for both you and your cat for many years to come.

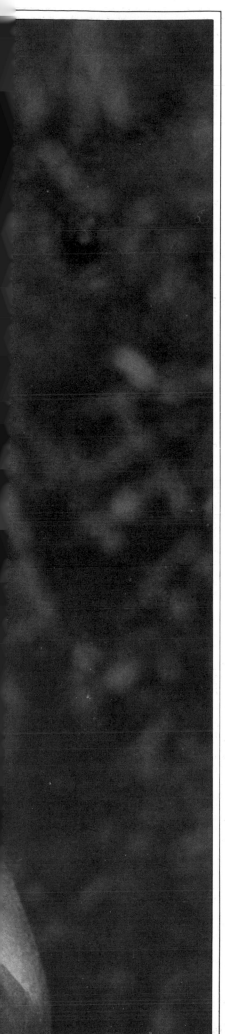

CHOOSING A CAT

Once your family has set its heart on having a cat, plan ahead before you rush out to get one. Ask yourself what you want a cat for. Is it to be a show cat or a pet cat? Male or female? Longhaired or shorthaired? What colour? Pedigree or mongrel? Let's look at these and some other questions.

Show cat or pet cat?
If you have never been to a cat show, you may not even consider the possibility of showing, but should you choose your kitten at a cat show, the breeder may persuade you to 'show just once'. Then, if the kitten takes home a prize, you may be hooked into the show circuit for good. It is quite possible to show an ordinary pet cat, but only in pet-cat classes; and, of course, you can own a pedigree cat without showing it. However, it would be sensible to decide which kind of life you want for your cat before you obtain it. If you do not want a cat to have kittens, you can have a pedigree cat neutered and still show it, but only in neuter classes. (Dogs, on the other hand, cannot be shown if they have been neutered or spayed.)

Male or female?
If you want to breed kittens, the answer to this question is obviously to buy a female. Remember, though, that if you hope to sell the kittens, you must breed from a pedigree female mating her with a sire of the same breed when she matures. However, breeding cats will not make you much money—it is largely a labour of love.

If you do not want to breed kittens, have your cat spayed at about six to eight months old, depending on the breed.

Never start with an entire male as a pet. For one thing it would be

Above: A tabby and white household pet is a perfect non-pedigree choice for all the family. Its short coat will be easy to groom.

Left: This little girl has chosen a Siamese kitten. It is a pedigree kitten, so that she can start on a show career, if she wishes to.

difficult keeping him happy at home without enough queens (females) to mate with, and for hygienic reasons you could not let him run free. He would also fight with the neighbouring toms (males) and get his ears bitten or worse! An adult tom is impossible to keep indoors as a family pet because of his strong urine, which he will spray round the house to attract the females. One does hear of toms living at home but this is exceptional. You should only choose a male kitten if you are prepared to have him neutered by the time he is about six months old.

Some people think neutered animals suffer a sense of loss or deprivation, much as if they were humans. This is not so; for them

mating is purely instinctive, and once the mating desire is removed they simply grow up differently, losing the urge to go out at all hours in all weathers and becoming content to rest by the fireside. They become more loving pets, too. This is surely better than being forced out at night by a sex urge that leads to fights and getting run over, not to mention adding to an already overgrown cat population. A pet cat must be neutered.

Neuters of both sexes are very lovable, but neutering a female is a major operation and consequently costs more than neutering a male.

Longhaired or shorthaired
This choice will depend not only on which kind of cat you prefer to look at, but on how much time members of the family can spare for grooming the pet. A longhaired cat is undoubtedly beautiful, but an hour's daily brushing and combing and untangling of knots may be needed to keep it that way; so only someone who is sure he or she wants to do all this work should have a Persian cat. It is no good if the novelty wears off after a few weeks! A cat may live for 20 years, and that means more than 7000 man-hours of grooming. If this thought makes you blench, you would be safer having a short-haired cat; there are many delightful kinds to choose from.

If anyone in the family suffers from asthma, a longhaired cat may bring on an attack and for that reason is best avoided. Some people suffer an allergic reaction near any cat, and for a few unlucky individuals all furred and feathered animals are taboo. Before choosing a cat visit cat-keeping friends to discover whether or not cats affect anyone in your family.

This is better than buying a cat only to find you must part with it very soon afterwards—a disturbing experience for the poor animal.

What colour?

Cats come in all colours except green. You can find black and white; brown; cream; shades of red; blues; and greys. There are also lots of exciting coat patterns, such as tabby, spotted, and pointed (the face, legs and tail a different colour from the main body). Then there are mixtures of all colours and patterns. But do not choose a colour to go with the decor or you may wish to change the cat each time you redecorate! Cats of any colour or pattern can be delightful. In fact, most people develop a loyalty to the colour or breed of their first cat, replacing that pet when it dies with another much like it.

Having looked through all the pictures and breed profiles earlier in this book and discovered a cat you consider ideally beautiful you may find there is none of that breed in your district, or even perhaps in your country. You may have to be very patient before you can acquire such a cat. Probably it is better to compromise and choose from what is available in your area; then at least the breeder is handy if you need to return for advice on aftercare problems.

Buying a pedigree cat

Once you have decided what kind of cat you want, you must look at the cost. Very fine show specimens can cost a great deal, but there is no point in paying a high purchase price unless you wish your cat to have a show career. Very often a pedigree cat with scarcely less perfect features than a champion's can be obtained for a fraction of a champion's cost. Such cats will make just as wonderful pets as top prizewinners. A breeder may be able to help you to find such a cat—but don't tell the breeder you do not want to show, and buy an imperfect kitten only to show it the length and breadth of the country under the breeder's prefix! On the other hand, it is a waste of money and a tragedy for the breed to buy a top show kitten and have it neutered without breeding or showing it. Take the breeder's advice in these matters, and never breed from inferior stock or you will only get inferior kittens.

Sometimes you find pedigree kittens in a pet shop, but more usually they are just advertised there and kept at the home of the breeder, who pays the pet shop commission for introducing buyers. Pedigree kittens are also advertised in the pets' column of local and some national newspapers. In such instances always visit the breeder's home and see for yourself the surroundings in which your prospective pet has been reared. Usually it is best all round if the kitten has been reared in the house with humans, even if it is put in a pen in the garden during the sunshine hours. Kittens raised in this way have grown used to

household sounds and so are unlikely to panic the first time they hear a vacuum cleaner or a postman arriving. Even if you choose a cat at a show it is probably a good idea to leave it with the owner for a day or two, collecting it after it has settled down again at home after the noise and excitement of the show.

When you arrive at the breeder's to choose your kitten, watch the whole litter for an hour or so if the breeder will let you, rather than making an instant decision. This will help you to choose a kitten with the right personality for you; some kittens are shy, some boisterous, some bullies, some loving, and so on. But studying the family can also provide clues to physical condition. Be suspicious of a kitten sitting quietly at the back while the others are joyfully playing—it may be a weakling or sickening for something, or having an off day. Do not choose the runt (the smallest or weakest) of the litter if there is one. It may look very sweet, but could spend much of its life at the veterinarian's at enormous expense to yourself. Select one of the outgoing, lively ones instead as a safer bet.

A healthy kitten should have bright eyes, shining coat and plenty of energy. However, like babies, kittens must have plenty of rest, so after chasing about for some time it is quite normal for them all to fall asleep in a heap. If there is any sign of illness, touch none from that litter. Either go elsewhere or come back another day to make sure. The first sign of sickness may be a visible third eyelid, which in kittens comes across the eye from the inner corner when things are not as they should be. The mother cat should also look healthy and well fed, and the home should be well looked after and spotless, not dirty or smelling of cat.

Remember that a very cheap pedigree kitten is usually a bad investment. Choose the best one you can afford.

Cats without pedigrees

If you cannot afford to buy a pedigree kitten it is easy to find a non-pedigree kitten in at least one of the following ways. First, one may appear on your doorstep! Many people have opened the door on a cold morning to find a sweet little bundle of fluff sitting there waiting to come in. Some

Above: With care and grooming this beautiful Chinchilla kitten could become a champion show cat.

might see this as an act of God. If not that, at least it is flattering to think that the little soul seems to have sought you out personally, and you may well find it hard to harden your heart and turn it away.

A second and more reliable source of supply is a pet shop. Usually it is non-pedigree kittens that find their way here, where perhaps they sit in the window looking adorable until someone with a soft heart comes along and takes them home. Usually the charge is small as the pet shop hopes to secure you as a customer, buying food and other items for the rest of the cat's life.

Thirdly, your local newspaper is likely to carry advertisements for cats or kittens offered 'free to a good home'. Some will have been born in the advertiser's home, but others may be unwanted presents. You should try to avoid taking a cat that has had too many homes and been moved around too much; this is always unsettling for a cat, and it may have become rather emotionally unstable as a result.

A fourth and unfailingly constant cat reservoir is one of the animal charities. Your local branches of the RSPCA and PDSA usually have cats and kittens looking for good homes. The charities have to destroy thousands of unwanted cats and kittens each year, but they try to place as many animals as possible. If you can offer a loving home to one or more animals, these organizations will be delighted to hear from you. Their addresses and telephone numbers are probably listed in your local telephone directory. Sometimes they ask for a donation in exchange for the cat or kitten, although this may be offered free.

If you lack the patience for rearing a kitten you may consider taking an adult cat, provided you have no other cat at home at the time. Adult cats are much more difficult to place than kittens, but they usually seem very grateful for the chance of a new home with a loving lap or a fireside. If you already have one adult, however, avoid introducing another or there will be jealousy. Remember that an adult will be set in its ways, so will need more patience and understanding than a kitten, whose behaviour you can generally mould as you please. Incidentally, rearing a kitten is much easier than raising a puppy.

The main objection to obtaining a mongrel is lack of information about its background. More often than not you know nothing about its parents or the care it has had. On the other hand, when you buy a pedigree cat from a good breeder, you can learn a good deal about the creature's heredity and environment. Because the breeder has studied cat nutrition and done her best for her cats from well before they were born you are more likely to have a healthier kitten and fewer veterinary bills if you buy from her than if you opt for a mongrel of dubious origin.

Is it old enough?
Whichever type of cat you choose it should be old enough to leave its mother. You can often check by examination. The kitten should have a full set of teeth or be at least eight weeks old. Pedigree kittens are usually 12 weeks old before the breeder will let them go. It is not just a question of being able to eat solids, but a matter of finishing their education with their mother! She will teach them how to eat, wash and use a litter tray and a scratching post. She will also show them how to play: making the moves they would need in the wild for fighting. She will teach them how to hunt for food: to lie in wait, pounce, and growl over a prey. By example she shows each kitten how to keep other cats away from its prey. Even a mother who is not allowed to go out into natural surroundings instinctively teaches her kittens these things, using spiders and toy mice, so that her offspring will be well equipped wherever they go in adult life. If kittens are removed from their

Above: Two kittens are fun! Here a Tabby-point and a Seal-point Siamese play happily together. It is a pity to part them.

mothers too soon, they will miss instruction that might one day assure their survival.

One cat or two?
Often two brother or sister kittens in a litter seem inseparable when you visit them in their own home. They play together, sleep together, and altogether seem to have more affinity for each other than for the rest of the litter. Very likely the breeder will hope to part with both to the same buyer—someone who has decided that two will be better than one. In several important ways they certainly are. When all

your family go out for most of the day, two cats will keep each other company. Also remember that one cat is fun but two are fun squared! When making your decision consider that if you take only one and later go back for another, they may settle in less well than if they go to their new home together. If you can afford it, have two straight away, particularly if there is more than one child in your family.

Parting with a cat
Perhaps this seems a curious topic to end our section on choosing a cat. However, it is a sad fact that unforeseen circumstances some- times mean people find themselves parting with the pet they had acquired not long before. If this happens to you, remember that

cats are sensitive creatures. Try to find yours an alternative home where a loving atmosphere prevails. Your obligation is not just moral—in many parts of the world it is a legal offence to neglect a cat: people who turn their cats out when the novelty of ownership wears off are liable to prosecution. (See also pages 152-153.) If a home cannot be found, then you must consider euthanasia (putting to sleep) rather than abandoning the animal to likely starvation. Naturally, you should make every possible effort to find your pet a new home before taking this last irrevocable step.

Below: This black and white household pet revels in the close attention of a devoted owner.

THE NEW KITTEN

You and your family decided that you all wanted a pet cat and were prepared to care for it for perhaps the next 20 years. You carefully arrived at a particular breed, colour, life-style, sex and future for your pet. You have actually chosen a particular kitten from among its litter mates for its glowing health, good looks and sweet temperament. Now it is time to think of what you will need in the way of equipment before your kitten arrives.

Feeding dishes and water bowl
For the sake of the health of the whole family your kitten should have its own feeding dishes and water bowl plainly distinguished from your own dishes, perhaps by consisting of brightly coloured polypropylene (a type of plastic that can be raised gradually to boiling point in water to sterilize). Stainless steel is also recommended. Always wash the cat's bowl and dishes separately from the rest of the washing up. Each meal should be served in a clean dish or on a disposable paper plate.

Always place the food and water containers in the same place, such as a convenient corner of the kitchen. If you are out all day, you may consider using an automatic hopper feeder, such as the Catamatic or you may prefer a timed feeder that can be preset to serve meals up to 14 hours later. Both are of British manufacture. An American design is the Step 'N' Dine, which has food and water bowls with a clear plastic cover that lifts off as the animal steps on the feeder and comes down again when the cat walks away, so covering the food from dust and flies until the cat needs some more. Only dry and semi-moist foods can be used in automatic feeders.

Above: This Persian kitten's owner is introducing her new kitten to the litter tray. Usually, house-training kittens is not difficult.

Left: Every kitten or cat should have its own place to sleep. There is room in this basket bed for the silver tabby kitten to grow.

Food
You will need to lay in a substantial supply of feed before bringing the kitten home for the first time. Include fresh, tinned and dried foods, so that the kitten has a variety. For the first few days limit the kitten to the foods it has been used to, but after that you can begin to introduce other interesting varieties. You may find your kitten prefers some proprietary foods to others. Just like people, cats require a balanced diet and you will find more about which foods to buy and serve in the feeding chapter starting on page 101.

Litter tray
Even if you plan to train it to use the outside garden your kitten will need a litter tray to begin with; you should not risk letting it out until it has grown accustomed to its new home. At first the best litter to use is what the breeder has been providing, and you can gradually change to another material if necessary. Probably the most efficient and convenient is the clay-type cat litter sold in most pet shops; some forms have a built-in deodorant. It is cheapest to buy cat litter in sacks of about 20kg (44lb), using a plastic scoop to ladle the litter from bag to tray. It is not advisable to use shredded newspaper as the cat is likely to continue to use any newspaper throughout the house.

House-training kittens is simpler than house-training puppies. In fact kittens who have grown up with their own mothers to show them what to do, will already be house-trained by the time you get them. A stray kitten placed upon a litter tray will instinctively use the litter. As its paws sink into the soft soil, the kitten will dig a hole and sit down in it, particularly if it has been some time travelling to its new home. In fact so clean are most cats and kittens that some people say there is no such thing as a dirty cat, only a dirty owner. Usually accidents happen only when a thoughtless owner has left no litter tray available. This is not to deny there are times when a cat is psychologically disturbed and shows its displeasure (of being neglected, for example) by defecating where it should not; but this is exceptional.

There are various types of litter tray on the market ranging in price according to design. Depending on the space and funds available, you can opt for a small shallow tray, or a considerably larger, deeper one. There are giant trays for breeders or people with more than one cat in the household and covered ones—'superloos'—for those who like their cats to have privacy. These trays may be expensive, but they certainly help to hide the used litter pan and their covers prevent cats from throwing the litter all over the kitchen or bathroom. The tops of the covered litter trays are removable for cleaning, and the United States boasts extremely sophisticated trays with built-in deodorizing hoods!

Some cats are so fastidious that they will not use litter once they have soiled it and the owner must change it completely or keep it picked over at least once a day. Many pet stores sell cheap plastic spoons for this purpose. Baking soda stirred into the litter pan will act as a deodorant, but effectively so only if it makes up one-third of the bulk of the cat litter. Beware of using disinfectants and deodorants sold for other purposes, because a surprising number of chemical substances are poisonous to cats. (See also page 116.)

If your kitten is to be kept indoors or confined in any way without full freedom of the garden it will need access to a litter tray all the time, but keeping this clean is not really a chore if you love the animal. Whichever litter tray or pan you choose will have to be cleaned regularly with hot soapy water and a chlorine bleach. Avoid the carbolic group of substances, creosotes, resorcinal and hexy-resorcinal as all these are poisonous to cats. The cloth used for cleaning out the litter pan should never be used for general cleaning about the house but kept specifically for the purpose. A pair of rubber gloves could also be set aside for the same reason.

Bed and blanket
Place and keep these in a quiet, warm, draught-proof place: next to a central-heating boiler is a

Below right: A covered litter tray, or 'superloo', is aesthetic and gives the cat some privacy. Below: Two types of perforated litter scoops, one with a disposable bag to collect the debris. Both will cope with the chore of cleaning the tray hygienically.

Bowls and Automatic Feeders

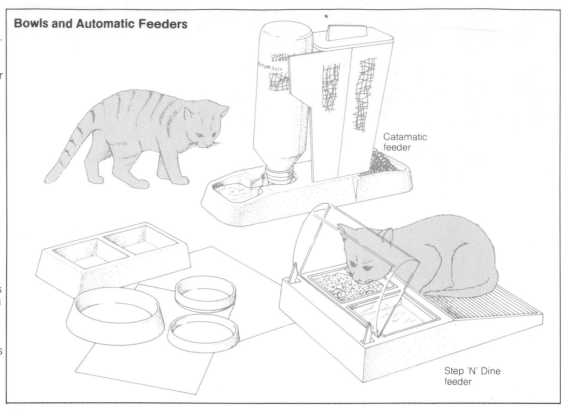

Catamatic feeder

Step 'N' Dine feeder

Above: These feeding bowls are suitable for food, milk or water. A place mat underneath will protect the floor from spillage. Such bowls should be reserved only for the cats; not shared with humans.

favourite location in homes that have one. A cat will sleep on your bed if you let it or with a child who has become a particular friend, but it should still have its own bed to which it can retreat with security any time it feels threatened.

Scratching post
Many people combine scratching post and bed in one in the form of a piece of cat's furniture called a cat tree. This is a useful item if you have room for it. The cat will love it, choosing the top perches to sit on and survey the world. It will feel safe up there away from strangers, strange dogs and the clasping hands of small children.

A scratching post is necessary for all cats to prevent them from

Above: The Catamatic is a hopper feeder for dry foods and water. Step 'N' Dine keeps the food free from dust and flies until it is required. Both are ideal if you are away from home during the day.

misusing the furniture. Its cost means a small outlay compared with re-covering the three piece suite! There are many on the market including ones made of cardboard, carpet on a pole, and carpet inserted in a plastic surround. There is even one made of bark, which is the most natural material for a cat to use. Outside in the garden the cat will employ tree trunks for the all-important task of manicuring its nails. The cat instinctively keeps its claws sharp for tearing prey apart ready for eating, and although most

Below: This Chocolate-point Siamese can retire to its own cat igloo for some peace and quiet.

household cats are fed food already cut up, cats remain as it were programmed to hunt, and the wise owner acts accordingly. A properly brought up kitten from a reputable breeder should be trained to use a scratching post already. If there was a post in the kittens' quarters on which to demonstrate, the mother will have shown her young what to do. Cats learn everything by imitation: hence the English word 'copycat'.

If you invest in a cat tree, let it be for sleeping, scratching and retreat only. Do not feed the cats up there: make them come down for food in the usual place.

Indoor cats may need to have their claws cut. (See the grooming section on page 110.)

Carrying box
It is a good idea to buy a carrying box when you buy your first kitten, so that you can collect the kitten in it and use it thereafter. Since the box should last the life of the animal, it is worth buying a good

Litter Scoops

one. You can obtain cardboard carriers that serve well enough for one or two journeys, but for long-term use you will need something more substantial. A good investment is the Hi-Flyer, an injection-moulded plastic cat-carrying box that doubles as a place for the queen to have her kittens, or can be used as a covered bed or as two beds. One of the beauties of this carrier is that there is no metal to add to the cost and weight; it weighs only 2.7kg (6lb) empty. It will take two adult cats for a short journey or one cat with a litter tray for a longer journey and it costs no more than a basket of the same size. Most pet stores stock it. (See also page 149.)

Most airlines in Europe do not allow cats in the passenger section of the aircraft and they would normally travel in a carrying box as cargo. In America, if allowed in the passenger section the carrier must be flat enough to go under the seat out of the way.

Exercise, toys and play

Cats that are allowed to roam free will exercise themselves chasing leaves, butterflies or other prey; climbing trees; running from the neighbourhood dog; and so on. When they come indoors it will probably be for a good rest by the fireside or on somebody's lap. Cats that are confined for one reason or another have less scope for exercise. These creatures include not only newly arrived kittens, but breeding stock, cats in boarding catteries and quarantine and any cat living in hazardous traffic conditions or a high-rise apart-ment. Encourage such animals to exercise by providing safe toys and setting time aside to play with them. Play is also a good way to establish a human-cat relationship.

Cats love to chase small movable objects such as a rolled up piece of silver foil or a small lightweight ball. They are also fascinated with any mouse-shaped object, whether it is made of fur or cloth. They like to hold it in their paws, throw it in the air and pounce upon it. You can sometimes obtain cloth mice filled with dried catnip. This is a perennial aromatic herb, which can be grown in most gardens. It is harvested on a dry day, just as the flowers are about to open and dried in the sun or a dry room. The stalks are aromatic, but the leaves and flowers are more so. The herb seems to have a psychological effect on cats, who just love the stuff; though you may find your cat less entranced by catnip in kitten-hood than when it matures. Adults will roll in it, eat it, sniff it and play with it. Their behaviour sometimes resembles a drunken man's. Close contact with catnip obviously sends cats into a 'high' but there are no known ill-effects. Incidentally, real fur toys are usually made out of rabbit skin and their animal smell lends these a special attraction.

Various toys can be hung by elastic from refrigerator and other door handles. The toys cannot be lost and they bounce around in a

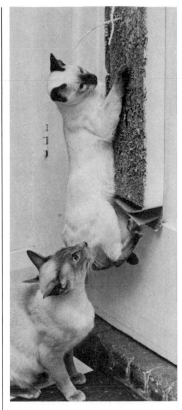

Above: Two Siamese cats using a cardboard scratching pad, one of many types that will prevent your cat scratching the furniture.

Above: Deluxe scratching posts combine a carpet-covered base and toys to bat around, as this house-hold pet demonstrates.

most inviting way when patted with an investigating paw. Sometimes spider shapes will excite the feline mind, which is always ready for a game of make-believe.

Many pet shops sell a variety of cats' toys and of course you can make you own. Toys with loose string or wool should be avoided, but empty cotton reels (spools) are ideal. Needles and pins are dan-gerous if swallowed and should not be left about. You can buy loose, dried catnip seeds and grow your own in the garden. The only disadvantage of growing your own is that the neighbourhood cats will

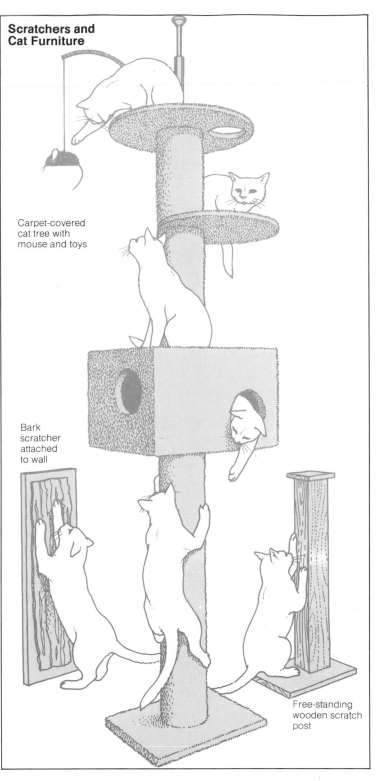

Scratchers and Cat Furniture

Carpet-covered cat tree with mouse and toys

Bark scratcher attached to wall

Free-standing wooden scratch post

Above: Bark is a natural substance for scratchers and free-standing versions are convenient for the home. All types will be well used.

probably decide to use your own garden as the local cat club's head-quarters.

Two kittens will play quite happily together with no toys at all, but as they do like to play 'tab' or 'he' all over the furniture, providing a cat tree for this purpose is a good idea if you can afford it.

Restraint

Because a playful kitten or cat may damage the furniture if unsupervised it is wise not to give your pet the run of the house while you are out. Instead, arrange to confine it to one room that contains

Above: Cat trees are fun if you have the space and more than one cat. The family enjoy this and the cats can retreat out of harm's way.

all the necessities, such as food and water, litter tray, a warm place to sleep and some form of amusement. Cats show an intelligent interest in everything that goes on around them and like to sit in a window watching the world outside: passing people and cars going by, birds, rabbits and perhaps a stray cat crossing their territory. From a safe place inside a house they often hurl insults at such an intruder from a half open mouth, while the tail thrashes from side to side in indignation.

If your cat is not to be allowed full freedom you must provide it with a supply of grass. Cats instinctively eat grass to provide their digestive system with roughage. A free-roaming cat will choose the rather coarse-bladed grass found in the unkempt part of a garden. Confined cats can have such grass grown for them in a pot. It is called cocksfoot grass and the seeds can be bought cheaply in pet shops. This grass takes about six weeks to grow and successive pots can be brought on. You can also obtain 'instant grass' packs with trade names such as 'Pussy Lawn'. You just add water and the grass is ready to eat in 7-10 days according to the temperature. It is worth the extra cost and cats love it. Ideal for apartment cats.

Fresh air

For kittens that cannot be raised with complete freedom to come and go as they please, an outdoor run will be beneficial. If there is plenty of wild life to be seen in the garden your cat will be happier outside than sitting indoors, and will appreciate the fresh air. The run can lead off the house or be a separate unit in the garden. A garden run should include provisions for sunbathing and for getting out of the sun, rain or cold as the cat's mood or the weather dictates. There should be a small house (with some form of heating for foreign shorthaired breeds) and as large a run as you can afford, with shelves at differing heights for exercise and amusement. Unlike dogs, cats in an outdoor run must have a wire roof, because they are great escapers.

Arrival of the new kitten

You have acquired all the basic equipment your kitten will need

Above: The big outdoors awaits this tiny Persian kitten. Making its first foray into the garden, it is taking an immediate interest in all the surroundings.

Indoor Grass

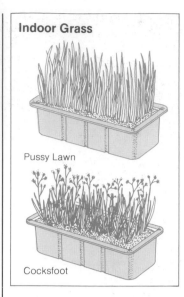

Pussy Lawn

Cocksfoot

Above: Cats kept indoors can have cocksfoot grass grown from seed or 'instant' grass packs are now available, such as 'Pussy Lawn', ready to eat in 7-10 days.

including the carrier to collect her (for the rest of this section I shall assume that the kitten is female). Now comes the big day when you bring her home and introduce her to the household. It is best to introduce her to one room at a time, starting with the room that contains her litter tray, food dishes and other items. If she has just had a long journey, the kitten will probably be wanting to use the litter tray.

All doors and windows should be shut and any chimney blocked up before the carrier is opened. It is wisest to let the kitten come out in her own time. Just open the lid and wait, perhaps making encour-

aging noises. At last she will jump out and begin to investigate, discovering all the places where she can retreat in an emergency, for example behind a boiler or refrigerator, under chairs or in cupboards. Resist the temptation to pick her up before she has finished smelling everything and getting her bearings. When she discovers the litter tray she may perform at once.

Below: Safety is combined with fresh air in this spacious run, complete with house for shelter and space for exercise.

It is unlikely she will be hungry, but once she sits down to wash you can be sure that she has made herself at home and you can then try offering food. Water should always be available and changed frequently. Regular feeding times should be established from the start and stuck to religiously. Offer no titbits between meals and serve all meals in the same place. This will encourage the kitten to learn that food served in the dining room is nothing to do with her. Feeding her before you yourselves eat will help to stop her begging food meant for others. Food not eaten in 20 minutes should be taken up and not offered again until the next mealtime.

Once the kitten has grown used to one room, you can gradually introduce her to others, but always allow access to 'her' room to avoid accidents. You can assure this by inserting a cat door in the door between the two rooms. Using her 'mini' door the cat can go from room to room without obliging you to keep getting up to let her in and out. However, do not allow your new kitten out of the house for several days; and even then make sure she knows where she lives in relation to the immediate surroundings. If these are safe and quiet you may decide to let your pet have full freedom and insert a cat door into an outer door of the house, so that she can come and go as she pleases.

First night

The first night in a new home will be the most traumatic for your kitten. She will be missing her mother and litter mates and be surrounded by strange smells, sights and noises. Comfort your kitten by holding her, stroking her gently and talking to her softly. This is the time to build up her confidence and begin to develop the loving relationship which you both hope will be the order of her life with your family from now on.

The first night is the time to decide whether your pet will sleep for the rest of her life in her own bed in the kitchen or in your bed or one of the children's beds. Left to the kitten, the choice would be to sleep with one of the family. In fact, her ideal would be all the family in a heap in one bed, cat style. She does not understand this strange human habit of each person going to a separate, cold, lonely bed, for she was brought up to lie in a heap, and knows that the centre of the heap is the warmest place. So if you allow her into your room, a smart cat will soon be in bed, not just on it. Be not deceived: once you allow her in for 'just one night', it will be a difficult task, indeed, to persuade her to sleep alone thereafter. Much better to harden your heart from the outset and put her firmly down in her own bed (with lots of fussing and stroking, of course), then turn out the light and shut the door. For a time she may wail for company, especially if she is a Siamese or Burmese; but the second night she will have received the message. On the other hand, if

Above: Handling a kitten the correct way will stop you getting scratched. This silver tabby kitten feels secure; its hind end is well supported by one hand.

she has spent the first night with you, she will take up to a fortnight to learn that you don't really want her and during that time she will spend the nights telling you where she is so that you can come and get her. You have been warned!

Handling
Normally it is wise to use both hands to pick up a kitten. Place one hand under the body behind the front paws to lift her and use the other hand to support the hind-quarters. In this way the kitten will feel secure and not struggle. If children are shown from the beginning the correct way to handle a kitten, they will not get scratched. It is when a kitten feels she is about to fall or lose her footing that she struggles to get a foothold and is liable to scratch someone in the process. Always support a kitten's hind feet so that she feels secure.

If destined for a show career, a cat can begin being handled at a very early age. You should hold it up high to examine it from all angles and position it on a table as it will be handled in the show ring.

Grooming
For a very young kitten brushing and combing generally turn into a game, with the kitten biting the brush and comb. Later she learns to appreciate that she feels better for grooming, and really enjoys it. Cats love routine, and regular grooming—like mealtimes and playtimes—helps to enliven the day. Full details of grooming procedure appear in a separate section starting on page 107. Fleas and other parasites are dealt with on pages 117-118.

Tricks
Some cats can be taught retrieving, shaking hands and other tricks usually credited only to dogs. Certainly, it helps if cats learn from an experienced dog trainer. But many a cat will sit up and beg

Above: Many kittens can be trained to do tricks. This Chinchilla Persian kitten is responding to its owner's instructions to sit up.

before a meal if you hold the plate of food above the cat's head. If you also ask: 'What do you say?' or a similar phrase each time, the cat will meow and you can then reward and so reinforce this behaviour by giving the food. Most cats like the taste of yeast tablets and would soon learn to associate the sound of your shaking the yeast tablet tin with the giving of titbits. A cat even seems to come to enjoy the routine of sitting up on its hind legs (or adopting some other pose) on command, before being rewarded with a tablet. It is wise to make this a routine performance repeated at the same time every day.

A well-run household is a happy household and when such routines are established you will find the cats present themselves at the right times in the right places for all activities. Visitors will be astonished that your cats are so beautifully behaved. They always thought you couldn't train a cat!

The cat's name
Your cat will learn her name as you repeat it each time you call her for food, grooming, playtime and so on. It is important for her to have a name that she responds to. In naming a cat, therefore, make sure you choose a name you can

shout over the housetops without embarrassment when she has strayed and you want to recall her. For this reason it is easier to shout vowels rather than consonants, and two syllables rather than one. If your cat is a pedigree animal your name for her will probably be much shorter and simpler than the grand official cattery name in which she will have been registered and under which you would present her at shows. Yours is the pet name by which she will be known to all the family. Teaching her to respond to this name could save her life in an emergency.

However, if you allow her out and she wears a collar and identity disc, this should not include her pet name: the thief could entice her away with that. The disc should carry only the owner's name, address and telephone number.

Inoculations
Once your kitten has settled down in her new home, have her checked by a veterinarian and given any inoculations that may be needed. The breeder should have supplied a certificate showing what injections, if any, the kitten has had before leaving home and there should be a note saying what other action should be taken and when. The veterinarian will want to see these certificates before he decides what else needs to be given. He will also say when you should bring your pet again, as an adult, for a booster injection.

Spaying
If you have not obtained your kitten for future breeding or showing you should have her spayed (or him neutered) when about six to eight months old, or earlier if the cat is one of the precocious Foreign Shorthairs: their females sometimes 'call' and males may spray as early as four months. These are perfectly normal functions for entire adults, but it is advisable to spay or neuter before these habits are established in a kitten kept just as a pet. (See also the section on breeding and rearing, which starts on page 121.) If a male is not spraying, it can be left until 10-12 months old.

Relationships
As one of the family, the kitten will probably develop different relation-ships—some closer than others—with human members of the group. If grandma is the only human at home while the others are at school or work, the kitten will talk to her and may curl up on her lap after lunch at the same time every day. The two will have that kind of understanding. When the children return from school, it may be playtime for the kitten, and time for teaching tricks with rewards. As she hears the children come in, the kitten will bound towards them, ready for this next part of her daily routine. Later on, or perhaps first thing in the morning, the grooming session takes place with maybe yet another member of the family who has a different but equally meaningful relationship with the little feline member. Lastly, at night comes the final cuddle of the day, eagerly looked forward to by kitten and owner.

Discipline
Physically punishing a cat for some misdemeanour is pointless: the creature simply does not associate the punishment with the crime and just thinks you are being unpleasant. The best way to show your displeasure is a loud 'No!' If your usual voice is soft and cooing, a harsh command should be enough to make the animal stop doing whatever it is that displeases you—at least while you are there! Many Americans swear by a water pistol if all else fails and I am assured that it is very effective, although British cat-lovers may think it unsporting. It should be aimed at the body, never at the eyes, where it might cause serious injury.

As with children, keep the list of forbidden activities short, but enforce discipline firmly. Remember, though, that a cat is a cat and no amount of trying to make it behave like a child will succeed. It can act only within its animal framework of instinct and intelligence and should not be punished purely for being a cat. Thoughtful owners will study cat nature and reach an under-standing of what can and cannot be expected from cat behaviour. If you or your family cannot tolerate normal cat behaviour, you probably should not have a cat.

UNDERSTANDING YOUR CAT

In order to enjoy your cat to the full, you must understand what kind of animal it is. This means discovering its needs, desires, instincts and, perhaps, neuroses. First, remember that a cat is not a dog and cannot be expected to behave like one. It is true that some cats trained by dog owners will retrieve, go for walks with the dogs, and even act as watchdogs about the house. Cats can also learn to perform certain tricks. But cats behave in such ways only when it is in their own interest and not conflicting with something they would rather be doing. Unlike dogs, cats never learn complete obedience. This is not because dogs have been domesticated longer than cats: cats are just made differently, with inborn, instinctive and unalterable behaviour characteristics peculiar to themselves. So remember too that a cat is not a child. It would be cruel to try to condition your cat to behave like a dog or a child.

Instincts
Feeding, scratching, hunting, playing, loving, curiosity, mating and sleeping are instincts that play important parts in a cat's life. Some of these are discussed here, others have chapters to themselves.

Scratching. Because your cat will scratch instinctively, it is better to provide a suitable place for this activity rather than leaving the cat no choice but the best furniture. Providing a scratching post as soon as you obtain a cat will prevent your pet becoming unpopular about the house. (See also pages 88-89.)

Hunting. No cat should be scolded for hunting: cats are biologically programmed to

Above: Indoors a cat will chase and jump at moving toys. This should be encouraged to keep your pet amused and exercised.

Left: Hunting is a natural pursuit for cats. Outdoors they will find plenty of things to stalk and chase, so keeping themselves fit.

indulge in this behaviour. One day when a friend's Siamese appeared on the lawn with a baby rabbit in his mouth, I remember my friend complaining: 'I have told him a hundred times he is not to catch rabbits!' She chastised the cat and removed the rabbit, provoking a grieved sound from the cat, who plainly felt he was right and she was unjust. I was ashamed of my friend and told her so. Despite her efforts she never altered her cat's instincts. Later he came to me for his holidays while she was away, and I was told he ate very little. In fact I had never had such a greedy cat. Quite clearly at home, surrounded by prey-filled corn fields, he ate out a great deal. Most of the time he was simply smart

enough not to let her catch him!

Some owners object to their cats bringing home trophies. People tend to see these as presents, but they most likely show no more than a strongly developed instinct to bring prey to the nest, even when there are no kittens to be fed. Without this parental instinct many wild kittens would die.

Mice and rats are one thing, birds another, but to a cat all are just moving prey; so you should not commend your cat for killing rats and mice and scold it for killing birds. If you are a bird lover it is wise to invest in a cat-proof bird table or a window bird feeder, so you and your cat can watch the birds from inside the house. Of course the cat will chatter at the birds and flick its tail from side to side, but both will be safe.

Playing. This instinct is associated with hunting but the cat is the only animal to play with its prey before killing it. It is therefore an important instinct that must be indulged at home. Toys for the indoor cat are a must and will keep it exercised and amused for hours. Outside cats will chase anything that moves and even play make-believe: chasing and pouncing on imaginary prey. During play on its own or with another kitten or cat there will be embracing, pawing, biting, chasing, pouncing, stalking, leaping, catching, rolling, kicking with the hind feet and neck hugging. All are good exercise for muscle tone, and the wise owner will make sure that the cat can enjoy some of these activities during its day.

Loving. Cats are naturally affectionate creatures and need physical contact with other cats, other animals or humans. They respond enormously to affection, hand stroking and cuddling and give a five-fold return in love and loyalty.

Curiosity. This is another essentially feline attribute. Cats are so curious that they will 'help' you pack or unpack any parcel. They love the noise of rustling paper and will take a great interest in what you are doing with it. Unfortunately some breeds, particularly Burmese, are also car-conscious and liable to jump into anybody's car, perhaps ending up miles from home. Sometimes they get returned, but not always. Because of their curiosity they will walk into any open door and regularly visit the neighbours, if allowed out. Some of mine have been reported not only calling on the neighbours but once actually getting into bed with them! If you are busy and often out, and at the same time allow your pets full freedom, you may find that they have two homes: while you are away they spend their time in their second home, returning to yours when you come back. Or you may find someone else's cat visiting you, walking indoors and making itself at home (if your cats will let it) and later going back to its owner. There are many stories of a cat enjoying double rations provided by two would-be owners.

Mating. This is one of the few natural-instincts best suppressed in most cats, simply because it accounts for the hundreds of thousands of unwanted kittens and cats that have to be put down every year. As we explain elsewhere in this book, having a cat sterilized is not cruel, and actually helps the creature to settle down to domestic life.

Sleeping. For most cats this may well rank in importance only after eating and loving. Members of the cat family sleep for approximately 65 percent of their life, and should not be denied the right to do so. Prevent children constantly waking up cats to play with them, and protect the cats from other repeated harassments. The whole family should recognize that cats need a lot of sleep somewhere quiet, dark and warm (or cool if the weather is hot).

Above: Cats will take a lively interest in everything. Here a Seal-point Siamese watches the world from a caravan window.

Even asleep, cats are not boring. Watch one closely and you will find its eyes, paws, ears and whiskers twitching. The dreaming cat is obviously reliving a hunt or some other waking activity. On waking, cats invariably stretch to their fullest extent, pushing one leg at a time away from them; then they often have a good wash to wake themselves up.

Cats love to sleep in secret places and even as kittens may disappear for a quiet snooze. I

remember losing a whole litter of kittens one afternoon. I was sure they could not get out of the house, but where were they? Eventually when it came near to feeding time, I saw one kitten emerge from behind the books on an open shelf of a bookcase. I expressed great surprise at seeing this little creature climbing over the books, and at the sound of my voice the others swarmed over too. Needless to say, I knew where to look on another occasion. As soon as you find one place, though, they discover another.

Cats' senses
Cats are generally reputed to have nine senses: touch; smell; taste; sight; hearing; temperature; balance; place; and time.

Touch. A kitten gains awareness of touch from early contact with its mother. Her tongue will wash the young kitten and she will move it towards her in the nest with her paws. So the kitten learns to associate its mother's tongue with a caring attitude; later in life stroking by a human hand becomes a substitute for licking by the mother. Petting and grooming are said to reduce tension by slowing down the heart beat. This is one reason why a cat will often start to wash when in doubt or after a nasty fright.

Touch is also the sense that comes into play when a cat chooses its sleeping place. Cats seem to be able to sense texture through their paws; they like warm, soft fabrics and will often refuse to stay on the lap of someone wearing a cold or slippery dress or suit of man-made fibre.

Smell. This is another sense that develops early in the nest. If kittens are moved from a familiar nest into a new one, they will shriek or cry so that the mother comes running; they know that the smell has changed. Once mother rejoins them in the new nest and reassures them with her own smell, they settle down again. Older kittens can see as well as smell their litter mates, so they are less perturbed when moved into a clean bed. Unlike puppies, kittens seem to be attached to one particular teat when breast-feeding in a litter, and it is probably the sense of smell that guides each kitten to its proper place. Because of their acute sense of smell cats will scrutinize closely every new object that comes into the home.

When a cat rubs up against a piece of furniture or a human leg, it leaves a scent or a mark on it. Similarly, two cats rubbing heads together will leave their scent on each other, so that they recognize each other next time they meet. If one cat in a household goes off to stud to be mated, she will return and be rejected at first by those who stayed at home because she will now carry the stud cat's smell, which is unacceptable to them. She will have to wash them and tell them how pleased she is to see them again before they will believe

Below: Sometimes a cat's curious nature gets it into some awkward situations. Here a bold kitten meets a goat for the first time.

that it is her and be prepared to welcome her. In the same way, your cat will know when you have been to a house where there are other cats; and while you were there the cats you met would have known that you were a cat owner. The scent that a cat emits may tell other cats far more than we realize about its sex, age and health.

It is probably the smell of a strange place that makes some cats detest moving house. They feel secure with remembered

Below: A kitten's introduction to touch is the mother's tongue. She grooms the kitten from head to toe and makes a game of it too.

smells and sometimes even dislike the furniture to be shifted. Some find moving home so traumatic that they go off their food and wander about mewing. A few cats even become aggressive, but this is unusual. Lots of loving and attention is the answer, and most cats eventually settle down again. Even so it is wise to keep them in for a few days to make sure they do not take off, forget where they now live and get lost. Intelligent, or perhaps rather emotionally stable or confident, cats seem to adapt faster than others.

Cats instinctively like pleasant smells and (in a litter tray or elsewhere) try to cover up the nasty smell of their own excreta.

Above: A Burmese on the defensive (left) has dilated pupils. A calm and composed silver tabby cat (right) has 'slit' pupils. Cats on the attack also have slit eyes.

The scents of certain plants fascinate many cats. Top on the list is the aromatic perennial herb catnip, which seems to give them a 'high'. Cats will instinctively roll in a bed of catnip, or play with toys stuffed with catnip or even with dried catnip leaves and flowers purchased in pet shops. Some cats are more susceptible than others, and adults like catnip more than kittens do. If you wish to grow your own, the seeds are *Nepeta*

cataria (it is the nepetalactone in the plant that attracts). Valerian is another plant liked by cats; and, left to themselves, cats will go round the garden smelling the flowers. This is not always to 'read' who has been in the garden that day; cats simply like lovely-smelling things. Perfume is another favourite.

Taste. Taste is linked to smell and a cat that cannot smell for some reason will often refuse to eat. Occasionally you will see your cat smelling something with its mouth open: this is known as 'Flehmening'. The purpose is to let scent particles reach the vomeronasal organ and so to discover more than the cat would learn merely by using its nostrils. Catnip, a stranger or a sexual stimulus will trigger off this reaction, which involves a combination of taste and smell.

Sight. Cats have acute eyesight, but are better able and more likely to see objects when they are moving than when they are still. A cat instinctively knows this, and will 'freeze' when it sees another cat; similarly, a mouse will 'freeze' hoping to be overlooked if a cat is approaching. In poor light cats can see better than we can, but they can see nothing at all in total darkness. Their pupils dilate to enable them to see more clearly when the light is dim, and form narrow slits in broad daylight. A cat's pupils also dilate when it is on the defensive, and contract when it attacks. Cats are not colour-blind as many people testify.

Many cats take a lively interest in other cats seen on television or home movies, and may even try to get onto the screen and join in the fun. Other cats simply seem to enjoy watching television; presumably they find its flickering images fascinating.

Hearing. Cats have acute hearing and can detect sounds too faint for

us to register. This explains the 'extra' sense that appears to tell your cat that someone is approaching the door or telephoning before you yourself hear a knock or a ring. The cat has simply picked up the first faint sound vibrations before you have.

White cats with blue eyes tend to be deaf (see page 44). But even deaf cats seem to be able to 'hear' with other parts of the body. This probably means that they sense sound vibrations as these pass through solid objects.

Cats have marked likes and dislikes in sounds. Some are said to like music. One boarding cattery I know plays music to its visiting cats at certain hours during the day to reassure them and make them feel more at home when they may be disturbed by the change of scene. Most cats dislike loud noises, and I remember one brown Burmese queen complaining bitterly in a very loud voice every time the telephone rang. Cats will avoid the dustbin area on garbage collection day, and make themselves scarce if any building or alterations are in progress. In fact if there is going to be much noise in your house (including wild teenage discos) it is probably kindest to put your cat in a room with every comfort as far away from the noise as possible. Cats not restrained in this way have been known to take off and not come home for days.

You will find that your cat is sensitive to the tone of your voice. This has practical applications, for it helps you control its behaviour, though of course less completely than that of a dog. Cats dislike shouting, so a shouted command may make your pet stop some activity that you dislike — cats will do almost anything for a quiet life! At the same time they enjoy responding to the sound of their name and your cat will generally come when called providing you resist the urge to call for no good reason. If there is some point in its responding (a cuddle, for instance) it will do so, but if there is no reward it is unlikely to come next time you call. If your cat has only just gone out, and suspects that your call means 'come along in now', it will completely ignore you. Cats are incredibly reasonable beings and do not fit in well in unreasonable households.

Cats love you to whisper to them and will purr with great gusto while you whisper sweet nothings in their ears. Because their ears are so sensitive, what you say is not nearly so important as the tone of your voice.

Temperature. This is an individual characteristic: some cats like it hot and some like it cold. The foreign, thinner coated cats like and need plenty of heat and will be found sunbathing on a hot summer's day, perhaps reclining on a bed of catnip, or lawn cuttings (which generate heat). In cold or temperate climates most cats prefer to sleep in a warm place indoors. A cat that is too hot will likewise find a cool

Above: A Tortoiseshell British Shorthair using its fine sense of balance to climb high into a tree, perhaps after a tormenting bird.

draught to sit in. Most cats that are allowed on the furniture (as such clean animals surely should be) soon learn that when a human rises from a chair, the seat will be pleasantly warm. In fact when you have to remove a cat from your lap to answer the door, it will be much less annoyed if you place it on the seat of your chair than if you plonk it down on a cold floor. You can pick up the cat when you come back and it will hardly know that you have been gone.

Balance. Cats have an extraordinary sense of balance which they need for climbing trees, roof tops and other — to us — perilous places such as ledges and window sills. This sense of balance helps cats attain places that are out of our reach and that of their natural enemies, dogs and foxes. A quick sprint and climb, and a pursued cat is safely high up a tree. It is quite probable that whatever tree a cat or kitten ascends, it can also descend. When we see a very tiny kitten driven to the top of a tall tree in fright because of a neighbour's dog, we are apt to panic and call the fire brigade. But if we let well alone, nine times out of ten the kitten will come down again of its own accord, although maybe not before dark, if its misguided would-be saviours set up a commotion below.

If a cat falls from low or medium heights its sense of balance ensures that it twists its body in the air and lands securely on its feet — an accomplishment that helps to

prevent injury. However, from a very great height a cat can also fall to its death.

Place. Numerous stories, some well authenticated, tell of cats travelling hundreds of miles from their owners' new homes back to the places where they used to live. Like homing pigeons, cats must have some sort of instinctive direction-finding ability that enables them to do this; following a scent trail could explain only a much shorter return journey.

Time. Cats appreciate routine. They like the same things to happen at the same times every day or every week. They expect meals to arrive at fixed times and are prepared to be around to eat them then. This makes life easier for us as well as them, except perhaps at weekends when we might prefer a break from routine chores. Cats enjoy being groomed regularly, too. In fact they like a well-ordered life, which is surprising in an animal that in many ways is a supreme individualist.

Maybe these nine highly developed senses help to explain why cats reputedly have nine lives.

Communication
Cats can communicate with one another, other animals and humans in two ways: vocally, and by body language.

Vocal language. Cat language is less formally circumscribed than ours. Cats simply make whatever noise appears appropriate to the occasion. An owner who takes the time and trouble to listen to, as well as talk to, her pets will readily come to understand the different nuances of sound they produce,

Above: A Siamese cat complaining vocally about something. Its devoted owner will be sure to know what it is all about.

and thus what each is 'saying' to her. So many people (myself included) swear that they and their cats understand each other, that surely this must be true. However, to enjoy this kind of understanding with a cat you must take time to know your pet and listen to it carefully. It is just the same as communicating with people: you have to listen to your husband or your children as well as talk to them if you hope for a two-way relationship. Without love, kindness, compassion, patience and observation you will gain no true understanding between you and your pet.

Once you start to pay heed to what your cat is saying, you will soon learn its basic vocabulary. Thus it may nag you vocally to 'come to bed' at bedtime: cats like retiring the same time each night.

Your cat will greet your daily homecoming with a special sound like a chirrup (what we used to call 'going into overdrive with its purr') when you pick it up to say, 'Hello, and what sort of a day have you had?' It is a sound reserved for greetings and scarcely heard at any other time.

Other sounds include purring, when the cat is relaxed; hissing, when uncertain; growling, when convinced you are intruding into its affairs or possessions; and various other sounds for: 'I'm hungry, what's for dinner'; 'Let met out'; 'Please open the door'; 'Can I come onto your lap'; and 'Let's have a game!' The complaining voice: 'Where have you been all day?' is quite distinct from sounds of anger or indignation. Siamese cats often protest about nothing in particular or because it is raining ('Why don't you turn it off?') or in anticipation of frightful things that are about to happen, such as a visit to the veterinarian.

We must also mention the silent meow. This is a seemingly sound-less vocalization in which the cat opens its mouth to tell us some-thing or make a request but no audible sound comes out. It is a very endearing gesture that usually gets results. Maybe in fact there is a sound that other animals can hear.

Some cats will always speak when spoken to, and appear to possess a vocabulary of small talk.

As an owner, you should always respond to a vocal greeting from your cat. Whenever I entered the house, I used to say, 'Hello, sweet-hearts,' to mine, picking them up for a quick cuddle at the same time. Once this has become a routine, you can be sure that they will always be at the door to greet you. Never feed your cats, no matter how overdue the meal is, until the formal greetings have taken place. They should never be allowed to think that food is more important than good manners.

Most vocal sounds are for communicating with humans. The main exceptions are mothers talking to their kittens, and mating vocalizations. The mother cat bleats after her kittens if they run away from her when she wants them nearby. She has other sounds, which they obviously understand, for 'Come and have lunch' or 'It's time for bed'. And later they learn from her to growl over a live mouse that she has brought in: this warning helps to keep their prey from being taken by other cats.

All of us are liable to hear the wailing sounds of females on heat or toms on roof-tops in the middle of the night. Owners of females need to know that when a young queen starts to roll on the floor and push her head along the ground, with her rear in the air, she is not insane or suffering, just calling for a mate. She has just discovered that she is female and is feeling rather sexy about it. If she is not to be allowed to have kittens you should take her to the veterinarian for a neutering operation; but wait until she has gone off call because if done while the cat is on heat she may call vocally for the rest of her life.

Above: A cat pleased to see its owner will move forwards with its tail held high in the air like this ginger and white pet cat.

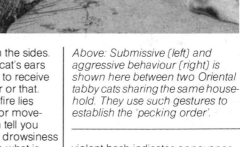

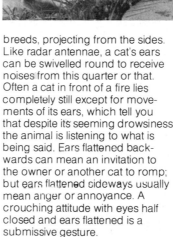

Above: Submissive (left) and aggressive behaviour (right) is shown here between two Oriental tabby cats sharing the same house-hold. They use such gestures to establish the 'pecking order'.

Body language. Apart from sexual vocalizing, adult cats usually communicate with each other by body language. This can involve movement of the tail, ears, paws, whiskers, eyes, head or body.

The tail is very expressive and may be held upright for pleasure and greeting or hung low and curled under in a fight. Cats show anger by lashing the tail from side to side, unlike dogs, which wag their tails when pleased.

Apart from cats with folded ears, cats normally wear the ears upright on top of the head or, in some

---

Below: A Burmese on the defensive. The back is arched, the tail is fluffed out and a cacophony of spitting and wailing rends the air.

breeds, projecting from the sides. Like radar antennae, a cat's ears can be swivelled round to receive noises from this quarter or that. Often a cat in front of a fire lies completely still except for move-ments of its ears, which tell you that despite its seeming drowsiness the animal is listening to what is being said. Ears flattened back-wards can mean an invitation to the owner or another cat to romp; but ears flattened sideways usually mean anger or annoyance. A crouching attitude with eyes half closed and ears flattened is a submissive gesture.

A mother cat will use her paws to hold kittens down so that she can wash them, or to prevent them straying. Cats also use their paws to pin down an enemy in a fight. A

violent bash indicates annoyance, possibly with claws unsheathed. But a gentle tap on the cheek or the nose with the claws well sheathed can mean: 'I love you'.

Whiskers change direction to suit various moods, and also twitch significantly.

Eyes may be wide open, showing interest in what you are doing; vacant, staring you out; or half closed in ecstasy while a cat is being stroked. Cats also seem to use their eyes for focussing on something that simply is not there. Or can they see things we cannot?

The head is used expressively for butting up to a person to gain attention, or as a loving gesture. Cats butt each other in this friendly way and it is certainly a signal of acceptance. The head is also used extensively in courtship.

The body itself can tell us much about what a cat is thinking and feeling. A cat turned sideways with arched back and fur fluffed up will be on the defensive, usually against another cat or perhaps a dog encroaching on its territory. A queen with kittens to protect may often take up this position. Aggres-sion, on the other hand, is signalled by a confident attack. The cat will move towards the intruder, expecting submission.

Sitting near a door with the head raised means: 'Please open the door, I want to go out.' Sitting near a door but pointing towards the floor may mean: 'There is a kitten behind the door,' or 'There's someone outside.' Some cats eager to get out jump up at the door handle, and many can open not only lever handles but round door knobs with a little practice. Others have been reported working a door knocker of the house where they live, then sitting back, waiting confidently for it to be opened. I have also known cats attack people who have come into the house without knocking or being let in in the usual fashion. The cat is acting as a watch-dog.

A 'tea-cosy' cat sitting on a chair or window-sill with paws tucked neatly underneath itself and tail wrapped round its body is an indication of a happy, relaxed, unthreatened cat. Sitting upright in a window shows that a cat is intensely interested in people, birds, and other passing forms of life. However, on seeing another cat enter its territory, the watcher will swish its tail, open its mouth and chatter in a threatening fashion, full of indignation.

If you have had to chastise your cat and its feelings have been hurt, the animal may register displeasure by sitting grooming itself with its back to you. This rebuke is meant to goad you into talking it round and making a fuss of it, to which the cat finally responds. This is often followed by skittish behaviour, for your pet will be glad there is no more unpleasantness and all is forgiven.

Moods and feelings
When a cat gets to know you as its owner, it will respond to your mood. If you are ill, the creature will sit with you on your bed all day,

Below: Outdoor exercise can be enjoyed even in unsafe areas by training your cat to a harness and lead, preferably an elastic one.

content just to be with you. If you are happy, it will catch your mood and invite you to have a little game. We should likewise respond to the moods of our cats. They need cuddling sometimes more than others. We should never be too busy to pick them up for a bit of attention, if it is required. Siamese and Burmese cats can be rather demanding in this respect. On a lovely day they may want to go for a walk, and they make it clear that they want you to go along as well. Don't always be too busy. Make time for togetherness. Of course many cats do not have the freedom to go out into a garden, but even if full freedom is not possible you and your cat can still enjoy a walk with harness and lead. Remember, however, that you are not walking a dog. The cat will not walk at your heel: it will probably lead the way. This is all right provided you don't let your pet rush up a tree, leaving you holding the lead at the bottom, or turn to face you and back out of its harness. Unless you are careful almost any breed will do one or the other, as cats are great escapers. Handled properly, the all-elastic kind of harness helps to make cat management easy as well as being comfortable for all shapes and sizes of cat.

The pensive mood finds your cat sitting in the window. 'Sometimes I sits and thinks, and sometimes I just sits' is very applicable to cats.

If a cat wants sympathy and has previously had a leg in plaster, it will suddenly start limping again to fend off a chastisement!

Much like children, cats are capable of feeling angry, possessive, jealous, hungry, tired, sick, stroppy, resentful, rebellious, disgusted and disdainful. They can also feel happy, playful, affectionate, loving, restful, friendly and thought-

Above: This White Persian has lifted herself up to her owner's hand in the hope of being stroked and petted. This is one way cats show their affection for owners.

ful. One thing cats (unlike dogs) never seem to feel is guilty. It is therefore useless to punish a cat, because it never associates the punishment with the crime. The creature just thinks you are being mean for hurting it. However, cats can feel embarrassed, for example after you have said 'No' or after it has had an argument with another animal. The cure for such embarrassment is compulsive self-grooming. When in doubt wash, is the cat's motto.

Anybody who has already owned a cat will be familiar with the phenomenon known as the 'mad half hour'. Early evening is often the time when a cat fully wakes up from its afternoon siesta in the sun or snooze by the boiler. In the wild this may be the traditional time to think about hunting for the evening meal. Anyway many cats now unleash a burst of super feline energy and rush madly all over the furniture, up the stairs and down again, and round and round in circles, leaping and pouncing on pretended prey. Make this a time for family fun and games, tricks and exercise. Harness the energy constructively. As they grow older most cats get more staid but will still occasionally indulge in a mad half hour. So don't expect them always to sit still and be quiet. Realize that they have to let off steam, particularly if they do not have a free run outdoors.

Cats like to play hide and seek. Yours will soon catch on if you hunt it and let out a shriek when you find it. Your cat will disappear once more, inviting you to hunt again. When you find it repeat the same sound of delight and surprise as before and off it will race yet again to another hiding spot. If you have more than one cat, you will find that they play hide and seek together. Some owners have reported that after their cats found objects their owners had hidden, the animals rushed out of the room so their owners could hide the object again. The cats themselves will suggest all sorts of games that will appeal to them. Be responsive. Cats usually love movement, so many games will be chasing moving objects, and apart from sophisticated toys they will enjoy most a small piece of silver foil rolled into a ball. They are also intrigued by the rustle of a screwed-up ball of cellophane unfolding itself. Whatever happens, try not to laugh at a cat: the creature will hate it. Seemingly a laughed-at cat senses an affront to its dignity.

Cats are capable of feeling bereavement when their owner or an animal friend dies or departs. Some cats will pine dreadfully on these occasions and seem entirely inconsolable. They will go off their food and creep about the house mewing piteously. There are stories of cats and dogs sitting on people's graves long after they have been buried. The first black cat we had and buried in the garden at only two years old had a tabby friend who came and sat on his grave every day for weeks. Then he suddenly disappeared.

Despite their individualistic nature, cats need companionship, particularly some breeds. There are stories of cats making friendships with individuals of many other animal species, even those that would normally be their prey. Because cats are so companionable they make exceptionally friendly pets. No one can be lonely if he or she owns a cat. But cats used to companionship can pine and die if deprived of it.

Training

The way you train your kitten will largely determine the sort of adult it will grow into. As kitten, so cat. So start as you mean to carry on. Do not allow a kitten to do things you would not want an adult cat to do. For instance it may be cute to see a kitten climb up you and sit on your shoulders. But if you encourage this, you cannot reasonably be cross with your pet when as a heavy adult it wants to do the same, perhaps while you have on only a thin cotton dress, or, in the bathroom, nothing at all! It is much better not to encourage this kind of thing from the beginning.

I can never understand people being less enchanted by a cat than by a kitten. It is true that young things are amusing, charming, entertaining and usually affectionate, but a properly treated adult cat should be all these things too, for many years. But a dull owner will produce a dull cat, and once a cat is ignored it will retreat into itself and become even more of a loner. If free to do so, it may even choose another home where it will be more appreciated. So treat your cat as one of the family, or do not try keeping a cat at all. Assuming that you do go ahead, choose a kitten from a breeder who has handled and played with the litter from an early age; otherwise all the kittens may be too timid. But timidity may also be acquired from the mother if she is wild and her experience has made her anti-human. Very young children should sit on the floor before being allowed to hold a young kitten, and trained not to squeeze it like a doll.

Disciplining a cat is really a simple process as your cat is more sensitive to your voice than to most other sounds, and will respond to 'No!' said in a sharp voice, if your normal voice is soft and cooing. Our first two Burmese cats were never allowed in the dining room; we figured they had enough house without that, and if they were fed before us anyway they would not mind being left out of the room while we ate. They took some persuading: each time the door opened for another course they sauntered in, and we had to remove them. They were not chased out because this would have become an interesting game. They were just told 'No!' and gently deposited on a Persian rug outside the room. Finally they got the message, and we had won. The interesting thing is that when the queen eventually had kittens, she trained them the same way. When they swarmed into the dining room, as kittens will when you open any door, she followed them bleating, and carried them out by the scruffs of their necks. I helped her, and they soon got the idea that the room was out of bounds.

Scratching the furniture or stair carpet can be handled in the same way. Similarly if your pets have their own cat tree or small scratching post and are removed to it whenever they scratch elsewhere, they will eventually respect your wishes. You must have patience,

but it will be handsomely rewarded.

Another habit that must be curbed from the outset is biting. If you allow a cat to bite, as it will when you start grooming it as a kitten, it may become quite vicious eventually. Instead of removing your hand (it will only get scratched in the process), put your hand further into the animal's mouth. You will find that your hand in its mouth prevents aggressive behaviour and the cat will back off. Teach children this trick if you can, though it takes nerve at first, for one's instinctive reaction is to try to take the hand away.

Cats do not hold grudges for long, and neither should you. Never let the sun go down on your anger, if for instance your cat has broken something valuable. This is seldom entirely the cat's fault. Make sure you tell it you love it again before it goes to sleep. Relationships are more important than possessions anyway. If you don't think so, don't have a cat!

People who live in the country and can give their cats full freedom are probably rare today, but some are lucky that way. I know one household with a Sheltie dog that frequently scouts the countryside, rounds up the cats like sheep and brings them home again.

Training, then, consists of lots of love and affection expressed in a soft voice, plus a firm 'No!' whenever cats scratch the wrong thing, go where they shouldn't, chew the houseplants or do whatever else is taboo in your household. Never hit a cat; a soft finger on its nose, like the mother cat's paw, is enough.

Social gatherings

For all their independence and individualism, cats love social

Above: Training is a trick to encourage good manners. Cats enjoy routines like this and your friends and neighbours will be very impressed. Daily routine performances with rewards add zest to a cat's quality of life.

gatherings. These are often unrelated to sexual activities. Free-roaming cats will form into groups and sit and watch each other. This may be in the sunshine or at night on the tiles. Then they go home (if they have a home to go to). If you have a large catnip patch in your garden, they are likely to use this as the local cat club's headquarters.

If the cats are not free to roam but there are many in one household, a hierarchy develops, with dominant cats, less powerful ones, and the weakest of all, which are completely victimized. A breeder will see to it that no cruelty arises and that the weaker ones are isolated for their own protection, but if it can be arranged that they can still see the others, they will be happier. (Cats love to watch each other, and in a well arranged boarding cattery or quarantine or breeding establishment, cats, although kept separately, can at least see other cats and so enjoy a measure of company.) If two queens are free running in a house and have kittens about the same time, these must be marked at birth because the dominant queen will steal the other queen's kittens if she can and mix them with hers. If the submissive queen objects, her own kittens must be given back to her and she will have to be separated so that the dominant queen cannot get to them. Again if the isolated queen

can still see the other it is better than being shut up in a room by herself without other cats' or her owner's companionship. Otherwise she may consider having kittens to be some form of punishment.

Abnormal behaviour patterns

There is no need to dwell much on abnormal behaviour patterns because your own cat should not display these if you have followed the procedures laid down in this book. However, you may take in a stray or otherwise acquire a cat with problem behaviour, so at least a few words will not be amiss.

Emotional upsets are rarer in cats than in dogs, perhaps because cats do not surrender themselves to man to quite the same degree. But cats left too much without the companionship of other animals or humans may grow so bored that they groom all day, wear out their fur and even bite their own flesh. This is a vicious circle because the more damage they do, the more they will groom to put it right. Wool sucking is frequently reported, and it may be the lanolin in wool, which smells like a queen's nipples, that attracts and soothes a young kitten if this has been removed from its mother too young.

Cats suffering bereavement may starve themselves to such an extent that they leave themselves open to infection. The cure is to give them a full-time companion for a while: a sick person or another animal, someone who can listen to their tale of woe. It is very important for cats to have someone to listen to them as well as to talk to them.

A sudden fright can cause some cats' hearts to show signs of failure. The animal may sweat profusely (not normally possible for a cat), shiver, salivate, and sit with pupils dilated. If you suspect that your cat has had a sudden fright like this, particularly if she is nursing kittens and trying to protect them, you will have to sit with her quietly and talk soothingly or she could collapse and die.

Some cats drool while being petted. This is not strictly a disorder but it may mean that their teeth or gums need veterinary attention.

By keeping a cat indoors we may be repressing its natural instincts so that the creature sublimates its desire for hunting by suddenly leaping out from behind a door or armchair and pouncing on your ankles, legs or arms. Discourage these antics by giving the cat plenty of organized play with moving objects.

Cats that are lonely, shut in, neglected and bored may defecate where they should not, in a last attempt to win their owner's attention or affection. Anyone suffering this problem and unable to spare time for the cat should find it another home where it will be loved. Occasionally there are physical reasons for urinating or defecating in the wrong places; a veterinary check will show if this is so. But the trouble is most likely to be psychological in origin.

FEEDING YOUR CAT

Much has been written about cats' nutritional requirements. Cats need a balanced diet containing proteins, carbohydrates, fats, vitamins and minerals; but about 30-40 percent should be *protein* — a higher percentage than is necessary for a dog. The best way to tell whether you are feeding the correct diet for your own cat is the animal's condition. A satisfactory diet will produce a shapely, healthy, bright-eyed, lively animal with normal stools. An unbalanced diet may cause diarrhoea, lethargy, moulting, spiky fur, scurf, dull eyes or obesity, although all these signs may be due to some specific illness or infection.

A cat's natural diet

Cats are designed primarily to eat raw meat and offal. They have canine teeth to penetrate and kill their prey and tear apart its flesh. A cat tears pieces from the carcass and swallows them whole. Cats do not have teeth designed for chewing. Therefore, it seems sensible to follow nature and serve either swallowable pieces or a large lump which the cat must tear into pieces with its canines and sharp cheek teeth. It can manage well with minced flesh and liquidized foods, and a combination of these forms of foods adds variety and interest. Some cats like the crunchy biscuit-type dried foods. They help to clean the teeth, but, if feeding these, take care that plenty of water is available.

In the wild a cat will eat small mammals, such as rabbits, rats, mice and voles; reptiles; amphibians; birds; spiders; and insects including flies and grasshoppers. Some cats also eat fish, caught by a sudden swipe of

Above: A cat has no chewing teeth; it tears its food with the large canines at the front and cuts it with the sharp-edged cheek teeth.

Left: A tabby and white household pet enjoying a bowl of semi-moist cat food, one of many types of prepared foods popular with owners.

the paw while standing on a rock overhanging the water. Yet cats seem to know instinctively that shrews, robins and bullfinches are not good to eat. But though a cat born in the wild may be able to survive, a domestic cat that has been turned out will not always fare so well. Indeed, it is cruel and an offence to turn out a domestic cat to fend for itself (see page 152).

Water

Fresh water should always be available in a clean bowl. Change the water frequently, even when the cat does not appear to use it, especially if a dog shares the drinking bowl (dogs tend to leave saliva deposits). A cat that does not drink indoors can often be

found drinking from muddy puddles. Perhaps some cats dislike our chlorinated tap water and we cannot blame them. But such animals may take boiled water or barley water. For lactating queens add a sodium citrate tablet to the water. It is worthwhile taking trouble to produce water that is acceptable to your cat because, if left to drink outside, it might choose puddles polluted by rodents or insecticides from garden spraying. If your cat will not drink water from a bowl you must add water to its food to prevent the risk of dehydration. The easiest way to add water is to serve some meals in liquidized form, which is usually acceptable.

Vitamins

Small amounts of these substances are essential to healthy growth. Fish oils, liver, seaweed powder, wheat germ, yeast, and raw or lightly cooked vegetables and milk are valuable sources of key vitamins and minerals. Serious lack of vitamins or minerals results in irreversible medical conditions and sometimes death.

Vitamin A promotes the growth of body cells and aids resistance to infection. It helps the eyes to work well in light of varying intensity. Cats are not able to synthesize this vitamin, which must thus be added to the diet in some way. It is found in egg yolks, fish-liver oils, carrots, green vegetables, grass and seaweed.

The Vitamin B complex includes vitamins promoting growth, healthy skin and eye function, and preventing various deficiency diseases. Milk, wheat germ, yeast and liver are rich in certain of these vitamins.

Vitamin C prevents the deficiency disease called scurvy. It is found in malt extract and green vegetables, grass and seaweed. This particular vitamin can be manufactured in the cat's body.

Vitamin D is known as the sunshine vitamin, because sunshine is needed for its synthesis. It promotes healthy bones, and cats can synthesize it by sitting in sunshine or in ultraviolet light. (Beware though, if you have a show cat, for ultra-violet light may fade the coat.) Fish-liver oil is rich in vitamin D.

Vitamin E promotes fertility and virility, and is plentiful in wheat germ and lettuce.

Carbohydrates
These are ene.gy-rich foods found in such things as grains and root vegetables, including potatoes. Carbohydrates are essential in small quantities, but favoured more by some cats than others. If your cat likes milk, you can occasionally mix this with cereals. If it likes sardines and other oily fish, you can add cereals or brown bread crumbs, which help to make the oily fish more palatable. If the cat dislikes carbohydrates, you can liquidize them (including table leftovers) and mix with minced fish, when they will usually be acceptable. It is not a good idea to mix cereals with meat, as this will sour the stomach.

Vegetables, fruit, grass
Some cats obtain green vegetables naturally from the stomachs of mice that they kill and eat. Domestic cats may have traces added to their food.

Fruits are not essential, but some cats are known to have a liking for various kinds, including melons, grapes, olives, asparagus and avocados.

Grass is beneficial and eaten by most cats who are allowed to roam free. In fact, they cannot extract its carbohydrate nutrients but use it for roughage, and as a source of vitamins. If they vomit up grass, as they often do, it brings with it fur balls, which would otherwise cause an obstruction.

Fats
Cats need small quantities of fats and will usually readily devour these in the form of butter, margarine, fish oils, or fat meat from table scraps. Most cats will readily lick a knob of butter mixed with enough yeast extract to colour it a light fawn, and this is very beneficial once in a while.

Protein
Protein provides the major part of a cat's food and can be served in the form of lean meat, fish, eggs, cheese, milk, vegetable protein and prepared pet foods. A diet of nothing but pure protein would leave a cat deficient in essential minerals and vitamins and give rise to kidney disease. However, protein should make up 30-40 percent of an adult cat's diet

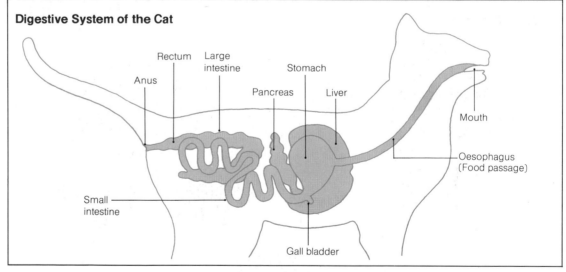

Digestive System of the Cat

Rectum · Large intestine · Anus · Stomach · Pancreas · Liver · Mouth · Oesophagus (Food passage) · Small intestine · Gall bladder

compared with about 18 percent for a dog. It is advisable to avoid meats unsuitable for human consumption, but if you have to feed them for one reason or another, use a different chopping block and knife from those used to prepare human foods.

Meat
All lean meats are suitable with small quantities of fat. Thus you can give beef; lamb; venison; cooked pork; kidney; heart; rabbit; kangaroo; chicken (not hormonized); chicken heads (raw to eat or play with); and liver. Liver is strange in acting as an aperient if eaten raw, but having the reverse effect if eaten cooked. If you remember this you can usefully employ liver to correct either constipation or diarrhoea.

Because battery hens usually receive food with hormones added they are not suitable as food for breeding stock.

Fish
Cats living wild will often catch fish and eat it, as your household cat will demonstrate if you leave the top of a goldfish bowl uncovered! Most cats like fish and most animal nutritionists agree that this is best cooked, although many cats themselves prefer it raw. Remove scales if the skin is to be fed; most cats do not object to being served fish with the skin on. All bones should be removed if the fish is to be served cooked. Kittens prefer fine-grained fish such as plaice, but coarse-grained fish such as coley (coalfish) is accepted by most adult cats.

Fish is a good vehicle for introducing fish oils, a small quantity of powdered seaweed (which makes the fish taste very fresh), and cereals, potatoes or bread crumbs in small quantities. Fish oils are most needed as a source of vitamin D in the winter months. Fish is best served moist, but not too liquid, and at room temperature, not too hot from cooking and not straight from the refrigerator.

Tinned fish is excellent for cats and most seem to like it. Offer sardines, mackerel or pilchards in tomato sauce—dried off with brown bread crumbs, bran, cornflakes or some other acceptable cereal. Many cats appreciate a jelly made of fish with chicken stock. Check that tinned tuna has added vitamin E (look for

Left: An Oriental-type cat eating grass. Most domestic cats will instinctively chew grass for the beneficial roughage and vitamins.

Above: A household pet lapping milk. Most cats will drink milk, a convenient source of valuable protein, calcium and minerals.

it on the label). Herring and some of the fatty types of tinned fish may act as aperients, so serve if you suspect constipation rather than when diarrhoea is in evidence.

Egg yolks
These are rich in protein and you can add them to milk for a delicious and nutritious meal, perhaps when time is short. A little glucose added to the mixture will give energy, although it is generally reckoned that cats cannot assimilate sugar.

Cheese
This is a rich source of protein and some cats will sit up and beg for a small cube of cheese. It would not form a complete meal on its own, but is an interesting addition and generally liked. Fish or chicken in a cheese sauce left over from the human table is considered a great treat.

Milk
Milk is a valuable source of protein as well as of calcium and other minerals. However, some cats cannot tolerate the lactose present in cow's milk, particularly some Siamese and Burmese. Where this is so, try goat's milk, milk substitutes, cream or a complete liquid food. Milk should not be watered down for kittens as they need concentrated foods. If a pregnant queen cannot take milk

add extra calcium to her diet in some other form, such as crushed calcium tablets or bonemeal. Cats that normally dislike milk will often instinctively take milk when pregnant.

Vegetable protein
Protein-rich vegetable foods such as soya beans are increasingly used in cat foods because they are cheaper than animal proteins. Most cats accept them, particularly if mixed with other forms of protein. Because cats are primarily carnivores (flesh eaters) they would not be satisfied with an all-vegetable-protein diet.

Prepared cat foods
Since the second World War, prepared cat foods have grown from nothing to a worldwide multi-million dollar industry. You can buy them canned, dried or semi-moist—this last type developed in response to an outcry about the dire results that followed eating dried foods without drinking plenty of fluid at the same time. Each type of food is convenient to use and between them the various types provide considerable variety. Each has its advantages.

Dried foods can be left down for some hours without deteriorating or attracting flies as readily as wet tinned foods do. Semi-moist foods are good to take when travelling or when you are in a hurry. Canned foods now come in such a wide assortment of flavours and ingredients that there is something for even the choosiest cat.

When prepared foods first made their appearance on the market, some breeders were much opposed to them as many seemed to give young kittens diarrhoea. Since then pet-food manufacturers have spent vast sums on research to produce affordable foods that cats find nutritious and palatable. Accordingly, it is now an exceptional home that does not use prepared cat food for at least one meal a day. Modern prepared cat foods are hygienic, safe to use, and labour saving. But some will prove more acceptable to your cat than others. Find out which it likes, then add them to its weekly menu, interspersed with fresh meat (particularly rabbit) and fish. If a certain prepared food should have adverse effects whenever used, it is only fair to write to the manufacturers and tell them. This kind of consumer contact helps them to keep in touch with what suits the feline population.

Diet supplements and treats
These are becoming increasingly available as commercial preparations. They include yeast tablets, chocolate drops (some cats adore chocolate) and vitamin

Types of Cat Food

1 Fresh food, which may be any lean meats, liver, chicken, rabbit or fish, is loved by most cats. It should be cut up, minced or left in one piece for the cat to tear up. Pet meat sold as unfit for human consumption has been known to be very dangerous.
2 Canned cat food is probably the most convenient for today's busy owners. It comes in great variety including meat, liver, chicken, rabbit and fish. It is hygienic, wholesome and usually accepted. Tuna fish should have Vitamin E added to be safe for cats.
3 Semi-moist cat food is easy to use, especially when travelling. Some cats prefer these soft pieces to dried or canned foods and there are a variety of flavours to choose from in most pet stores.

4 Dried cat foods combine cereals with meat, liver, rabbit or fish. They are much liked by some cats for their crunchy consistency. More water must be given with dried foods and they can be soaked overnight for a change in taste.
5 Frozen pet foods are readily available in pet shops. They add variety to the cat's diet and are easy to handle. Try them all.
6 Milk is a valuable source of food, if your cat likes it and can tolerate it. Some cannot. It must not be diluted. Egg yolks can be added for an extra special treat.

7 Water should always be left down. It must be changed every day or more frequently in hot weather or if shared with dogs.
8 Cat treats may be vitamin or yeast tablets or chocolate drops and are useful as rewards when training to do tricks.
9 Vegetables and cereals are both necessary in small quantities and may be soya bean products, root vegetables, potato or green vegetables in variety, liquidized or finely minced. Seaweed powder can be sprinkled on the food for a source of vitamins and other valuable trace elements.
10 Fish liver oils come in handy containers, sometimes with a dropper attachment. They are useful added to fish and are a ready source of vitamin A.

Left: This display shows examples of the main types of cat food that owners can choose for their pets. The dry complete diets should be mixed with water or given dry with water available.

pills. In small quantities they can be useful and used for trick training, but giving them too freely will create dietary imbalances.

Table manners
Each cat in the household should have its own dish. But because the cat may remove some of the food to tear it up, it is advisable to put a place mat under the bowl; this will save the carpet or kitchen floor from getting messy. Some cats are so greedy that they are best fed little, but often. Otherwise they tend to bolt a large meal only to regurgitate it a few minutes later. Once a small quantity of food has gone down and stayed down, you can offer a further supply.

When there is more than one cat feeding the household, make sure that the slower eaters and the shy ones get their share of food, and that the bully does not wolf its own rations and then start on its neighbours'. If this happens, it is a good idea to feed the shy cat in a special place where it can eat uninterrupted. Remember, too, that active cats may need extra food. The idea that a working mouser need not be fed is a

fallacy: it will hunt better if it is well fed by its owner!

Some cats are sensitive to being left for undue lengths of time and sulk or refuse to eat if the owner has neglected them at home or by leaving them in a boarding cattery for too long. The same may happen in a quarantine establishment where there may be too little personal attention. Usually, once home again with their beloved owners they will start to eat again and make good any lost weight.

As I mentioned in the section on training, it is a simple matter to train a cat to sit up and beg for its food by holding the dish above its head. It will enjoy this routine and look forward to the little ritual before a meal. Visitors will be impressed by your beautifully behaved cat, who says 'please' so nicely!

Feeding dishes
Whatever food or drink you serve, it must be presented in individual, clean bowls or dishes, washed between each meal or refill. Bowls or dishes should also be sterilized periodically. Never use these containers for any other purpose,

Above: Twin feeding bowls are convenient for both cat and owner. When offering complete diet dried foods, one bowl can be filled with water to ensure that the cat has the necessary supply close by.

Below: Kittens feeding from a shallow bowl. Young kittens just learning to eat solids should be given four small meals a day rather than fewer larger ones. Two meals should contain milk.

and store them separately from those intended for human use. Lovely ceramic, stainless steel or plastic dishes are on sale in most pet shops, and you should consider such items a necessity rather than a luxury for each cat. Always offer the dishes at the same time and in the same place, usually in the kitchen for convenience. It is a mistake to offer food all over the house, and, like children, cats appreciate routine: it makes them feel secure.

How much to feed
Cats have a small stomach in relation to their weight and therefore need more than one meal per day. They should have small, nourishing, concentrated meals. As with people their metabolism varies, so one cat may need more food than another. On average 30gm (1oz) of food per kg (2.2lb) of body weight will be enough to keep a cat healthy, though breeds such as Burmese seem to need more. The average pet female will need about 250 kilocalories per day and the average pet male 300 kilocalories per day. The amounts and kinds of food that cats need depend largely upon their age, condition and level of activity.

Kittens
Very young kittens will need four meals a day: two with milk and two of meat. The meat can be scraped steak or fine-grained plaice. The milky meals could include some finely textured cereal, egg yolk and milk, a complete liquid food or one of the weaning milks developed specifically for hand-rearing and weaning young kittens.

Queens
Once a queen is pregnant she will need more to eat—but not so much *larger* meals as *more* meals per day, because cats have a small stomach. She will need at least half as much again as usual. A queen may go off her food just before kittening, which may be the first sign that she is about to go into labour. She seems to know instinctively that she will soon be eating the afterbirths.

Once the kittens are born she will need twice as much as usual and it is said that it is impossible to overfeed a lactating female. If there is a large litter, feeding may seem an unending task, particularly with some breeds. Once the kittens begin to eat a little for themselves, although still suckling, her appetite will probably abate a little. Anything put down for the kittens will be readily devoured by the queen. Perhaps she instinctively realizes that if she eats the same as they do, her milk will mix better in their stomachs than if she and they have quite different diets.

While she is feeding the kittens she should not be emaciated, but in perfect health. If she is too thin, she may require building up with more food or more nutritious delicacies. The kittens should be

plump, not thin. If they are thin, the mother cat may not have enough milk, in which case you should supplement hers with milk fed by bottle, and wean them on solids earlier than normally.

Working stud cats
Stud cats also need generous rations, for mating as well as kittening is hard work. Give extra protein and good doses of vitamin E to promote virility and fertility: besides meat, stud cats still need their vitamins, minerals and carbohydrates. While one stud will want to eat before servicing a queen, another may go off his food as soon as the queen arrives and refuse to eat until he has serviced her. Each individual stud will differ and a pattern will be established. Visiting queens usually prefer to mate before eating, then are ravenous!

Neuters
Neuters need less food than stud cats which are working, but they should be fed twice a day rather than once to add extra interest to their lives. If a neuter puts on too much weight, it is eating too much and its rations should be

cut down, although it will not like this. It may be overeating because it is bored. A more exciting play time will take its mind off food and make for a happier cat and a happier owner. After all, without play or outside hunting a neuter does not have too much else to think about!

Old cats
Geriatric cats need less food than other adults just like their human counterparts. As with overfed neuters it is better to reduce the size of the meals rather than cut out one meal altogether. Eating gives old cats something to do and they find pleasure in keeping up a lifelong routine; also they enjoy the special attention associated with the serving of a meal. If they have lost some teeth they will enjoy liquidized and minced meals more than chunks of raw foods. If they seem to go off their food, they may have gum or tooth trouble and need to see a veterinarian. Often an old cat takes on a new lease of life after a visit to have a tooth out.

Children should not pull and worry old cats; let them live out their days peacefully, but tempted

Above: Spoon-feeding a kitten with a complete liquid diet. Sick cats can also be fed this way; the extra care and attention given could ensure their survival.

with little delicacies they have always been partial to: just a little sign that they are still loved and appreciated.

Sick cats
Cats which are sick or injured may need, and will certainly appreciate, special attention. If a cat's coat is messy, sponge it clean: a cat hates having soiled fur and will be very pleased that you have taken the trouble to clean it, if it is unable to do so itself. When ill, cats often give up and die without such little attentions from their owners, willing them to live. This is probably truer of cats than of any other animal.

Diets for diseases
Some specific diseases require special diets, but these are best prescribed for each cat individually by a veterinarian, who is best placed to weigh up the situation and advise accordingly.

GROOMING YOUR CAT

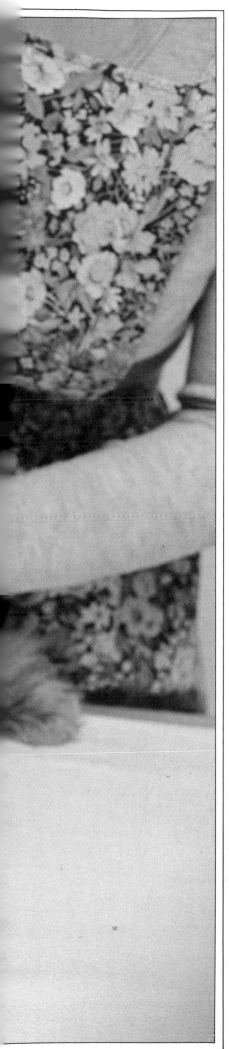

Grooming means taking daily care of the cat for its health and beauty. The purpose is to tone up the muscles; remove dirt, grease, dead hairs and dead skin flakes; and stimulate blood circulation, thus improving the condition of the hair and skin.

Many cats seem able to groom themselves successfully, but the majority appreciate and enjoy a little help from their owners. If there is more than one cat in the household, they will often indulge in mutual grooming sessions. It is a case of: 'You wash my back and I'll wash yours'. The mother cat will wash the new-born kittens thoroughly, both to keep their coats clean and to stimulate the circulation and the production of urine and faeces. Washing appears to be an instinctive process, as newborn kittens will begin to make ineffective washing movements at about three weeks of age, and by the time they are six weeks old, most kittens will be making a pretty good job of it. Very often the first sign of a queen coming on call (into heat) is the way she washes vigorously all over, particularly in the vaginal area.

The Oriental Foreign Shorthairs with their short coats and long noses, and consequently long tongues, are especially efficient at self-grooming. But their long-haired cousins have long coats and short noses, with correspondingly short tongues, so are less able to cope. Thus we find that some need help with grooming, and all should enjoy it.

It is best to develop a daily routine, possibly grooming just before feeding your cat, so it gets used to have a little combing, brushing and loving session, which appears to be rewarded by

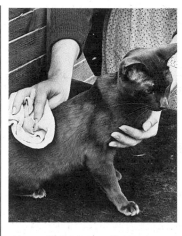

Above: Polishing an Oriental Shorthair with a chamois cloth, a simple daily routine that will keep the coat healthy and shining.

Left: Combing a Blue Persian (Longhair). Longhaired cats need regular grooming to remove loose hairs and prevent knots forming.

a good meal. An important part of these sessions is removing dead hairs to prevent hair balls forming in the stomach, which could well happen if the cat were allowed to swallow all the loose hairs in its coat. In nature, where cats have to fend for themselves and hunt for food, the hair balls so formed are regurgitated with birds' feathers and rodents' skins. So the cat owner should not be alarmed if her pet throws up what looks like a long grey sausage on the carpet. It is only a hair ball. But in domesticity, hair balls tend to accumulate in cats' stomachs, particularly among the longhaired varieties. If not regurgitated, the balls may form solid intestinal obstructions that at worst must be

removed surgically. Prevention by daily combing is plainly better than cures as drastic as that.

The daily grooming session can establish a psychological link between the owner and the cat: a bond of dependence forged by an enjoyable regular routine throughout the life of the cat. This practice should start when your pet is a kitten, and continue in whatever condition the cat finds itself. Kittens consider it a great game and will try to bite and fight with the brush or comb; queens appreciate a little attention to the parts they cannot reach during pregnancy; stud cats, living in their own quarters, look forward to this little daily attention from their owners; ill cats appreciate a clean-up, when unable to do it themselves; and elderly cats find contentment in being looked after by their owners at a time in life when interest in much else has waned. Thus grooming serves the well-being of the cat both physically and emotionally and owners will find this little devotion adding a new dimension to their relationship with the cat.

Eyes
Equipment required: cotton wool, salt solution.
The normal eye is clear and alert. If the third eyelid begins to come across each eye from the inner corner, there is something wrong. It may be an indication of a temperature, or an early sign of infection. A single visible 'haw' (third eyelid) may indicate an accident to one eye only. If the condition persists, a veterinarian must be consulted. If the tear ducts are blocked, the tears have to course down the cheeks and may leave a discoloration from the eye to the nose. This mark must

at the entrance of the ear. These result from ear mange-mites or *Otodectes cynotis,* which are contagious among dogs and cats. Ideally the cat should be isolated from other animals until cured.

You can remove the encrustations of wax and mite dirt with a cotton-wool bud dipped in liquid paraffin or ear-mite solution, but some of the solution will then have to be poured into the ear daily. It is important to see that the cat does not shake its head and throw the contents out before these have had a chance to penetrate into the deeper parts of the ear. Help this penetration by massaging the warm liquid into position before letting the cat's head move. Then the second ear can be attended to. It is not wise to poke down beyond what can be seen. Ears should be inspected once per week and attended to daily when necessary.

Teeth

Equipment: A hand, or wooden spatula, for opening and examining the mouth. Discoloration of teeth or gums, pale gums or bad breath indicate that veterinary attention is necessary. There may be tartar on the teeth, which can be removed by a veterinarian. Loss of appetite may be due to sore gums. Dribbling may be a sign of poison or ulcerated mouth. The best way to open the mouth is to tilt the head back with one hand and open the mouth with the forefinger of the other hand. Mouth and teeth should be inspected weekly.

Nose

Equipment: Cotton wool and salt solution.

Any sign of a runny nose, sneezing or a nasal discharge is a warning that something requires attention. Since respiratory infections may be serious it is best to consult a veterinarian right away. However, if powder has been used for grooming, check that the cat is not allergic to this preparation. Isolate any sneezing cat from others.

Claws

Equipment: Claw scissors or guillotine clippers; scratching post. Cats normally scratch against trees or a scratching post to sharpen and clean their claws. It is wise to supply a suitable post so as to distract them from using the furniture. An outdoor cat gets its claws trimmed naturally by walking on roads and paths, and also by scratching tree trunks. Indoor cats may find that their claws grow unduly long and get caught up in the carpets and upholstery. The claws should be shortened at the tips only. This is done by sitting the cat on your lap with its back facing you. Use one hand to hold up a paw pressing on the pad of the foot and the top of the foot to make the claws spring forward. You can then clip the claws with the scissors or clipper held in your other hand. The end of each claw is dead

Above: Wiping around the eyes with moistened cotton wool will remove tear streaks and may prevent any infection in this sensitive area.

Left: The outer parts of the ears can be cleaned carefully with a cotton bud if wax builds up, but avoid probing too deeply.

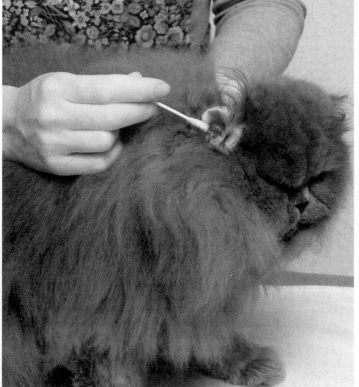

be removed with cotton wool dipped in a salt solution (one teaspoonful to a pint of boiled water, cooled; equivalent to 18 gm of salt in a litre of water). A (usually brown) discharge from the eye may also be a sign of respiratory infection and a veterinarian must be consulted. Eyes should be looked at once per week or bathed more often if necessary. Blocked tear ducts may have to be unblocked surgically.

Ears

Equipment required: cotton-wool buds; liquid paraffin; ear mite solution. If there is any trouble inside the ears, the cat may scratch them. This may be an indication of ear-wax or ear mites. If mites, dark waxy specks appear

Basic Grooming Equipment

1 Dual-purpose bristle and wire brushes for general grooming. Care should be taken when using the wire side, as hard brushing can strip the coat.
2 Pure bristle brush, with short, soft bristles, especially good for shorthaired cats.
3 Rubber brush with short flexible filaments, and rigid plastic type for general grooming.

4 Blunt-ended scissors for cutting through mats (in a longhaired coat).
5 Toothbrush for brushing up the coat of a longhaired cat around the ears and eyes.
6 Cotton-wool buds for cleaning the outer parts of ears.
7 Wide, flat tail comb ensures each hair on the tail of a long-haired cat is separate. Also known as a slicker brush.

8 Specially shaped scissors for trimming the claws.
9 Fine-toothed comb for short-haired cats—smooths the coat and removes fleas and dirt.
10 Wide-toothed comb for removing tangles in the fur of longhaired cats.
11 Metal dual-purpose comb with wide- and medium-spaced teeth, ideal as general purpose groomer.

12 Non-toxic baby shampoo, safe for cleansing.
13 Bay rum spirit conditioner; removes grease from the coat
14 Surgical spirit essential for re-moving stains from pale coats.
15 Cotton wool for cleansing eyes, ears and nose.
16 Non-toxic grooming powder or baby powder gives body to the coat. Sprinkle into the fur and brush out completely.

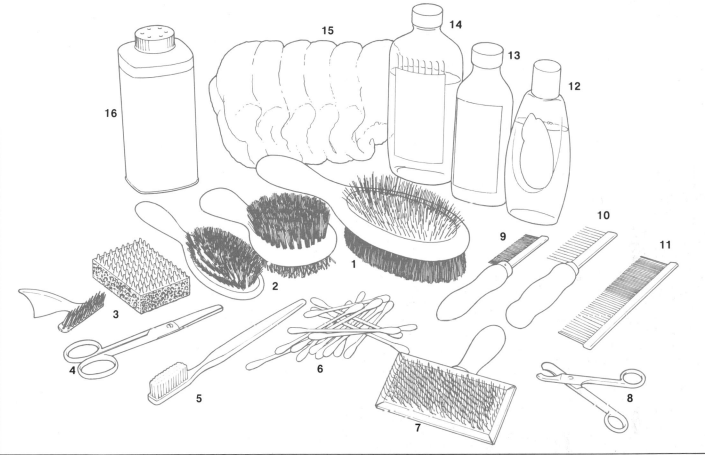

Trimming Claws

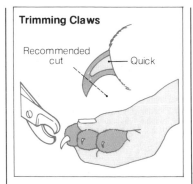

Recommended cut

Quick

Above: Check your cat's claws every month and trim the tips as shown here. Outdoor cats usually wear down their claws naturally.

tissue, and, like the end of your fingernails, can feel nothing; but the pink part or quick should not be touched as this contains the nerves and blood vessels bringing a blood supply to the claw. The scissors or clipper must be sharp so as not to split the claw. A monthly check on the length of the claws should be sufficiently frequent. It is unethical and inadvisable to de-claw a cat.

Right: Grooming a shorthaired cat with a rubber brush to remove dead hairs and stimulate the blood circulation in the skin.

Coat

Equipment: Brushes (pure bristle is best as it creates little static); combs; shampoo; grooming powders; cotton wool; ear plugs; Elizabethan collar; towels; bran; surgical spirit; silk cloth; chamois leather cloth.
Combing regularly helps to keep the coat free from dirt and para-sites. It is best to start at the head, gradually moving towards the tail, and paying particular attention to behind the ears, and to chin, hind legs and underparts—especially in a longhaired cat. If mats have formed here they must be teased out with a blunt-ended knitting needle or, if too dense, cut out carefully with blunt-ended scissors. However, this will spoil the cat's appearance for the show bench.
If the cat is subjected to hours of pulling in an attempt to rectify a neglected coat, the owner should not be surprised if the cat loses patience and becomes bad

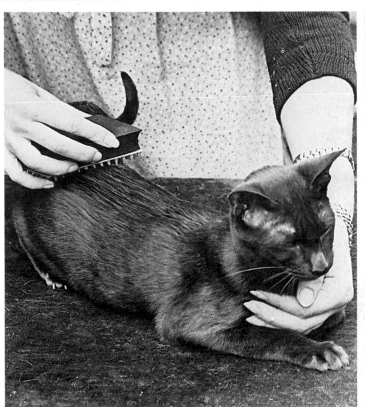

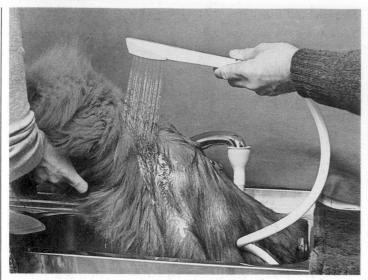

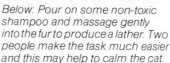

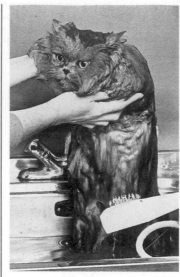

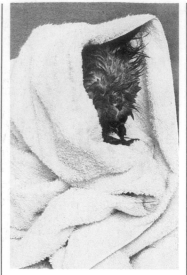

Above: First stage in shampooing a longhaired cat. Soak the fur with warm water, keeping the head dry. If necessary, plug the cat's ears with cotton wool.

Below: Pour on some non-toxic shampoo and massage gently into the fur to produce a lather. Two people make the task much easier and this may help to calm the cat.

Above: After shampooing, rinse the coat under a gentle stream of warm water. Be sure that every trace of shampoo is thoroughly rinsed out of the fur before drying.

Above: Wrap the cat quickly in a warm rough towel. With the cat on your knees, rub briskly but gently to remove excess moisture. The face can be cleaned separately now.

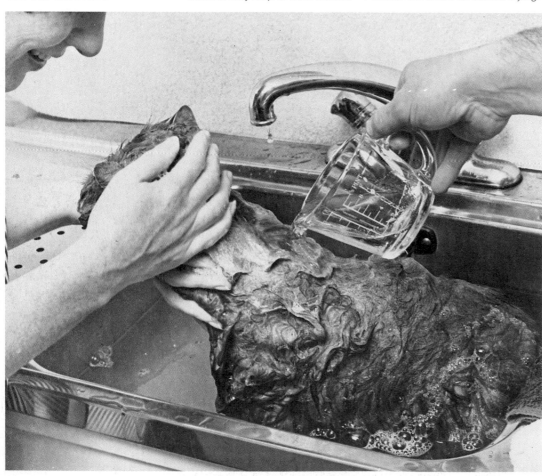

domestic hazards of which cat owners should beware.

Shampooing your cat
Shampooing is really a task for two people. First get cat, people and equipment into the room and close all the doors and windows. Wear plastic overalls in case of accidents. The kitchen sink is the best place to work in because bathing can then be carried out at table height. A rubber mat in the bottom of the sink will prevent the cat's paws slipping and so give it confidence. Fill the sink to a depth of 5-7.5cm (2-3in) with water at the cat's blood heat 38.3°C (101°F). Plug the cat's ears with cotton wool in case it struggles. Then lower the cat into the water and hold it by the scruff of the neck. Soothing words will help to keep the cat calm at this stage. Next the fur should be gently wetted all over with a sponge, except for the head, and the shampoo rubbed gently in all over the body to produce a lather. Some cats purr while this is being done as it is warm and comforting. If your cat hates standing in the sink you can put its forelegs on the draining board. After two or three attempts it is usually possible to work out the best method.

After shampooing the cat, rinse thoroughly with warm water. A spray attachment on a short hose is particularly effective, as long as the pressure is gentle. It may be necessary to give a second shampoo, as above, but make sure that the final rinse removes all traces of shampoo from the coat.

Remove the cat from the sink and cuddle it in a large, warm towel. Meanwhile the face can be washed by the second person using warm, wet cotton wool. Any stubborn marks on the face can be removed with surgical spirit taking care to keep it well away from the eyes.

Some cats enjoy being dried by a hair dryer, but many are

tempered. It is better not to have a longhaired cat if you are not prepared to undertake two half-hour combing sessions each day.

When the head, back and tail have been combed to perfection, the cat should be turned over on its back to complete the underparts and legs. If this is done regularly from kittenhood, the cat will enjoy it and not struggle. The first combing should be done with a wide-toothed comb to remove tangles, followed by a medium- or fine-toothed comb to separate each hair. The coat can then be finished with a brush.

Gentle stroking along the lie of the fur, with a non-greasy hand of

course, is often the best grooming treatment of all for the shorthairs. To add further shine, the coat can be polished with a silk handkerchief or a chamois leather. When brushing shorthairs brush along the lie of the fur, but in a long-haired cat the coat can be gently whipped up so that each hair stands away from the body and the ruff makes a wide frill or halo round the head. The tail should also be brushed up and gently shaken, holding the tip. When every hair is separate and stands away from the body, the cat is said to be in perfect show condition. It is not possible to attain this condition in one session; it is the

result of twice-daily grooming, all the year round.

A show cat may need to be shampooed a week before the show if the cat is at all dirty or greasy. Such marks will show up particularly in paler-coated cats. Make sure to choose a shampoo that is non-toxic to cats, especially one that contains no bleach or carbolic acid. A soft soap, such as a baby shampoo, is best. Cats are susceptible to many things that people and dogs are not, therefore it is necessary to be very careful in choosing preparations for grooming cats. In the United Kingdom the Feline Advisory Bureau produces a leaflet on the

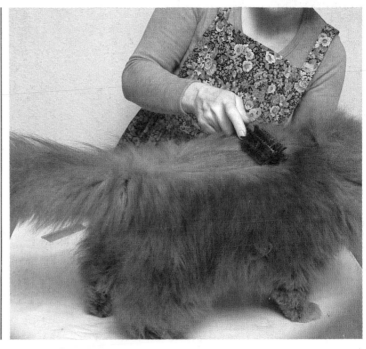

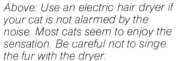

Above: Use an electric hair dryer if your cat is not alarmed by the noise. Most cats seem to enjoy the sensation. Be careful not to singe the fur with the dryer.

Right: If you are grooming for a show, brush in some non-toxic or baby powder to add body to the coat. Ensure that the powder is brushed out and add the finishing touches for perfect show condition.

Right: When the fur is very nearly dry, use a wide-toothed comb and then a brush to fluff up the coat so that the hairs are standing away from the body.

frightened by the noise. One person can hold the cat, with four feet on the ground or table, while the other plays the hair dryer gently through the coat, taking care not to get too close or to singe the fur. The cat should then be put into the airing cupboard or left inside a container near a fire. It is essential not to let the cat out or leave it in a draught until the coat is thoroughly dry. When this is very nearly dry a gentle combing will help to separate the hairs.

The bath will leave the coat very soft. Thereafter until show day, give the coat a daily powdering with a non-toxic baby powder or fuller's earth, rubbed well in, then well brushed out again. This puts body back into the fur and helps to keep every hair separate. Not a trace of powder must be found on show day.

Dry cleaning your cat
Dry cleaning cats with short dark coats is a suitable alternative to bathing, unless the cat is particularly greasy. A bran bath is the usual method. Put 0.45-0.9kg (1-2lb) of bran into the oven and warm it to rather more than hand heat. Then stand the cat on a newspaper laid over a table or kitchen top. Now massage the warm bran into the fur with your hands. Most cats love this motion and the warmth engendered by a bran bath, and will purr continuously. When all the fur has been processed by the bran, move the cat on to a clean piece of newspaper and comb out the bran. Afterwards the coat should really gleam. A bran bath is not recommended for longhaired cats; particles of bran not removed could cause the formation of painful knots in the fur.

BASIC HEALTH CARE

Keeping a cat in perfect health means providing correct food, grooming, housing, and inoculations at the required intervals as well as a constant show of affection.

Correct feeding
This involves giving enough food of the right kinds, mixed in the correct proportions, enriched with dietary supplements as necessary and offered at intervals that depend on the age and condition of the cat. Titbits between meals are not a good idea, however amusing to the owners and their friends. A cat should know by repetition when and where to expect meals, and will then usually present itself at the right place at the right time.

Grooming
Regular daily grooming is essential for the health of all cats, twice daily being ideal. A well-kept cat should have a glossy or shining coat with visibly separate hairs and no tangles. There should be weekly attention to the eyes, ears, teeth and claws. (See also pages 107-111).

Housing
All cats should have a place of their own. A pet cat needs a bed in a warm, dark, draught-proof corner of a room, while a breeding queen needs her own quarters (See also pages 121-129.) If your pet is a Siamese or Burmese it may need warm bedding or even a heated bed, for these breeds feel the cold more than others. In fact, if allowed to, they will frequently prefer to sleep with their owners or any other cats or dogs in the household. From their viewpoint this is quite practical: most cats are adept at

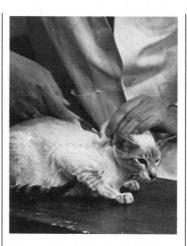

Above: A veterinarian injecting a vaccine as part of a routine series of inoculations recommended for all domestic cats.

Left: A sick cat will respond well to human affection, and keeping it warm and clean will aid its rapid return to full health.

moving out from under, if rolled upon. All cats should have a choice of a warm or cold area of bed to lie on, so that they can move over to the cold part if they get too hot, or vice versa. In hot climates air conditioning may be required.

Inoculations
The most prevalent serious diseases can be prevented by the right injection at the right time. Kittens receive some immunity from their mother for the first eight weeks of their lives. After this, they need their first jabs for feline enteritis, a widespread and potentially fatal disease, and against respiratory diseases. In each case your veterinarian will provide a

certificate which you may have to produce when your cat goes to stud or to a boarding cattery.

Loving
No cat is completely happy without some individual attention from its owner. For its psychological well-being it needs to be stroked and petted and talked to at some time during each day. Most cats will amply respond to any attention they receive and will reward their owners with a lifetime of devotion. Someone once said, 'There are no dull cats, only dull owners.' An interested owner will produce an interesting cat.

Nursing the sick cat
A healthy cat will be alert and friendly, with clear shining eyes and clean shining fur. It will purr a great deal. Any deviation from this norm means that something has gone wrong. The trouble may be an injury. Some cats are very accident prone, but their reputation for having nine lives reflects an ability to recuperate from the most amazing mishaps. However, nursing plays a very important part in recovery. This can be even more important in illness due to disease. A sick cat easily gives up the will to live, unless a human friend is prepared to take the trouble to nurse it back to health.

Water is more important than food to a sick cat and it must not be allowed to become dehydrated. Even when unable to eat or lap, the sick cat can take water administered by eye dropper or by a curved foster-feeding bottle. You can also drop small pieces of raw meat to the back of the throat, but avoid struggling with the cat as this

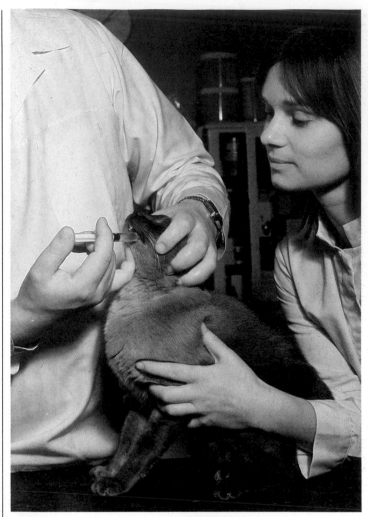

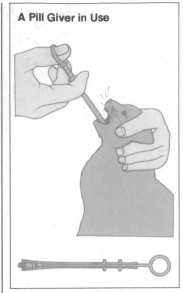

A Pill Giver in Use

weakens it. If the animal can lap or eat in the normal way, you can serve concentrated beef essence; an all-purpose food for invalids; beaten egg; soup prepared in a liquidiser; or some other highly nutritious substance. In critical situations your veterinarian can inject sterile hydrolyzed protein directly into the bloodstream. Hold the head up if you have to give food and drink; then introduce the bottle or dropper into the side of the mouth and towards the back. Gently sponge the mouth clean afterwards.

When dispensing medications supplied by your veterinarian you may have to give pills or capsules; put drops into the eyes or ears; fasten an Elizabethan collar; apply a bandage; or take and keep records of your cat's temperature. It is as well to learn how to do such things in advance.

Liquid medicines can be administered by feeding bottle, syringe or dropper. You can crush a pill or empty a capsule and mix the resulting powder with a small knob of butter or with a piece of sardine or some other highly smelling food, then drop the 'doped' food to the back of the cat's tongue. You can even buy a pill giver designed to help you introduce pills to the back of the cat's mouth without getting your fingers bitten. You simply open its mouth with one hand, insert the pill giver with the other and then push the plunger forward.

Above: Commercially available pill givers consist of a plastic tube split at the end to hold the pill. A plunger pushes the pill out at the back of the throat.

Left: A veterinarian using a syringe (without needle) to give medicine. He holds the cat's head up and introduces the syringe into the side of the mouth.

Below: Taking a cat's temperature rectally. Ideally, two people should collaborate to do this; one to restrain the cat, the other to introduce the thermometer.

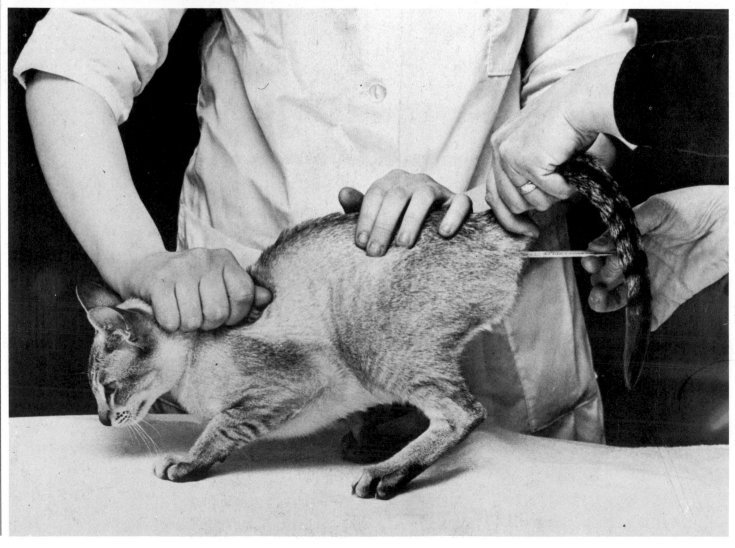

Taking a cat's temperature may require two people. One holds the cat's head and front feet, the other introduces the thermometer into the rectum, having first lubricated it with petroleum jelly. The second person may also have to hold the rear feet.

Eye drops are put into the eye while the head is lifted and kept still. Again, it may be necessary to hold the front paws or wrap the whole cat in a bath towel first to stop it interfering with what you are doing.

Here are a few more chores you may have to perform for a sick cat. If it is bedridden—perhaps immobilized by a fracture—you may have to turn it from time to time to prevent bed sores. If there is diarrhoea, you must clean it up. If the cat is off its feet for some time you may have to trim its claws (cut the tips only, not into the quick).

Sometimes the veterinarian may recommend a steam bath. The best way to give this is to put the cat into a plastic-coated wire basket, cover the top and sides of the basket with a towel and stand it in the vapour rising from a hot bath of water. In this way, the cat breathes in some of the vapour, which helps to relieve nasal congestion. Any mucus round the nose, eyes or mouth must be sponged away with damp cotton wool. Do not add any inhalant to the steam bath without veterinary instruction.

Sick cats often try to run away and hide, but you must not allow them to do so. Place a sick cat in a dark quiet place, with warmth if required, and talk to it reassuringly from time to time without undue fussing. If the disease is transmissible you must keep the cat isolated, and enter other homes containing cats only after changing your shoes and clothes and washing your hands.

After the illness has subsided, restrict the diet until the patient's stomach can again cope with normal food. Most sick cats do not groom themselves but will appreciate their owner taking the time to do so.

Common accidents
Most road accidents involving cats happen at night or in the early morning. To avoid this risk keep your cat in at night if you can. Cats that have been neutered or spayed (and that should be all cats not being used for breeding) will be quite happy about this. If used for breeding, they will be confined to quarters anyway.

Abscesses These tend to occur in free-ranging cats and are the result of fighting with other cats or, less commonly, from bites from rodents such as rats, mice or squirrels. Cats confined for breeding purposes seldom have abscesses.

Signs and symptoms:
Swelling under the fur, hot or hard and painful to touch. The swelling is caused by bacterial infection.

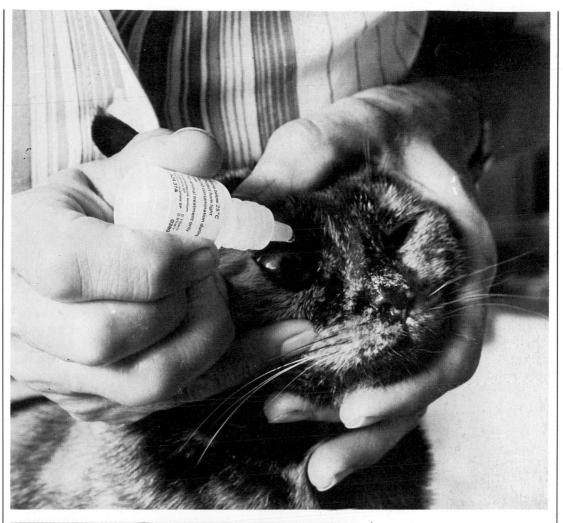

Above: Eye drops can be given at home, but it is important to hold the cat firmly or wrap it in a towel to prevent it struggling while you administer the drops.

Left: An abscess on the cheek shows clearly as a swelling. Simple abscesses may be treated at home, but this one needs expert veterinary attention.

What to do:
Hot fomentations can be laid on the bump to localize the pus it contains. Cut away long fur if this prevents access to the swelling. When the abscess comes to a point, it must be lanced (slit) with a sterilized scalpel. As the pus begins to ooze, you can gently squeeze the abscess to extract all the liquid. When the wound is empty, clean with hydrogen peroxide. But do not allow the wound to close up until all the pus is out, which may mean daily removal of the scab with repeated squeezing until the wound is quite clean. It will then heal normally. If the cat has a temperature as well as an abscess, take it at once to the veterinarian.

Swelling of one or both ear flaps may be the result of a blood blister called a haematoma. This requires the attention of a veterinarian, who will drain and fix the ear flaps flat to prevent crumpling. The veterinarian will also check the ear region for any underlying infection or irritation as a primary cause of the haematoma.

Fractures Fractures are often sustained in road accidents; or by falls from high windows, buildings or trees; or by heavy objects falling on a cat. Thus fractures are most frequent among free-ranging cats and are commonest in legs, jaw, pelvis and spine. People who keep cats in high apartments should have the windows wired over because it is not unknown for a cat to jump out of the window after a bird.

Signs and symptoms:
Bones sticking through fur
Bones at wrong angles
Inability to move or eat
Limping gait
Irritability at being touched
Complete or partial paralysis

What to do:
Call the veterinarian or take the cat to his surgery as soon as possible, disturbing the cat's body as little as possible.

If the wound oozes much blood, stem the flow with a pad or bandage. If the mouth is bleeding, hold the head lower than the body and facing downwards, so that blood does not run down the

Below: Preparing a cat for an X-ray. Veterinarians will generally take them to reveal the exact nature of accidental injuries, particularly for broken limbs.

throat. If the body is bleeding, the head should be higher than the body. The veterinarian will repair the fracture and may plaster or bandage as necessary.

Burns These are generally caused in the home by spillage of hot liquids, electrical appliances (as with kittens chewing through electric cord) or chemicals.

Signs and symptoms:
Hair pulls out or is lost spontaneously.
Signs of burns are visible at contact points.
If burning is extensive, shock, collapse and unconsciousness will be apparent.

What to do:
Call the veterinarian for advice, having ensured safety from further burns by disconnecting electric cord, moving the cat or removing the source of further burns in the case of chemicals. In severe cases, symptomatic treatment such as artificial respiration and warmth should be applied, but since the treatments for the various types of burns vary with the cause, it is difficult to give any blanket advice. In cases of chemicals on the skin, these are best removed by bathing the cat in a suitable mild shampoo, and it is important that cats should not be allowed to lick the burns for fear of

swallowing the chemicals, thus causing internal damage. In this respect, an Elizabethan collar may be helpful. As with human burns, treatment may require intensive hospitalized care, which can only be provided by a veterinary establishment.

Poisoning Cats may eat houseplants (some of which may be poisonous) if they have no access to grass. It is always recommended, for indoor cats, to grow special grass in trays to satisfy their liking for vegetable matter.

Drugs of any sort should, of course, never be left lying around the house; cats are known to be

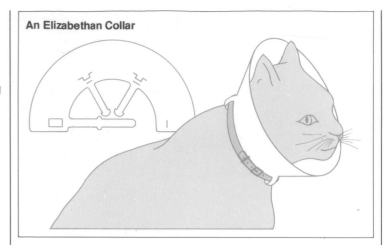

An Elizabethan Collar

Above: This commercially produced Elizabethan collar is made of flexible plastic. It can be folded and clipped around the cat's neck to prevent it from licking medicated or sore areas.

particularly sensitive to such commonplace drugs as aspirin. If it is suspected that a cat has ingested drugs of any sort, the name of the preparation or the purpose for which it was prescribed should be advised to the veterinarian, who should be contacted immediately. Guidance can then be given. Unfortunately, cats in the process of exercise tend to come into contact with paraffin (kerosene), turpentine and sump oil in garages and outhouses, and seem particularly attracted to car antifreeze, all of which are potentially dangerous. Such materials should never be left around, and should be hosed away with a detergent if spilled accidentally. Also, a wide range of chemicals such as coal-tar derivatives (wood preservatives, disinfectants) can be hazardous, as can household disinfectants, fly sprays and mouse and rat poisons. Again, where urgent treatment is necessary, a sample of the material or an exact description of the contents of suspect packets is of great assistance to the treating veterinarian.

Signs and symptoms:
Salivation
Convulsions
Tremors or fits
Vomiting
Pain
Weakness or dullness
Excitability
Death

What to do:
Cats may be made to vomit, providing this is done within minutes of swallowing the suspect substance. After, say, 30 minutes, there is little point, for the toxin will have been absorbed. The best emetic is a crystal of washing soda pushed straight down the cat's throat, which will be effective within seconds. Alternatively, a strong salt-and-water or mustard-and-water solution may be given by the method described for administering liquid medicines.

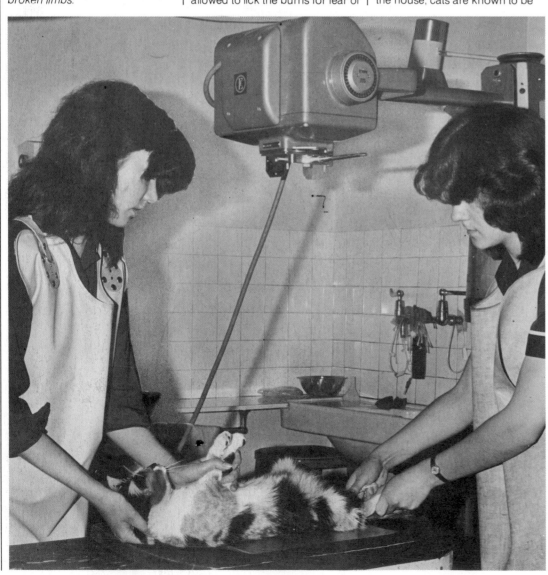

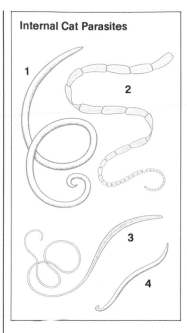
Above: The principal internal parasites that can affect cats. The drawings show the basic shapes of the parasites and are not in scale with each other. The most common species are listed.
1 *Roundworm (Toxocara canis and Toxocara leonina)*
2 *Tapeworm (Dipylidium caninum)*
3 *Whipworm (Trichuris sp.)*
4 *Hookworm (Ancylostoma caninum)*

Parasites
Various small organisms live on or in cats. Where large numbers occur in a cat they may impair the animal's health. Most spread from one cat to another via faeces or fur; a few may pass into kittens through the mother's milk.

Internal parasites
Roundworms Ascarid roundworms found in cats are thread-like, off-white creatures 5-13cm (2-5in) long. They live in the gut of the cat and may be coughed up or passed in faeces.

Signs and symptoms:
Severe coughing
Distended stomach (particularly in kittens)
Diarrhoea
Dull coat and eyes
Ravenous appetite
Haws up (third eyelid visible)

What to do:
The veterinarian will almost certainly prescribe a piperazine compound, the dose depending on the size, age and weight of the cat. It is advisable to dose kittens and cats every year, giving a second dose two weeks after the first, but a sick cat should never be wormed, as this could be fatal. Also you should worm queens before they go to stud and not after, when pregnant. Studs should be wormed regularly. Cattery hygiene is very important in the control of worms.

Hookworms These have particular significance because they suck the cat's blood from

their position anchored inside the intestines. Anaemia can therefore be a symptom of this parasite, which is much more common in the United States than elsewhere.

Tapeworms These are segmented flatworms. A tapeworm lives in the gut with its head attached to the cat's intestine. From the tail end of the tapeworm segments full of eggs drop off and are passed out from the cat with its faeces.

Signs and symptoms:
Small rice-like segments, sometimes still moving, appear on the fur around the anus. They show up better on dark-coloured cats than on light-coloured ones.

What to do:
Fleas are the intermediate hosts in the tapeworm cycle, so that flea eradication must go hand-in-hand with oral dosing against tapeworms. Other tapeworms are transmitted by mice, voles and rabbits which may have been eaten by free-ranging cats. Therefore hunters should be wormed regularly. There are various drugs which will rid the cat of tapeworms easily and with the minimum of side effects, but these tend to have to be repeated because of the animal becoming re-infested. It is recommended to seek advice from your veterinarian on the best dose.

Coccidia These are microscopic unicellular organisms that inhabit the intestine and to which a variety of symptoms are attributed. They are rarely a major problem except in certain localized catteries in various parts of the world.

Signs and symptoms:
Persistent intermittent diarrhoea
Loss of weight and condition
Blood in faeces

What to do:
Scrupulous attention to hygiene is essential and particularly safe disposal, such as incineration, of soiled litter. Drugs are available from veterinarians to eradicate the coccidia.
A unicellular organism called *Toxoplasma*, considered to be a natural parasite of the cat, is thought to be particularly hazardous to pregnant women.

External parasites
Fleas These are hard-backed, brown, wingless insects, flattened from side to side. Cat fleas live in a cat's fur and feed off their host's blood. They occur only in temperate and tropical climates and are virtually unknown in northern regions such as much of Scandinavia. Cat fleas will bite a dog or a human but will seldom stay on either, much preferring a cat host. They are mostly found round the back and bib. Heavy

flea infestation can lead to anaemia, eczema and other troubles.

Signs and symptoms:
Dermatitis (eczema)
Scratching
Restlessness
Skin feels gritty
Visible manifestation: fleas run and jump

What to do:
There is a wide range of insecticides effective against fleas. They are ideally used in powder or aerosol spray form, and may be supplemented by use of an impregnated flea collar, though feelings about the safety of these are very mixed. Cats can be bathed in cases of most severe infestation, although cats are especially susceptible to insecticides in shampoo form. Therefore it is essential to rinse thoroughly.
Fleas breed off the host, and scrupulous attention to de-fleaing bedding and furnishings with which the cat comes regularly into contact should be given. Ordinary household insecticides are

Below: A veterinarian giving a cat a thorough inspection. He will be particularly careful to check the fur and skin, which could be harbouring various parasites.

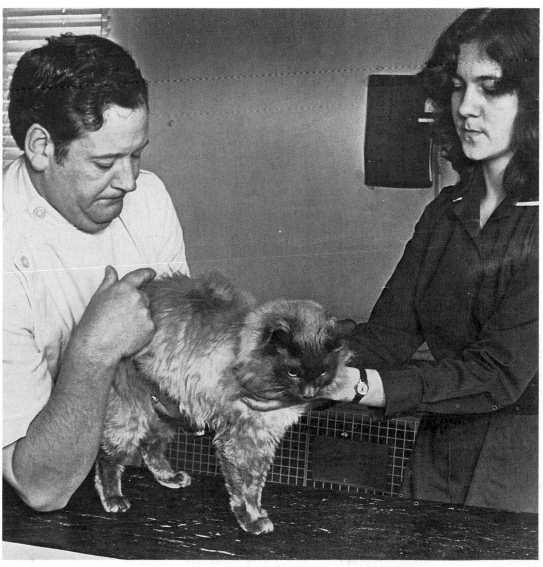

satisfactory for this purpose, but should not be applied with the cat in the room, nor without advice from your veterinarian regarding safety factors.

Lice These are pale grey, wingless insect parasites, flattened from top to bottom. Lice attach themselves by their mouths to the skin of the cat. They lay eggs which they glue to the hairs of the cat, and spend their entire life-cycle on one host.

Signs and symptoms:
Scratching
Visible evidence: you may see lice on the cat's head, and their nits (eggs) attached to some of its hairs.

What to do:
Give the same treatment as for fleas (above), but repeat weekly because lice are very difficult to eradicate. Take care to comb out all visible nits. You can also pick off lice with eyebrow tweezers and drop them into disinfectant.

Mange mites These can be conveniently lumped together, and there are three main offenders: *Cheyletiella* — which affects all parts of the body and readily transmits to human beings; *Notoedres* — head mange, which causes scabs and hair loss and intense irritation to the cat around the head; *Trombicula* (harvest mite or chiggers) — usually found on the lower parts of the body, particularly the legs and feet, in certain areas, usually agricultural.

Signs and symptoms:
Vary from nil to extreme irritation
Signs of hair loss
Secondary scabs
It is not usually possible to see mites without a microscope, except for *Trombicula*, which are just visible to the naked eye.

What to do:
Exactly as for fleas.

Ear mites (*Otodectes cynotis*)
These mites live in the ear canals of dogs and cats and can be transmitted from one to the other.

Signs and symptoms:
Vigorous scratching
Head shaking
Ears twitching or at odd angles
Head held on one side
Brown or reddish blobs of wax on insides of ears

What to do:
It is possible to detect ear mites by probing the outer ear (only the visible part) with a cotton wool bud and examining the debris under a magnifying glass. The mites themselves show up as tiny, moving white objects, while their excreta appear as a reddish brown debris. If a severe condition exists, the veterinarian may completely wash out the ear, then prescribe drops for you to administer daily. The cat should object only mildly provided you make sure that the drops are at

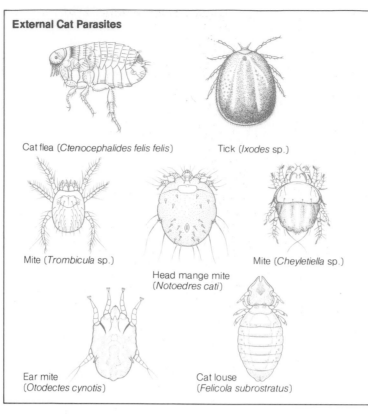

External Cat Parasites

Cat flea (*Ctenocephalides felis felis*)

Tick (*Ixodes* sp.)

Mite (*Trombicula* sp.)

Mite (*Cheyletiella* sp.)

Head mange mite
(*Notoedres cati*)

Ear mite
(*Otodectes cynotis*)

Cat louse
(*Felicola subrostratus*)

Above: The principal types of external parasites that may be found on cats. The species and severity of infestation vary throughout the world. In some areas parasites carry diseases.

Below: A veterinarian using an auroscope to look into the deeper recesses of the ear. Such inspection may reveal ear mites, a bacterial infection or blockage by a foreign body.

room temperature. Massage the liquid into the lower ear before releasing the head; otherwise the cat will shake its head and eject the liquid before it can do its job.
Treatment must continue for several weeks and the ears need regular inspection thereafter if you are to guard against a recurrence of trouble. In an emergency, warm liquid paraffin can be administered to each ear. This will soften ear wax and thus help in its removal from the ear. If one cat or dog in the household has ear mites, it is likely that any others will have to be treated.

Ticks These usually only affect cats that roam in rural areas. A

tick fastens on to a cat's skin with its mouth and feeds by sucking blood. Cats are seldom aware they have ticks.

Signs and symptoms:
You can see ticks hanging from the body of the cat. They may be white and flattish when first attached, or grey, fat and pea-sized when engorged with blood.
In some parts of the world, notably the scrubby East coast of Australia, ticks can infect cats with a fever that causes partial paralysis of the hind legs and eventual death if not treated. The disease is transmitted by a toxin secreted by the salivary glands of the tick.

What to do:
Avoid pulling off ticks without preparation — the head tends to remain embedded, producing a septic lesion. Dab the tick with a small amount of chloroform, alcohol or surgical spirit. Then remove the tick carefully with tweezers. Match or cigarette-lighter flames should not be used to remove ticks as these could burn the cat's fur.

Infections
Ringworm This is a fungus infection spread by spores and disfiguring the coat by producing bald patches that are more obvious in shorthairs than in longhairs. It is highly contagious and can be contracted from and by cats, dogs, rodents or people.

Signs and symptoms:
Bald, scaly patches
Scurf in the fur

What to do:
The veterinarian may be able to confirm the presence of ringworm by using ultraviolet light, in which the lesions glow green, or by microscopic examination of the scales. Treatment may involve bathing, or administering lotions and tablets. If you have to let liquids soak into the skin, first clip the hair for maximum penetration. It is essential to isolate the animal from cats, dogs and people. Handle the cat with protective rubber gloves and other clothing and meticulously wash or replace the cat's bedding and other items with which it often comes into contact.

Rabies This is invariably fatal to mammals and man. This disease must be reported to the health authorities. It is caused by a virus that attacks the nervous system, and it spreads by bites or saliva from infected animals. The incubation period is highly variable, but rabies usually manifests itself in the cat within two months of contact. Cats can contract it from each other, from dogs or from wild animals such as foxes, skunks and raccoons. Geographical isolation and strict quarantine laws have protected the UK, Australia, New Zealand and Hawaii from outbreaks, but rabies is widespread in much of the world.

Signs and symptoms:
Behavioural change, eg ferocity
Salivation
Dilated pupils
Incoordination
Convulsions
Paralysis
Death

What to do:
Outside the rabies-free areas of the world, any bites from wild animals should be suspect and the cat rushed to the veterinarian to be checked. Cats allowed to run free where rabies occurs should be given a vaccine at 3-4 months old, with boosts every year or two years.

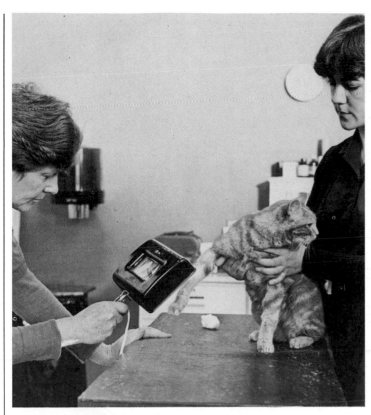

Above: Using a 'Wood's lamp' to check for ringworm, a highly contagious fungal infection of the skin. Under the ultraviolet light that the lamp produces the affected circular patches glow green.

Feline viral rhino-tracheitis (F.V.R.) This disease is also called cat' flu and pneumonitis. It involves severe congestion of the nasal passages and is highly contagious, especially to kittens. Preventive vaccines are available.

Signs and symptoms:
Sudden onset
Coughing
Sneezing
High temperature
Conjunctivitis (red, sore eyes)
Discharge from nose and eyes
Lack of appetite
Lethargy

What to do:
It is not necessary to rush to the veterinarian every time your cat sneezes, but if some of the other symptoms are present, no time must be lost. Waiting a week could be fatal. If only one cat in the household shows the symptoms, it must be isolated from the others; even if the cat is cured, it could become a carrier to infect any other cat. After veterinary treatment, the cat should be kept at an even temperature to avoid chills; even then permanent damage may have been done and the cat could suffer nasal congestion or 'snuffles' for the rest of its years.

Feline infectious enteritis
(Known, too, as feline panleukopaenia, cat plague and distemper) This is the chief killer disease of cats. Early inoculations are almost 100% effective and all cats and kittens should be done.

Signs and symptoms:
Listlessness
Pain
Subnormal temperature
Loss of appetite
Diarrhoea
Vomiting
Collapse
Severe dehydration
Sudden death

What to do:
It is best to send immediately for the veterinarian. If he is delayed, try to introduce a little water and glucose into the cat's mouth without a struggle, and keep in a dark, quiet place. Without the specific preventive antiserum, death could follow within 24 hours. Kittens are naturally immune for the first few weeks, through their mother. The veterinarian will advise type of vaccine and age for vaccination. If death ensues, it is wise to wait for six months before introducing a new kitten to the household, unless previously vaccinated.

Feline leukaemia Feline leukaemia or lymphosarcoma is a fatal cancerous condition of the blood, caused by a virus. It occurs in epidemic proportions in some breeds, so it is wisest to buy kittens from leukaemia-free catteries.

Signs and symptoms:
Wasting away
Lack of appetite
Collapse
Sudden death

What to do:
There is currently no cure, and euthanasia (painless killing) is advised for pet cats and essential for breeding establishments as they could be a health hazard to other cats. There is currently no evidence that this virus is a risk to humans, as was once thought.

Kidney disease Kidney disease is particularly likely to occur in old cats.

Signs and symptoms:
Excessive water intake
Excessive urination
Bad breath
Listlessness
Repeated vomiting
Lack of appetite
Weight loss

What to do:
Conditions affecting the kidneys tend to be irreversible. Once the kidneys have started to degenerate, they need more and more water to flush out the same amount of body waste. Hence there may be accidents around the house. The cat should not be blamed for being dirty: it can no longer hold its water. Drugs may prolong life, but kidney disease is progressive and finally fatal, so it is possibly kinder to have the cat put to sleep painlessly before it loses all its dignity.

Bladder troubles Two fairly common conditions are cystitis (involving an inflamed bladder) and urolithiasis (urinary obstruction). The first is usually due to infection; the second to crystals in urine blocking a male cat's narrow urethral canal. Cystitis causes pain and frequent urination. In urolithiasis blood may appear in urine as the cat strains to pass urine through a blocked canal, and back pressure from a distended bladder may damage the kidneys.

Signs and symptoms:
Small quantities of cloudy urine passed
Urine may be bloodstained
Obvious pain
Possible inability to urinate
Weakness
Loss of condition
Total collapse

What to do:
Urgently get in touch with your veterinarian. He will probably give an antibiotic injection for cystitis, and surgically or manually try to remove any obstruction blocking a male cat's urethral passage. If left unattended, such obstruction could be fatal. At home the cat should be encouraged to drink plenty of fluids, with barley water instead of tap water. To prevent urolithiasis in male cats, avoid giving diets that produce crystals in the urine. Dry food should only be fed to cats which normally drink a lot of water. Keeping the litter tray clean will encourage a cat to use it more often, thus helping to prevent the build-up of crystals in the bladder.

Temperature-induced illnesses Heatstroke This affects cats of all ages when they are subjected to extreme heat without sufficient ventilation. This may happen at cat shows, in a closed car, or if the cat is moved to a tropical climate. During heatstroke, the cat's temperature may rise to 41°C (106°F).

Signs and symptoms:
Vacant expression
Prostrate posture
Heavy panting
Increased pulse rate
Vomiting
Unconsciousness

What to do:
Ideally the cat should be immersed in cold water to reduce body temperature. If this is not possible, lots of fresh air, perhaps with a fan, or an ice-pack or cold water face wash and body massage will suffice. Then take the cat to a veterinarian.

To prevent heatstroke in a car, have drinking water always available and fit ventilators to all windows, particularly if animals are to be left in the car unattended on a sunny day.

Hypothermia This is a drop in body temperature, perhaps fatal.

Signs and symptoms:
Decreased pulse rate
The cat seems cold to the touch

What to do:
If kittens seem cold to the touch, they are in danger of dying of hypothermia. Hold in your hand until they warm up, then place on an electric or other warming pad. An infrared lamp may be used; hot water bottles tend to cool too quickly but may be used in an emergency. Hypothermia is a particular problem when the queen has died during kittening, and her kittens are no longer warmed by her body. In such cases provide artificial heat for the first few days of life. Old cats, like old people, may be subject to hypothermia. Their age reduces the efficiency of their body temperature control mechanism, keeping their body temperature low, especially when their surroundings are cold. Artificial heat is required to reduce the risk of chilling and death.

Psychological disorders Some cats object to being left alone a great deal, or to a new cat in the family, or a new human addition to the family. These cats may express their feelings by odd behavioural patterns.

Signs and symptoms:
Spraying in unusual places
Spraying on owner's possessions
Defecating in the house
Aggressive behaviour

What to do:
The important thing is to find out what the cat is objecting to. Like many a disturbed child, a disturbed cat is seeking attention because it thinks it is being neglected or displaced in your affections by someone else. This is quite natural and once you renew your attention and show of affection the problem will usually clear up. If the cat is objecting to being left all day without human companionship, the best thing is to provide it with a dog or cat as a faithful companion.

BREEDING AND REARING

Left to themselves all cats will decide to go in for breeding. However that is hardly a good idea. Because they multiply at a tremendous rate we should be overrun with cats and unable to find homes for their innumerable kittens. To preserve the species at what we consider its best, only the healthiest, finest-looking and best-natured cats should be bred from. Such selective breeding for health, appearance and temperament has made today's pedigree cats superior to any that have gone before. Of course, there is a risk that inbreeding will encourage the development of hereditary defects, but responsible breeders will guard against this.

The average non-pedigree cat is usually let out at night and nature is left to take its course. In this case the kittens may be of any colour and type according to the colours and types of the sire and dam. There can even be more than one sire to the same litter of kittens, in which case the resultant mixture may be very colourful. Cross-breeding produces mongrel or alley cats which are very robust, and the pretty ones are usually offered homes. But if you want a specific type and colour spectrum you must restrict breeding to certain pedigree animals that can be relied upon to give the correct results when mated, according to its genetic make-up.

Keeping a queen

It is best to start by owning a queen of the chosen breed. A queen is an entire female. Beginners should not also try to own a stud (an entire male) in the hope of mating them, as this is extremely impractical (see page 128). When the queen is ready,

Above: A new born kitten, still wet from the fluid in the amniotic sac in which it was born. The mother licks the kitten dry.

Left: A silver tabby mother with suckling kittens. Moving to the nipples is an instinctive reaction for the newly born kittens.

send her to a stud of the same breed. She may be anything from six months to two years old, but even if she is an early developer wait until she is a year old so that her body has a chance to mature. The foreign breeds usually 'call' much earlier than the other shorthairs or the longhairs. 'Calling' is the term given to queens who come into oestrus (on heat)—that is, who are ready to mate. The term 'calling' is used in cats because most of them are exceptionally vocal at this time. Their loud plaintive cries, intended to attract any passing male, are accompanied by rolling on the floor, head down and rear end in the air, and rubbing their legs against their owners and the furniture. Foreign breeds have been known to 'call' as early as four months whereas some longhairs and other shorthairs may be one to two years old before their first call. The average age would be the first spring after reaching adulthood at eight to nine months old.

Persians in particular have a 'closed season' from October to March, whereas many foreign cats will call all the year round. Cats of any breed usually settle down to a pattern, which may be every other week for some Orientals to twice a year or anything in between for others—the cycle is individual to each cat.

Calling coincides with a vaginal discharge of clear liquid which the queen removes with her tongue. Another sign of oncoming oestrus is therefore frequent washing, particularly in this area.

It is possible for a queen to have as many as five litters in two years if she calls frequently, but it is best for her to be limited to one litter per year. Some queens go on producing year after year. Others dry up naturally at about eight years old or continue to call and mate but no longer become pregnant. When you want to stop her producing kittens have your queen spayed (if necessary).

Pre-mating preparations

When you first see signs that the queen is ready to mate you must keep her in or she will choose her own husband within an incredibly short time. The cat will be anxious to get out of the house, pacing up and down by the windows and jumping at the door handles. Children are often tempted to oblige by opening the door for a cat that is obviously desperate to go out. To avoid this temptation and the accidental slipping out as humans come and go, it is best to fit a room with a cat-proof wired-in run attached to sleeping quarters or to build a special house and run in the garden where the cat can be confined. This should be prepared well in advance of the queen's first call.

These queen's quarters will be invaluable later for confining the cat and her kittens so that they do not get trodden on or moved by the queen to unsuitable places. Keeping her in such a nursery will also make sure the queen does not escape to stray or get killed before the kittens have been reared — a disaster that would leave the owners with the onerous task of hand-rearing. In cold and temperate climates a source of heat should be available, particularly for foreign breeds, so that the quarters may be used all the year round.

Look around for a suitable stud of the same breed while waiting for your young adult queen to call; the breeder who sold her to you may have some good suggestions to make about this. You might wish to consult the pedigrees of several studs and compare them with the queen's own pedigree. The stud should be a champion and fairly experienced if he is to mate a maiden queen. A more mature queen can be sent to a young stud. The stud should be chosen to complement the queen and excel in any points where she is lacking. For instance if her only defect is poor eye colour, choose a stud with superbly coloured eyes. You can sometimes assess him by his kittens seen on the show bench. Some studs always throw kittens with good eye colour regardless of the queen's potential.

Book the stud in advance, and give the stud's owner some idea of when to expect the queen. You can judge a suitable date if you keep records of her calling cycle, once this has started. Some cats go off call if moved too quickly. It is better to wait a day or two until the cat is really ready than to send her or take her to stud as quickly as possible. If she goes off call whenever she is moved, it may be necessary to arrange with the stud's owner for her to stay with the stud until she comes on call again. This will not be possible unless the stud has a double stud house with room to have a queen in waiting.

It is usually wise to visit the stud in advance, not only to see the stud but to inspect his quarters. They should be clean and roomy, preferably with a queen's department with her own fresh-air run and some heat for the queen if she is used to it at home. Otherwise she may catch a chill during her stay.

Mating procedures
The queen must always be taken or sent to stud in a cat-proof container, for however gentle or docile she is at home she is liable

Left: A queen assuming the mating position with the hind legs. Accompanied by head rolling on the floor and plaintive cries (to attract the attention of male cats), this is a sure sign of calling.

Below: A queen (left) and stud cat getting to know each other before mating takes place. This familiarization period is an essential part of the mating ritual; if the queen is not ready she may hiss at first.

Below right: Queen and stud cat in mating position. The stud mounts the queen from the rear and grasps the back of her neck with his mouth. Immediately after mating the queen will roll excitedly and may even attack the stud cat.

to go berserk at the first smell of a stud cat, particularly when she is calling. The ideal arrangement is one where she can enter the queen's quarters without going through stud territory before her box is opened. Usually a wire partition separates the queen from the stud so that they can see and smell and get to know each other before mating. The queen will usually hiss and spit at her suitor at first sight, particularly if not absolutely ready. This is quite normal and nothing to worry about.

As soon as they start billing and cooing and rubbing together through the wire, it is safe to let the queen out to be mated. A non-slip mat is usually provided in the stud's half of the stud house and the queen instinctively runs there. The stud grabs hold of the back of her neck and mounts her from the rear. At her climax she throws him off and rolls violently in circles on the floor. She may even attack him, so he wisely jumps up and out of the way.

The queen may be mated more than once while with the stud. If both are allowed to run together there will be many matings in one day. But more matings do not necessarily mean more kittens. Once is sufficient and a litter of 10 is known to have been produced from a single mating.

Of course owners as well as cats have their affairs to settle. Financially this means you pay a stud fee that includes not only the service fee but a proportion of the costs of keeping the male at stud throughout the year plus the queen's board and lodging, which may last some days if she is not ready to be mated on arrival. The stud owner will usually also insist that the queen has been inoculated, so her certificates should be produced on arrival. The queen's owner should likewise be able to inspect the stud's certificates.

The pregnant queen
When she returns home the queen may still be calling, so you

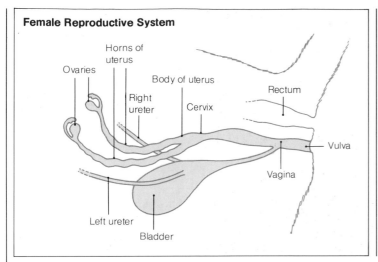
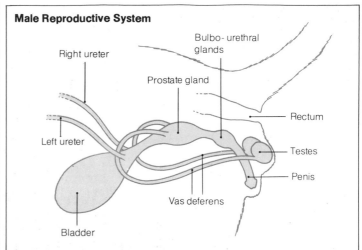

must keep her in until she stops. If she calls again in a few days or weeks, you will know that the mating failed to take and she must return to stud. The stud owner may give a free mating this time but is not bound to do so and is entitled to charge a fee to cover boarding.

If the mating has taken, there will be a period of blissful quiet. The queen will still rush about, but now appears very pleased with herself and is the picture of health. You should add extra vitamins and calcium to her diet at this time (see page 105). About three weeks after mating her nipples will turn pink and the queen will roll again but without any vocal

accompaniment. Eventually she will begin to look plumper and start nesting all over the house. She will appreciate help with her grooming at this time particularly with the parts she may have difficulty in reaching. Using blunt-ended scissors, cut the fur around the nipples of a longhaired queen before she kittens so that the fur · does not get wet, and dry in hard spikes, scratching the kittens' eyes. The fur may also be cut short around the vagina of a longhair before kittening.

Confine the queen to her own quarters during the last week, having made her a perfect kittening box lined with plenty of clean newspaper. She will have a

lovely time shredding it into a comfortable nest for her babies. A cardboard box will do. Even better is a wine carton with a top-opening lid and the compartments removed. Use a sharp knife to make a round hole at one end to let the queen in and out. The hole should be 10cm (4in) above the floor and 15-20cm (6-8in) in diameter. Place the box in a dark, warm, draught-proof corner. If it is winter the whole box can stand on an electrically heated blanket pad, or other form of flat source of heat. The queen's teats should be examined a day or two before the birth and massaged gently with corn or other edible oil.

Giving birth

Birth will occur 63 days after mating in some breeds, 65 days for Siamese and other foreign breeds, or up to 73 days for Egyptian Maus. Anything from 61-70 days can be considered normal if the queen is not otherwise distressed. Most queens like to have their owners present when they kitten, particularly the first time. This can mean either sitting up all night with your queen, perhaps several nights running, or taking her to your own bed so that both of you get some sleep! If you place the prepared kittening box on the bed beside you the queen will usually stay in it and kitten there, especially if you hold her paw and make reassuring noises. You can return the kittening box to the queen's quarters after birth.

Most cats have their kittens quite naturally with no mishaps. Each kitten comes in a 'plastic bag' called the amniotic sac. This has to be broken so that the kitten does not suffocate. Usually the queen bursts the sac. If she fails to do so, or neglects the kitten, perhaps because another is already on the way, you can safely break the sac with clean fingers or a tissue, wiping mucus away from the kitten's mouth and nose. It will then be able to breathe and will probably make little squeaking noises that immediately cause the queen to take fresh interest in it. She will lick it all over and draw it towards her to keep it warm. It may even move towards her teats instinctively and try to suckle.

If the kittens come in quick succession you should certainly help, but if they are well spaced the queen may prefer to do all the work herself. This will include biting off the umbilical cord about 10cm (4in) from the kitten to separate the kitten from the placenta, which attached it to the womb and came away during birth. If the mother fails to sever the cord, you must do so. Take care not to cut it too close to the kitten, nor to pull it away from the kitten. You can use scissors, or pinch with thumb and forefinger, pulling towards the kitten. After some weeks the remaining piece of cord withers and falls off. The queen usually eats the nutritious remains of the placenta, known as the afterbirth. If there are many kittens the queen may not want to eat all the afterbirths, and when you see she has no more interest in those that remain, remove them.

Birth problems

Sometimes a queen fails to produce any kittens hours after starting labour (a condition where the muscles in the flanks contract at regular intervals). If this happens and she is becoming exhausted, call the veterinarian. It may be a breech birth (that is, the kitten is presenting hindquarters first) or something else may be wrong. Provided the queen is not distressed, however, it is best to leave well alone and let things happen naturally. It is unlikely that deformed kittens will be born, but if in doubt have the veterinarian examine them and put malformed kittens to sleep painlessly. Do not try to drown them yourself. Any with cleft palates will make a shrill, unpleasant noise easy to distinguish from the soft squeaking of normal kittens. Often the queen will lie on such kittens to silence and smother them, and this is the best thing that can happen to them. The queen is usually very good at telling which kittens to rear and which to discard.

Kitten care

When all the kittens are born, you can lift them out of their box on

Above: A pregnant queen. The nipples show clearly and the cat is suitably plump. During this time she seems very contented and glows with perfect health. She should be given extra calcium and vitamins to ensure sturdy kittens. Pregnancy lasts 61-70 days.

Below: The mother licks one of her kittens immediately after birth. This is an instinctive reaction to clean the kittens of the amniotic fluid. Once clean, the kittens will be drawn close to the mother's body for warmth and they may start trying to suckle straight away.

the pad of newspapers, prepare a clean bed in the box, and return the kittens one at a time. The queen may object to this but will soon realize that what you are doing is sensible, and curl up with her kittens purring her satisfaction. Now she can safely be left for some hours to enjoy her babies, although she may also appreciate some warm milk, a commercial whole-food diet usually mixed with milk or other warm drink (but see the chapter on feeding, as some breeds are allergic to milk). Put the drink in a deep bowl and hold it so she can drink while in the kittening box; some cats refuse to leave their box for hours, but will drink or eat anything offered while they remain there suckling their kittens.

Eventually the mother will leave her box to visit the litter tray, which should always be nearby. From now on such visits offer you the best times for changing bedding. If possible shut the queen out of the room for the few minutes this takes, or she will rush back to the nest at the first vocal sign that her young are being disturbed. Once they are all settled down in new, clean bedding, you can let her

back into the room, and she will curl up with them in the clean bed. The bedding will have to be changed once or twice daily for the first week as the queen will probably still be losing a certain amount of blood.

Changing bedding is the best time for sexing kittens, although they often screech when suddenly picked up. Sexing is done by holding the kitten in one hand, all four feet on the hand, and lifting the tail with your other hand. The illustration on this page shows sexual differences.

After a few days the queen will get hungrier and hungrier, and some people say it is impossible to overfeed a nursing queen. She should have as much nourishing food (with added vitamins and minerals) as she can eat. She will appreciate regular grooming during this time and if the kittens have any infection around the eyes her whole underside should be washed with baby or other cat-safe shampoo and the kittens' eyes cleaned with damp cotton wool—a fresh piece for each kitten—before they are placed back together again.

Should the queen call before the kittens are fully weaned, she must be carefully confined with them. But if she loses her milk, has no milk, has been allowed out and fails to return to attend to her maternal duties, or has died giving birth (a rare occurrence), the kittens will have to be reared without her. Sometimes it is possible for another queen who has milk to take over the kittens, and this is the best way as she will also wash the kittens and keep them warm. If you cannot find a foster mother you are faced with hand-rearing, a very time-consuming but most rewarding process.

You will need a foster-feeding bottle and a substitute milk formula. The kittens will require feeding every two hours, night and day, for the first week, so no one should attempt this without the patience to see it through. And feeding is only part of the task: the human foster mother must also massage the kittens' bellies to stimulate urination; wipe their rear ends clean with damp cotton wool; change the bedding twice a day; and keep the kittens warm. There are various electrically heated beds or panels on the market for this purpose. A hot water bottle is not recommended as you would have to replace it every four hours. There is a non-electric pet bed warmer on the market but this lasts only eight to ten hours before needing attention. A bed heated at one end only is a good idea, as the kittens can move to a hotter or colder section as required. When hand rearing, you can drop some of the night feeds in the second week, then feed only every four hours for the third week.

Rearing kittens
After giving birth to a lovely litter of kittens, your queen will hardly

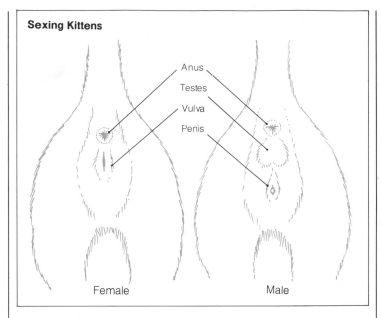

Sexing Kittens

Anus
Testes
Vulva
Penis

Female   Male

Above: The differences in young male and female kittens, easiest to discern in the first few days of life. The vulva and anus are close together in the female kitten; the anus and the developing testes and penis are clearly further apart in the male kitten.

Below: Contented kittens growing strong on their mother's milk. They will suckle for about three weeks before being weaned onto other foods. While the mother is feeding her kittens she will consume vast quantities of food, which should be nourishing.

move out of the kittening box for the first week, except to feed herself and attend to her toilet. She will curl up with them, purring, letting them suckle and washing them, completely satisfied.

At about 10 days old the kittens' eyes will begin to open, and the kittens will start to move around in the box. If there is a litter tray near the breeding box, the mother will nudge them into it after feeding them and instinctively they will know what to do. They usually start using the litter tray before being weaned, provided you have been thoughtful enough to provide one for their use. Normal kittens will eat some of the litter in the tray or any other dirt lying about, which apparently may help them to populate the gut flora with bacterial organisms vital for digestion.

They will be content with only mother's milk to begin with but if she is lacking in milk they will not plump up as they should and you must think about supplementing her milk with a foster feeding bottle. The smallest who are not getting a fair share will be the first to accept the bottle, and the queen will eagerly devour whatever contents are left. In fact she should be

little at a time and slowly.

If the queen has been taught to sit up and beg for her food before the plate is put down, continue to do this and the kittens will follow their mother's example as soon as they can stand on two back legs without tumbling over. If the mother was not trained to do this before, now is a good time to start and they can all learn it together.

Even when the kittens are all feeding themselves and seem independent of their mother's milk, leave them with her until they are at least ten weeks old, preferably 12 weeks for the foreign breeds. During this time the mother has a chance to 'finish their education'.

Kitten education
When the kittens start crawling out of the nesting box, using the litter tray and eating food other than from their mother, their education begins in earnest. The mother must teach them a dozen things before they leave home; and a wise breeder teaches them to be loving little companions by handling them frequently and affectionately. Those destined for a show career should be handled as a judge will handle them, so that they are used to the routine by the time they go to their first show.

One of the first things kittens learn is how to wash. They may copy mother or perhaps it is instinctive, but their first ineffective movements are fascinating to watch. They move their paws to their mouths to lick, and then pass the paw over the ear.

The next thing they learn is how to play. They sit up and box each other using the paws. If one falls over, the other knows instinctively to pounce on it. Usually play concerns two kittens only, then one of them will break away and pick on one of the other kittens. They will also try to play with mother, who holds them down with one paw and washes them whilst they try to escape, but she is cleverer than they are. Then she moves her tail, and a kitten pounces on it; she moves it again, and others join in. Then she can relax, knowing their interests are near the nest. She is more anxious as curiosity leads them further afield. They will graduate to chasing moving objects supplied by the breeder. The moggie-play-pole and the cat-bat are group toys that the whole litter can enjoy, and any rattle ball on elastic attached to a door handle will give hours of exercise and amusement.

If there is a cat tree in the house or the queen has a thoughtful owner who has provided shelves at different heights in the breeding area, it will amaze you how quickly even the tiniest kitten will climb to the top shelf. He may squeal when he gets there and find the way down not so easy, but the mother or the breeder will soon come to the rescue. And so they learn to climb and with it to use the same posts for scratching their claws, just as mother does. If there is no cat tree, any scratching post of

offered a bowl of the same kind of milk. A week later this can become a milky baby cereal, served to the mother near the nest. If you use the same sounds as the mother has been used to, when you serve feeds to the kittens, they will soon associate these sounds with food and come running. Their language lessons will have begun. The kittens will copy their mother and stick their noses in the mixture; some will walk right into it, then squeal to find their feet slipping! The queen will soon clean them up. Eventually they will all get the hang of how to lap and will look forward to their porridge at regular intervals. In between they will still be suckled by their mother.

At three weeks they can be given one meal of raw meat, rabbit, chicken or fish, finely minced or chopped, four hours away from the cereal meal. If the kittens seem constipated you can use sardines and brown bread crumbs mixed with a little hot water into a mash.

After four weeks give two milk and/or cereal meals and two meat or fish meals each day, adding one drop of halibut oil per kitten daily, and making sure all kittens get fair shares. If any kitten is greedy and eats too much, so that it regurgitates the food soon afterwards, feed it separately, a

Above: Feeding a very young kitten with a curved foster feeding bottle. By taking the thumb on and off the open end it is possible to control the flow to the kitten.

Below: It is better not to disturb kittens in the first week except to change the bedding daily. Thereafter they need to be handled regularly to socialize them.

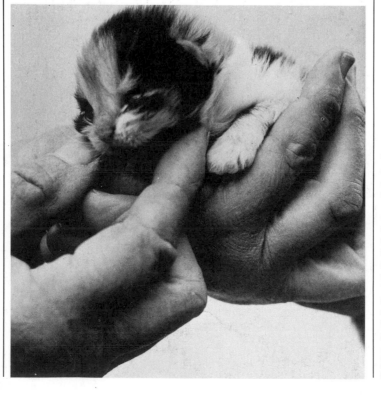

leg, sticking their little claws in to gain a foothold. Other kittens will be picked up very gently by other members of the family, stroked and fussed and talked to. The kittens will have discovered people and laps!

She will teach them to hunt, pounce, and protect their catches from others by growling over them, throw them in the air and eat them. She will teach them which humans to trust and love and which to avoid. She will tell them about dogs, if she has ever met one, and about all the other inmates in the household.

When the family are busy and have no time to sit, the kittens will be shown by mother which are the softest chairs and they will stake their claims, but mother will be the boss cat and have the first choice. If allowed upstairs, they will soon discover that beds are softest of all and that people in beds are warm too. Their owners may even allow them in bed as fur-covered little hot-water bottles to keep them warm! The purring on these occasions is really deafening and the kittens' faces betray their excitement. While nursing the kittens, the family can make a first attempt to groom with a brush and comb. All will be considered a game at first but a human can follow the mother cat and hold the kitten down with one hand, while wielding the brush or comb with the other.

If the queen is allowed out on hunting trips, she will now bring home mice and other small creatures. (None of the cat species regurgitates food from the stomach for their offspring, as do many other animals and birds.) She will growl over them in front of her kittens, showing them what to do when they are lucky enough to catch something themselves. This will interest and excite them enormously. Later on she will bring in live prey and deliberately let it go in front of them. They soon catch on and chase and pounce inexpertly. The mother will catch it again and throw it up into the air once or twice, while they look on enviously. They will practise on toy mice that the owner has thoughtfully provided, and soon become quite expert. If allowed out, they may even catch their own first mouse or at least a beetle or spider before they are sold. Thus their education continues and it has been shown that cats that have been taught how to hunt and kill prey by their mothers become more efficient mousers themselves.

As the kittens grow, they exercise well by chasing each other and playing 'he' or 'tab'. In this way they cover a lot of ground, leaping all over the furniture or up and down the stairs indoors, or round the shrubs and up the trees in the garden, if allowed out. They must have space somewhere to exercise and play.

Thus they will grow up into intelligent, healthy, agile, accomplished cats, with beautiful manners—a credit to any cat-loving home.

Above: The mother carries very young kittens by holding their heads gently in her mouth. As they grow older they become too heavy to be carried safely in this way.

Right: Kittens instinctively play together, which develops the muscles they will need later for hunting. The home provides endless opportunities for games.

wood, cardboard or natural bark can be used. The handyman of the home can sometimes be persuaded to design one specially to fit your own circumstances.

If the nest is heated at one end, the kittens will soon have found this out and the foreign breeds will be in a heap at that end. The smart ones discover that the middle of the pile is the warmest and you wonder how they can still breathe. Other warm places in the home are gradually discovered: the boiler in the kitchen, the airing cupboard, a sunny window sill or a warm radiator. Warmth plays a large part in a kitten's comfort.

When evening comes and the family sit down, the kittens may be brought in for a little socializing. Mother will jump up on to a lap and the kittens will try to follow, probably climbing up someone's

Keeping a stud

Keeping a stud pedigree cat is for professional breeders only. You should have experience with two or more queens of your own before considering it. Remember that managing a stud cat is no light undertaking, but calls for a deep and abiding love of cats—your own and other people's. Handling their visiting queens requires much patience, understanding and general cat know-how. Stud management is also expensive, done properly, as the stud cat should have his own quarters and the best of food. Another snag is odour: many people loathe the peculiar smell of an entire male cat. Consequently the family and the neighbours, if any, must be considered.

It is also important to find out if the cat fancy can absorb another stud cat of your chosen breed: perhaps there are already too many with insufficient work between them. A male cat is very unhappy if he is not given enough work to do, and if there is no demand for his professional services it is kinder to have him neutered. Never let a stud cat run loose to mate with all the local queens. He will get more exercise but he may catch a disease, suffer injury in fights, get run over or become lost so that he is unavailable when needed to receive a visiting queen.

To keep a stud permanently confined, you need the largest accommodation that you can afford, with room inside for the cats to mate, and waiting room for the owner. A large fresh-air run will make sure the stud cat has plenty of fresh air and exercise. Shelves 15cm (6in) wide fixed at different heights around the sides of the run will provide the cat with all the exercise he needs. The best-arranged stud houses combine a queen's compartment inside with her own individual run outside. They can both share the same escape run. In this way the queen's coming and going does not have to be carried out through stud territory, although of course queens must always arrive at stud in a cat-proof container and be released only when all escape routes have been closed.

Vinyl flooring is ideal for inside the stud house; vinyl should also be carried up the walls above spray height and sealed with a half-moon beading. A washable mat or rug in the centre of the stud's area will provide comfort and a surface that feet can grip during mating. In some climates it may be essential to provide stud and queen with heated beds or to install infra-red dull emitter lamps or another form of safe heating over the cat beds. In the tropics you may well need air conditioning instead. A light in the stud house enables feeding and mating to take place at night if necessary. All electrical wiring should be installed outside the stud house, entering only at the point of use. Concrete runs are best for ease of cleaning, with wire

raised about 1cm (½in) above the concrete to facilitate swilling underneath. Pots of home-grown grass and catnip will be much appreciated by both queen and stud.

To be successful in the cat fancy a stud cat must be a champion or potential champion of its breed, for only the very best are in demand by owners of pedigree breeding queens. Understandably, these people want to win prizes with their kittens and so build up their 'prefix' or cattery name.

The successful stud will be in peak condition all year round. This calls for a prime diet of best raw meat, chicken, rabbit and fish plus extra vitamins, minerals, egg yolks and also milk if he can take it

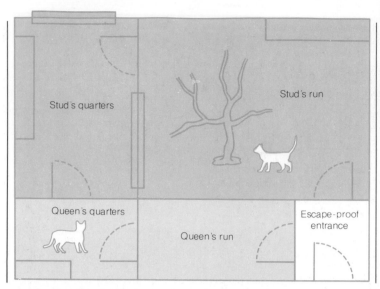

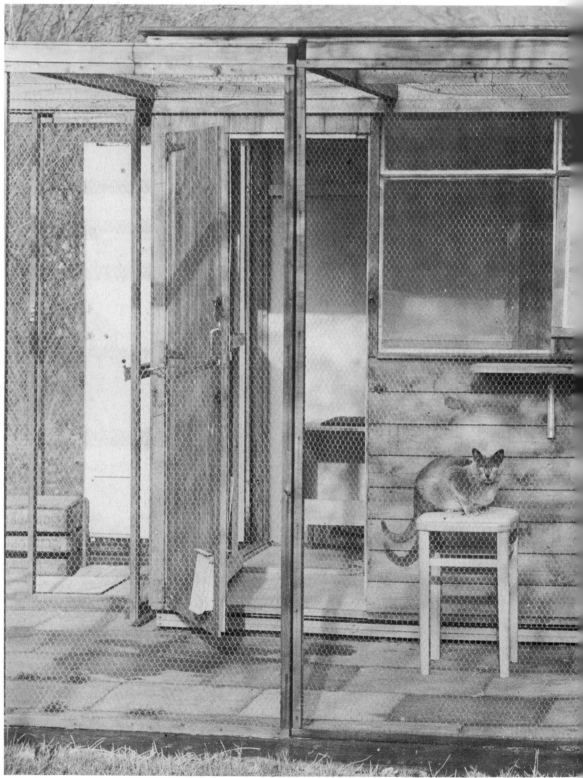

(some cats cannot). He will cost a lot to feed but each stud fee will include a proportion of his upkeep all year round. He must receive inoculations as required and the visiting queens' owners will expect to see the relevant certificates.

Using a stud

A male cat may become ready to mate a female as early as six months old or not until he is two years old. Readiness appears not to be breed related, but to vary with individuals; some precocious males of the foreign breeds have

mated with their sisters while still together in a litter. A male can be put to stud once he becomes a 'proved sire' by having mated a queen who has subsequently given birth to kittens. Some breeders limit the number of queens to be served the first year; others may limit matings at all times. Nature is usually the best judge, however, and so long as the cat appears to be thriving and getting enough to eat there should be no harm in letting him mate as many days a week as he wants. A research cat, a ginger tom, is said to have mated 17 times a day for months on end before a three-week break when he refused to look at another queen. But after this brief vacation he happily went back to work as usual.

It is unlikely that a stud cat will be overworked if well fed. If he goes into a decline it is much more likely to be for some other reason such as ill health or lack of human companionship. The cat who does not get enough work may be a more difficult problem. He could pine away or get bad tempered. His services can be advertised but if there really is no call for him he should be neutered. You can have this done at any age although it may take six months for him to drop the spraying habit.

A successful stud who is kept at work can go on for years, even to 16 or 17, but some studs eventually lose interest or, more likely, you find that the queens who come to be mated no longer 'take', or become pregnant. When this starts to happen to a stud he can spend the rest of his life as a household pet or you can use him simply to keep the queens happy when they are calling but not required to produce kittens.

At the start of his career you should mate a young stud only to experienced 'easy' queens: ones who know the ropes. This will build up his confidence. Save maiden queens for later, when he is experienced. If a young, timid stud gets an hysterical, 'difficult' queen the first time, he may develop a complex. Even experienced queens are sometimes troublesome and sorely try the patience of both stud and stud owner, perhaps due to a bad start in their sex life. You may have to steady the queen by hand, or it may be best to leave the couple to run with each other and sort out their own problems. Some cats will only mate if no human is present.

When the queen arrives, it is quite normal for her to spit at her intended if she is not quite ready, or if she has gone somewhat off call because of the journey. He usually doesn't mind too much because he knows that she will change her tune in due course. He waits patiently, wooing her with his voice until she rolls and coos back at him. When the stud owner feels the time is right, she will open the door of the queen's apartment and the queen will run out on to the mat and assume a mating posture. The stud will straddle her, take her by the scruff with his mouth and proceed to penetrate. He may thump her hindquarters until she lifts them to the required level and moves her tail to one side. She may waltz about a bit, moving round in circles, or actively try to throw him off. He will hang on, however, until her climax and until he has ejaculated, when he will jump clear.

After this she will roll round

furiously and may even attack him if he fails to get out of the way; a shelf about 46cm (18in) high should be provided for the purpose. Immediately the stud owner can make a fuss of the stud and tell him what a clever fellow he is, but no attempt should be made to handle the queen until she has calmed down. With any luck the queen will return to her own quarters voluntarily or with a little persuasion and the couple can then be left for some time to clean themselves up. They will usually enjoy each other's company and eating meals at the same time, and if the queen remains for any reason for any length of time after she has gone off call, the couple can run together and will often be found curled up together in one bed or enjoying mutual washing.

When it is time for the queen to go home, the stud's owner gives her a mating certificate showing the dates on which matings have taken place and the date kittens can be expected. The stud's owner also gives the queen's owner a copy of the stud's pedigree and asks for news of the result of the mating in due course. The stud's owner received the stud fee when the queen arrived. This fee varies with the breed, popularity or awards of the stud; the type of stud quarters; and the location. It should reflect the stud service and the queen's quarters and length of stay, and include something towards the stud cat's annual maintenance. If the queen does not 'take', some stud owners offer a free mating but they are not obliged to, and would certainly charge a boarding fee for the queen. The stud fee is never returned whatever the outcome, but if a stud persistently fails to impregnate his queens he should be withdrawn from stud.

A stud's life

The life of the stud cat can be lonely, as most stud cats are not allowed into their owner's house. This is mainly because of their quite natural habit of spraying what human noses consider a foul-smelling liquid. In fact this is the stud's 'visiting card', designed to attract the queens and left on inanimate objects to designate the stud's territory. Forced through this habit to live in his own house away from the human household and other cats, the stud is nonetheless an affectionate animal needing his share of attention. The stud owner must take time to groom him and make a fuss of him, perhaps when changing his litter, cleaning him out and feeding him. Between duties he would enjoy the companionship of a female who is not calling, or even a neutered male placed in the queen's compartment. Two studs together will only fight, so never try this combination; but two studs in houses 18m (about 60ft) apart will enjoy watching each other. However, only very experienced breeders will be able to cope with more than one stud cat.

Left: An ideal stud house layout with separate queen's quarters and run. She can be installed safely behind wire until ready to mate.

Left: This stud house is large and airy, with shelves at different levels for interest and exercise. The cedarwood frame is maintenance-free. The stud cat awaiting his next queen is a Blue Burmese.

HISTORY AND GENETICS

The first evidence of cats being domesticated is in archaeological remains as early as 2500 BC in Egypt where literally hundreds of thousands of cats have been found mummified. Cats were also known in China from 1000 BC and later in Japan. People esteemed the cat as a rodent officer protecting the silk-worm industry, the granaries and old manuscripts from damage by rats. Egyptian paintings and Pompeiian relics depict cats, which were either striped or spotted tabbies. The Egyptians even made gods of cats and all sorts of magical powers were attributed to them. So much so that by the Middle Ages, the Church, in an attempt to bring the people back to God and to suppress the interest in magic, persecuted both cats and their owners. This may account for the way bubonic plague swept through Europe and Asia in the mid-fourteenth century, because there were very few cats left to keep down the rats, which brought the plague with them wherever they went. By the end of the eighteenth century, the value of the cat in keeping down vermin was once again realized and the cat was re-instated in its place by every domestic hearth, symbolizing the perfect household pet.

It was not until the end of the nineteenth century that interest in the cat, to the extent of holding cat shows, began. People were beginning to realize the differences between the coat colours and patterns. As the science of genetics was formulated and grew, so cat breeders became interested in 'creating' new breeds and new colours or perfecting the ones that they had; and today we can change head shapes, eye colour, hair type and coat colour, and even perpetuate deformities! No matter

Above: An Egyptian bronze figure (dated after 30 BC), one of many images that show the respect given to cats by the Ancient Egyptians.

Left: This colourful British Shorthair litter is the result of mating two cats with genes for different colours in their make-up.

what we do, however, the cat will always be a cat. It will never be anything else. And what a blessing that is, for there can hardly ever have been anything so worth preserving as the cat—a perfect piece of creative genius. If it disappeared, the world would be a poorer place.

Since the 1914-18 war, the science of genetics has really got into its stride, and it is now possible to predict that within the next decade or two, every conceivable cat will be produced in any colour, coat pattern and coat type. Whether this will be prudent in all cases is another matter but it will undoubtedly be possible.

The following discourse is purposely non-technical. Anyone

wishing for a more scientific and detailed education in genetics is referred to the books mentioned on page 154.

Health and stamina
It is pointless to start a breeding programme with anything but very healthy stock. Any weakness in constitution will be doubled up in a line breeding programme. Therefore your foundation stock must be the best that you can afford both of its breed and in health.

Sex and colour
The cat has 38 chromosomes consisting of 18 identical pairs and one pair that is different. The different pair is for the sexes, male and female, and nature provides for equal quantities to be born, although in any one litter there may be more males than females or vice versa. Some breeds seem to have a preponderance of male kittens, and some coat colours are linked to sex, so that whereas you can only have males that are black, brown, blue, lilac, red or cream (in solid or other coat patterns), females can be black, brown, blue, lilac, red, cream, tortoiseshell or blue-cream, and their dilutions. In other words all the tortoiseshell cats and the tortie-and-white (calico) cats are always female, in all the colours and their dilutions. Occasionally a male cat will be born with tortie (or blue-cream etc.) colouring, which is achieved by the cat having an extra chromosome; but the cat in this case will usually be sterile.

Genes
Genes determine the characteristics of the cat in every field, and there are literally thousands of genes on every chromosome, all

Left: An Exotic Shorthair, the result of mating longhaired cats to shorthairs to get a cobby type body, round face and short hair.

Above: A Seal-point Colourpoint, produced by mating recessive long-hairs to shorthairs with Himalayan coat pattern. It took ten years!

having their specific location on the chromosome. There are genes, not only for coat colour and coat pattern but for temperament, eye shape and colour, body type, hair type, reproduction, and every other characteristic. During cell division, the gene reproduces itself exactly with great precision. When very occasionally, over perhaps hundreds of years, a gene does not reproduce itself exactly or misplaces itself to a different location on the chromosome, the gene is said to be a mutant and the resulting kitten a mutation.

Body types

There are two basic body types, the cobby shape with a round skull, typified by the show quality Persian and the Exotic Shorthair; and the finer boned, lithe, slender type with a wedge-shaped head, as seen in the Angora and Balinese

longhairs and Siamese, Colour-point and Oriental shorthairs. Every other cats is somewhere in between. Some are found as 'natural breeds' from various geographical locations, others are deliberate attempts by breeders to 'create' new breeds by mating different types together to produce something combining features from both. Occasionally a new type has occurred as a natural mutation and we get the Manx cat, without a tail or with various degrees of shortness of tail; the Japanese Bobtail, with a different kind of curled tail; the folded ear cat (the Scottish Fold), which was a natural mutation in Scotland as recently as 1961; and the polydactyl cat, with extra toes. With the exception of the Scottish Fold, these other mutations occurred so long ago that no one now remembers the dates but they were perpetuated

Above: A Scottish Fold. The folded ear is a natural mutation that has been perpetuated by selective breeding, notably in the USA.

Below: The front paw of a poly-dactyl cat, showing six toes instead of the usual five. Some affected cats may have seven toes.

Above: A Seal-point Siamese. The slender Oriental type of cat was found occurring in the East in Himalayan and other coat colours.

Left: An elegant Blue-eyed Angora, one of the longhaired breeds with a fine boned, slender type of body and wedge-shaped head.

because they were geographically confined and inbreeding intensified the characteristics. Manx is a recessive gene; folded ear is a dominant gene; and the polydactyl gene is also dominant over normal toes. (See page 135.)

Coat colour and pattern
The various coat colours and patterns as shown on pages 10 to 15 are all inherent within the cat species and it was only a matter of time before they were produced. It is doubtful whether they would all have come to light if left to themselves, with random matings of the cat population, because some colours are dominant over others and the recessive colours would

always have been at a disadvantage, unless once again the line breeding came about by being confined within a geographical location. This could have happened with the Korat and the Siamese. However, now that breeders are beginning to understand about selective breeding, all possible colours can be produced, within all coat patterns, and in each body and hair type or mixture of types. What constitutes a breed, therefore, is becoming more and more uncertain. In view of this experimental age, it is evident that the Governing Bodies of the Cat Fancies worldwide will have to get together and reassess the whole situation, finalizing eventually a new system of classification that will be acceptable to all, and based on sound principles of genetics rather than on whim and opinion.

Eyes
It is thought that most cats in temperate regions had hazel eyes—a good camouflage for them in the undergrowth; this leads one to suppose that the red and cream

coloured cats with amber eyes originally came from desert regions, where their colouring would have added to their chance of survival. On the show bench, however, other more dramatic colourings are sometimes desired by the fancy breeders; red cats with green eyes are produced, for instance, and very attractive they are. The science of genetics has made this possible.

Temperament

The genes for temperament vary with the different breeds and it is noticed that when one breed is crossed with another the resulting 'breed' has an intermediate temperament as well. Thus when some of the Siamese breeds are crossed with longhairs, the resulting Himalayan coloured longhairs are less aggressive than the original Siamese, less vocal and less destructive. It is interesting that temperament can be manipulated in this way along with other features.

Head shape

During this century, the Persian cat has been changed from a long-nosed cat, with consequent long tongue, which it needed to cope with its long fur, to a short-faced cat, with consequent short tongue, which is not nearly so efficient for its own grooming. The reverse has happened with the Siamese. This started life at the end of the nineteenth century as a short, round-faced animal, judging by early pictures of cats on the show bench. Selective breeding has now produced a very long, racehorse type of head, with very long tongue, more than adequate for grooming its very short coat. Fashion in each case has dictated these changes and some may think that it was not always in the best interests of the cat. In the case of the Peke-faced Persian, for instance, the shortness of nose in extreme cases produces breathing problems, blocked tear ducts and even difficulty in feeding. New breeders should beware of experimental breeding, therefore, and concentrate on improving not only the looks but the practicality of each cat within the various breeds.

Feature fixing

The way to fix a feature that you desire, is to take a female that has one or more of the features you wish to fix and mate her to a male with similar features or others that you wish to introduce into your own strain.
Out of the resulting kittens, you discard those not showing the desired features, and mate the others together or back to their parents. Again you keep the ones showing the desired features, and sell off the others as pets. When the next generation is old enough, you mate again with each other or back to the foundation stock. In this way a strain is built up all carrying the desired features. By discarding the others, some of these features will become 'fixed' and will appear in all future offspring. Care must be taken here

Above: Bicolour Rex cats from the USA. The curly or rex coat was a natural mutation that appeared in various locations. There are two genetic types: Cornish and Devon.

Right: A Seal-point Snowshoe, a Himalayan patterned shorthair with an added gene for white spotting deliberately introduced.

not to introduce outcrosses, which will undo all the work you have built up. In this connection, it is better to have more than one programme going at the same time, then cross over to the other strain built up similarly either by you or by another breeder attempting the same programme. This is not always as easy as it sounds because you sometimes come across a feature that is different because it is recessive or sex-linked. The red colour in cats, for instance, is sometimes sex-linked, and the dilute colours are recessive to the dominant colours.

Dominant and Recessive Characteristics

COLOURS

BLACK *dominant over* **Blue**	**BLACK** *dominant over* **Chocolate**
CHOCOLATE *dominant over* **Lilac**	**CHOCOLATE** *dominant over* **Cinnamon**
RED *dominant over* **Cream**	**WHITE** *dominant over* **All other colours**
TORTOISESHELL *dominant over* **Blue-cream**	**TORTIE-AND-WHITE (Calico)** *dominant over* **Dilute tortie-and-white** **(Blue-cream and white)**
SOLID COLOUR *dominant over* **Siamese**	**SOLID COLOUR** *dominant over* **Burmese**
SIAMESE *dominant over* **Blue-eyed albino**	**BLUE-EYED ALBINO** *dominant over* **Pink-eyed albino**
PIEBALD (Mostly white) *dominant over* **Solid colour**	**TICKED TABBY (Agouti)** *dominant over* **All other tabbies**
TICKED TABBY *dominant over* **Black**	**MACKEREL TABBY** *dominant over* **Classic or blotched tabby**
WHITE SPOTTING *dominant over* **Solid colour** **(There is also a recessive white spotting)**	**WHITE UNDERCOAT** *dominant over* **Solid colour**

Above: The completely tail-less cat is the result of genes for skeletal deformity. Manx mated to Manx gives a high percentage of prenatal deaths.

COAT TYPES

SHORTHAIR *dominant over* **Longhair**	**SHORTHAIR** *dominant over* **Hairless**
WIREHAIR *dominant over* **Normal hair**	**NORMAL COAT** *dominant over* **Rex coat**

OTHER FEATURES

FOLDED EAR *dominant over* **Normal ear**	**MANX TAIL** *dominant over* **Normal tail**
POLYDACTYL (Extra toes) *dominant over* **Normal toes**	

Dominance

In considering a dominant with a recessive feature, if both cats show the dominant feature, all the offspring will also show the dominant feature. If both cats display the recessive feature, all the offspring will display the recessive feature. If a cat with a recessive feature is mated to a cat with a dominant feature and all the kittens show the dominant feature, it is probable that the dominant cat is not carrying the recessive feature. However, if the offspring are half displaying the dominant feature and half displaying the recessive feature, this will prove that the cat displaying the dominant feature also carries the recessive gene. This will be a very important discovery for future matings with that cat. A table of dominant and recessive features is shown on this page. Armed with these charts, the breeder can decide how to go about building up a strain within a breed, or creating a new breed, new colour variety, or new combination of coat type, coat colour and eye colour. It may take many generations and much hard work (the creation of the Colour-point longhair, for instance, took ten years!) but it will be very rewarding when you see your cats taking championship honours on the show benches of the world.

Above: Butterfly markings on the back are characteristic of the inherited classic tabby coat pattern, which comes in all colours.

Summary

So we see that every characteristic of the cat is capable of manipulation today and it is to be hoped that today's and tomorrow's breeders will be very responsible in their creative skills. Let us aim for beautiful cats that are also practical. Do not let us perpetuate monstrosities and deformities or ugly cats. The cat deserves to be the wonderful creature it is, in all its various beautiful forms.

9

SHOWING YOUR CAT

Showing cats is a marvellous hobby for young or old. It brings together people with similar interests and can prove extremely exciting. As an educational hobby, showing deserves to be encouraged in the young. It also helps to give breeders scientific insight into what cats inherit from their parents.

The best way to start is to visit a local cat show and study the exhibits. This can be a most enjoyable day out for all the family. If it is an all-breed show, there will be many glamorous creatures like those illustrated in this book.

If what you see makes you want to own a pedigree cat, you may find such kittens for sale at the show, and, if not, most exhibitors will have kittens at home or know where to find them. They are usually pleased to help a novice start and may guide you through your first experience of purchasing a kitten, showing it and eventually breeding from it. You may have to wait some time for a show quality kitten of a rare breed, but the waiting is worth while; there is no point showing or breeding from an inferior specimen.

If you intend to show but not breed, it is kindest to have the animal spayed or neutered. (Unlike spayed or neutered dogs, altered cats may be exhibited.) This gives you a choice of male or female. Otherwise your first purchase must be a female because only an experienced breeder with several queens (entire females) should attempt to keep a stud (an entire male). You will learn why in the chapter on breeding, starting on page 121.

If you wish to pursue cat breeding seriously, you must have your own prefix, or cattery name,

Above: A proud young owner with her prize winning Female Siamese kitten at an Exemption Show held in the United Kingdom.

Left: A steward at the Supreme Show holds a Silver Tabby British Shorthair kitten while the judge writes her report on the cat.

which will apply to all the kittens bred by you. You must register this name with the governing council or cat association operating in your own country before the kittens are born—in fact, it is a good idea to act as soon as you decide to take up breeding seriously. A prefix might make an excellent Christmas or birthday present. Given common sense and the ability to gain a practical knowledge of genetics you should find it possible to produce champions and even to become a famous breeder.

The advent of showing
People have been holding cat shows only during the last hundred years or so. The first

official show in the UK was at the Crystal Palace on 13th July 1871. The first in the USA is reputed to have been at Bunnels Museum, New York in March 1881, followed by one at Madison Square Gardens, New York in 1895.

Shows are now held in Australia, New Zealand, the United States, every country in Europe, South Africa and Japan on a regular basis. Mexico had its first cat show in 1978 and Hong Kong its first in 1979. The largest shows are in the United Kingdom, with over 2,000 entries at the National Cat Show.

Persians form the largest classes at American shows, followed by Himalayans, Siamese, Burmese and Abyssinians in that order. Chinchillas are the largest single group of longhair exhibits at Australian shows, where Orientals are very popular. Somalis have reached Australia but are not yet numerous; neither are Rex, Korats and British Shorthairs. In the UK the Persians (Longhairs) are most numerous, followed by Siamese and Burmese.

Most shows have classes for household pets—that is, non-pedigree, sexually altered cats. A kitten found on a doorstep or a free gift from a friend might become a winner in these classes, particularly if prettily marked. Some of the larger shows offer prizes for household pets in categories such as 'any colour longhair', 'best black shorthair', 'most attractively marked ginger cat', or 'cat with the sweetest disposition'. To qualify as a household pet for showing purposes the cat must be of unknown or unregistered parentage.

The United Kingdom, New Zealand, Australia and South

Africa feature one-day shows where cats are placed in numbered pens and the judges go from pen to pen examining them. In the United States and mainland Europe shows last one, two or three days; pens are highly decorated with curtains, cushions and winning rosettes from previous shows; and the judging takes place elsewhere. Stewards collect the cats for each class and take them to a judging ring, often in another room.

Showing in the UK
The first step in entering a show is to obtain a list of shows for the coming season from your local governing body. Write for a schedule of the chosen show about four months in advance and return the entry form promptly, correctly filled in and with the correct entry money.

The schedule gives particulars in all the classes in the show, the venue, names of judges, club and show officials and officiating veterinarians, together with the name and address of the person to whom entries should be sent and the date by which all entries must be posted. At the front of the schedule is a list of rules and regulations.

The schedule is divided into Longhair, Shorthair (sometimes split into British and Foreign), and Siamese sections, with a separate section for Household Pets if they are included in the show. The classes are split into Open classes, Miscellaneous or Side classes, and Club classes. Sometimes all the classes for one section are grouped together, other times all the Open classes are first, followed by the Miscellaneous classes for all breeds, and finally the Club classes.

The schedule will tell you what it costs to enter each class and what prize money is given. At many shows rosettes or medals are given instead of prize money for the Open classes and these awards will be placed on the pen at the show.

At the back of the schedule you will usually find a list of cups and trophies offered by the club holding the show and by supporting clubs. Some are points cups awarded at the end of the show season for the cat gaining the most points in the category covered by the cup, points being won for first, second and third places, etc. Other cups are awarded for specific wins or good points in a cat at the show.

The following abbreviations are usually found in the schedule:

LH	Longhaired
M	Male
F	Female
SP	Seal-point
CP	Chocolate-point
BP	Blue-point
LP	Lilac-point
TP	Tabby-point
RP	Red-point
AC	Any Colour
AV	Any Variety
AOC	Any Other Colour
AOV	Any Other Variety

Types of Classes (UK)

Open classes
Open to all exhibitors, not just to members of the club holding the show. Any cat which is registered, and whose parents and grandparents are also registered, is eligible to enter the Open class for its own breed, sex and age, irrespective of whether or not it has won any prizes before. If eligible it must be entered in this class.

At a Championship or Sanction Show there are Open classes for all breeds catered for by the show, with separate adult Open classes for males and females in all breeds with Championship status. Adults are cats nine months of age or more on the day of the show.

Kittens under nine calendar months have separate Open classes for all breeds. Kitten classes for popular breeds may be split into males and females or be divided by age.

Neuters, which are castrated males or spayed females, always have separate Open classes of their own.

Any cat is eligible to enter only one Open class with the exception of full Champions or full Premiers, who may enter in both their ordinary Open class and the Champion of Champions or Premier of Premiers class respectively, these classes also being considered Open. They may enter these classes instead of the ordinary Open class, but only full Champions and full Premiers are eligible.

The Open classes are the most important ones, as here the cat competes against all others in the same category of breed, sex and age.

Miscellaneous or Side classes
Open to all exhibitors but without the importance of Open classes, they are generally split into categories for cats which have won a certain amount, have been bred by the exhibitor or otherwise, or come from specific areas, and are again divided into sections and into cats, kittens and neuters, e.g.
Debutante: For cats (kittens, neuters) which have never been exhibited before.

Maiden: For cats (kittens, neuters) which have never won a first, second or third prize.
Novice: For cats (kittens, neuters) which have never won a first prize.
Special Limit: For cats (kittens, neuters) which have not won more than two first prizes.
Limit: For cats (kittens, neuters) which have not won more than four first prizes.
Adolescent: For cats between 9 and 15 months of age.
Junior: For cats (neuters) under two years old on the day of the show.
Senior: For cats (neuters) two years and over on the day of the show.
Veteran: For cats (neuters) seven years and over on the day of the show.
Radius: For cats (kittens, neuters) residing within a certain distance of the show.
Visitors: For cats (kittens, neuters) residing more than a certain distance from the show.
Supporters: Sometimes held for cats residing further than radius but not so far as visitors from the show.
Breeders: For cats (kittens, neuters) bred by the exhibitor.
Novice Exhibitor: An owner who has never won a money prize.
Aristocrat: A cat with one or more Challenge Certificates but not a full Champion.
Charity classes: All cats and owners are eligible but entry fees are donated to a cat charity.

Club classes
Put on both by the club holding the show and other cat clubs, to be entered only by members of the club sponsoring the class.

Household Pet classes
For unregistered cats of unknown pedigree, split into Open, Miscellaneous and Club classes. At a small show the Open classes may only be split into Longhaired cats and kittens and Shorthaired cats and kittens, whereas at a large show they may be divided into several colour categories. Household Pets are expected to be neutered when they are old enough, so there are no separate classes for neuters.

Early application is necessary because some shows are oversubscribed, especially in the United Kingdom, and entries are taken strictly in rotation.

Filling in the entry form
The classes you may enter may not be very clear for your first show and it will help you if you consult the breeder from whom you bought the kitten or an experienced cat show friend or cat club member.

Sometimes there is one form for all breeds, but at larger shows there are usually separate forms for the Longhair, Shorthair and Siamese sections, often on different coloured paper. Household Pets always have a separate entry form. Study the form carefully; the following notes may be helpful.

1 Before you start to fill it in get out your cat's registration or transfer certificate. The cat's name, sire, dam, sex, date of birth, breed number, registration number and breeder's name must be filled in on the form exactly as they appear on the certificate. Failure to do this may mean your cat is disqualified after the show when the catalogue is checked. In the case of the experimental breeds, these may only be shown in the Assessment classes. Fill in the cat's details on the form, and enclose details of the provisional standard on a separate card to be displayed on the pen. Cats with no provisional standard can only enter an Exhibition.
2 Now select your classes, checking your cat's eligibility for each, and write them in the correct space on the form. There is sometimes a separate space for the open class number, and if so, make sure you write it in there. Put all the class numbers on the same line, not in a column down the form. At most UK shows you must enter in at least three and not more than 12 classes, although some shows reduce either or both of these numbers. As you fill in the class numbers mark them on the schedule so that you can remember which ones you entered in, and do not forget to make a note of which cat you have entered if you have more than one.
3 Look up the entry fees for each class in the schedule: there are sometimes higher fees for the Open class and usually reduced fees for club members. Make sure that you enter the correct amounts in the spaces provided.
4 Many shows offer double pens, which cost more than the ordinary benching. These are in short supply so are usually only allowed for adult males and neuters: do not ask for one for your kitten or any cat which does not need it. If you wish to book a double pen fill in the amount on the form, other-

Types of Cat Show (UK)

There are three distinct types of show in the United Kingdom:

1 Championship This is run under the strict rules of the Governing Council of the Cat Fancy (GCCF) and Challenge Certificates are awarded. Open classes are provided for all breeds and in the case of breeds with Championship status separate classes are provided for male and female adults.

2 Sanction Conducted under the same rules as a Championship Show with the same classes provided but no Challenge Certificates are awarded. It is a dress rehearsal for a Championship Show.

Some Championship and Sanction Shows cater only for a particular breed or group of breeds; these are called Specialist Breed Shows.

3 Exemption Held under the same basic conditions as the above shows but many of the rules are relaxed. For instance, the classes do not have to be split up as they are at Championship and Sanction Shows, so that all the Siamese adults of different colours might be put in the same Open class at a small show. Exemption Shows are often run as part of an agricultural show.

In addition to the three types of show described above, special exhibitions of pedigree cats are sometimes held, often in conjunction with a cat club meeting. These cats are on display and no judging takes place.

Pet cat shows are often held at agricultural shows or similar events. Household pets may be exhibited at these, but no cat which is registered with the GCCF may compete at anything other than a Championship, Sanction or Exemption Show. Classes for non-pedigree Household Pets may be held at all three official types of show but not all shows have room for such classes.

wise fill in the ordinary benching fee. If you are booking a double pen and are entering more than one cat in the show, do not forget to indicate which cat it is for.
5 If you are putting a cat on exhibition look up the fee for this and enter it on the form. All details of the cat must be filled in as above.
6 There may be additional spaces for entrance tickets, club subscriptions, etc., so if you wish, fill these in also.
7 Now add up the benching, entry fees, etc., and check your arithmetic. Write a cheque for the correct amount and make sure that it is payable to the right account.
8 If you live a long way from the show you may be able to obtain an early pass, enabling you to leave the show half an hour or an hour early. This must be booked with your entry, and if it is being permitted there will be a space to mark on the entry form. Not all shows permit this.
9 On the back of the form fill in the names of clubs of which you are a member.
10 Fill in your name, address and telephone number. If you wish to help at the show fill in the appropriate space, but if you have never helped before do say so.
11 Before signing the form, check everything again and see that your cat complies with all the rules and regulations.
12 Sign the form and date it.
13 Send the form off as quickly as possible, and certainly by the closing date, or your entry will not be accepted. Many shows do not have room for all the entries they receive and many have to be returned, so the earlier you can send your form in, the less risk there is of yours being one of the unlucky ones. Make a note of the

date you post your entry in case there is any query.
14 Remember to enclose your cheque with the completed form: no entry will be accepted unless it is accompanied by the correct entry fee.
15 Enclose a stamped postcard addressed to yourself on which

---

you have written 'your entry has been accepted.' If you do not do this you may not know whether or not your entry has reached the show manager until you receive your tally just before the show.
16 Also enclose a stamped, self-addressed envelope marked 'tally' in the top left corner. This is for the show manager to send you the following items: a tally (a small disc, usually white, with your cat's show entry number on it), vetting-in and pass-out cards, and entrance ticket (if paid for). At some shows these items are handed out at the entrance to the show, and if so this will be stated in the schedule. In the latter case there is obviously no need to send a tally envelope. The entry number cannot be allocated to the cat until the show catalogue has been compiled, so your tally and cards will not arrive until a few days before the show.

If, for any reason, you have entered your cat and find that it will be unable to go to the show, inform the show manager if possible. If the cat is unable to attend due to illness and you send a veterinary certificate stating this, to reach the show manager at least seven days prior to the show, your entry fees or part of them may be refunded.

Never enter a cat that is unwell or pregnant, and make sure your cat is inoculated well in advance of the show. Once your application is accepted groom your cat daily until show day, and acquire the show equipment you will need. Preparing a cat for a show career involves handling it regularly from kittenhood. If several people handle it the animal should grow used to strangers and remain calm when scrutinized by judges. Groom daily and feed correctly so

that your exhibit will be in prime condition for each show. (For grooming see pages 107-111).

Show equipment

If you are exhibiting in the United Kingdom you will need a white show blanket, white litter tray, white feeding dish and white water bowl. This uniformity is designed to help the judges judge cats only on their merits, uninfluenced by those of their surroundings. You will also need a length of white ribbon or hat elastic (tally elastic) to tie the cat's number around its neck. All these items can be purchased at some shows or from specialist mail-order firms. A bottle for carrying water is also worth including, and in cold climates a hot water bottle to go under the blanket will keep the cat cosy, but it will have to be changed every four hours.

The exception to anonymous show pens in the United Kingdom is the Supreme Cat Show. This was inaugurated in 1976 as an attempt to give an opportunity for winners at Championship shows to compete against one another in their own breed divisions. The awards in this show are Supreme Cat, Kitten and Neuter. Judging at this show is in show rings and the cats may be exhibited during the day therefore in decorated pens.

If you are exhibiting at this show you will want to make the most of your show pen to show the cat off to the public. You will choose curtains and a cushion to match or contrast well with your cat's coat or eyes. Some pens carry other ornaments—even flowers or necklaces around the cat's neck. Tastefully done, all these enhance the show scene for the visitor. Exhibition pens—pens containing cats not entered for competition—

may be decorated in all countries. Such pens contain cats for sale, cats as advertisements for breeders' stock, or new varieties.

Last-minute preparations
Have everything ready the night before the show. This means collecting all the show equipment just itemized; cat food and litter; and travelling container labelled with your name and address on one side only, so that it can be left anonymously under the show bench. Make sure that the cat is confined indoors so that it is not missing when you are ready to leave. Don't forget your own clothes and picnic.

Choose comfortable shoes for show day; there will be a great deal of standing and walking about. Do not put the show blanket in the carrier for the journey: there may be accidents. Keep the white blanket for the pen itself and use an old familiar one for travelling. Finally, never take a cat that is off colour; you may spread infection.

If the show is a long way from home, you may have to stay in a hotel for the night. First of all make sure that the hotel of your choice will accept cats. In this case, take a room with a private bathroom and put the cat litter tray in the bathroom. If the cat normally sleeps with you, it can still do so. If you leave the room, you should either put a notice on the door saying, 'Please do not enter, live cat at large' or, if you have room, take along a wire cage with a roof to it, approximately 91cm × 61cm × 61cm (36in × 24in × 24in), and place the cat in this, with a litter tray while you are out of the room. This will be for its own protection as well as for your peace of mind. These cat cages can be purchased; they fold flat for storage and travelling.

Remember to take along enough food for your cat for the whole trip. Canned foods or semi-moist are ideal for these occasions. I remember staying in a de-luxe hotel once in an English county town. In our rush to pack everything, we had forgotten the cat's food. We asked for the restaurant to send up four ounces of lean, finely chopped raw steak on a flat dish. The meal arrived on a silver salver with great ceremony and when we finally received the bill, we found that the cost of 'chopped fillet steak' from that restaurant was astronomical!

The next day, the hire car which had been booked to take us on to the show broke down and the owner of the car hire company kindly sent along his own Rolls-Royce. After all this star treatment, the cat just had to win, and in fact my Brown Burmese male obtained his third Challenge Certificate on that occasion, making him a full Champion!

Helpful hints for show day
On show day get up and set off early because 'vetting in' usually starts about 8 a.m. This is a medical check to make sure every cat

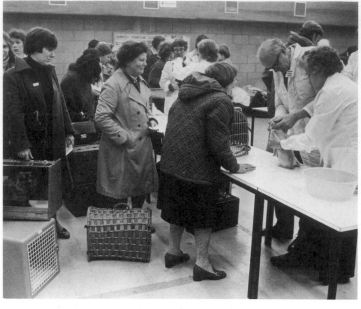

Above: Anxiety shows on the faces of owners during 'vetting in'. All cats must pass this health check by a veterinarian before the show.

admitted to the hall is healthy. If for some reason your cat does not pass the vetting in, it must go home again. Once past the veterinarian your cat can be penned. You can then feed and water it to make the pen ready for the judging. About 9.30 a.m. remove all food from the pen and tidy it, changing the litter if necessary. Place your cat's travelling container under its show bench so that your name and address cannot be seen by the judges.

Exhibitors must now leave the hall so that judging can begin, although many show halls have galleries from which it is possible to view the judging and to see how your cat handles. During the judging you may take the opportunity to see something of the town and eat your picnic or take a meal in a local restaurant. Usually you will be readmitted with the public at about midday. You can then see how your cat has fared.

Catalogues for the show are usually sold when the hall is cleared, and you may then buy one to check the details of your cat and the classes you have entered in. If there is any mistake ask to see the show manager quickly. If your cat has been missed out of a class or is in the wrong one it may be possible to rectify this before judging has finished in this class.

The classes in the catalogue are in the same order as in the schedule and the cats generally have consecutive numbers in their Open class order. Occasionally you will find that the adult males and females have been penned alternately to lessen the risk of full males upsetting one another by being in adjacent pens.

The first time a cat is mentioned all the details of sire, dam, date of birth etc, are given, and there is a list of other classes in which it is entered. In subsequent classes no details are given beyond its number, name and owner and sometimes a reference to its Open class number.

Sometimes classes are split if there are many entries. Two or more may be amalgamated if there are very few entries, except Open Championship classes.

There may have been a change of judges since the publication of the schedule. These must be published in 'Cats' magazine. All judges' changes must be displayed on a board just inside the hall.

At the back of the catalogue, after the classes, will be a full list of cups and specials offered by the club holding the show and supporting clubs. At the very end there is a list of exhibitors' names and addresses in alphabetical order, usually with the pen numbers of the cats they are showing.

While you are still restricted to the side of the hall or gallery overlooking the hall read through the catalogue and make a note of any cats you wish to look at in particular. You may be thinking about a stud for your queen or considering buying a kitten from a particular breeder. It is most annoying to get home, read the catalogue, and then wish you had thought to look at a certain cat at the show but omitted to do so.

Below: After 'vetting in,' the cats are put into their allotted pens by their owners, who will then vacate the hall for the judging.

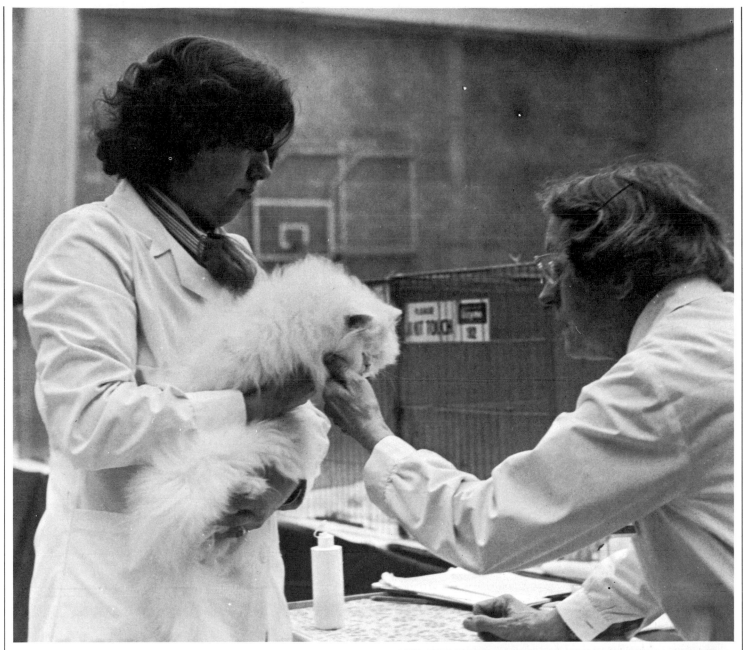

As the slips go up on the results board, mark the results of your classes in the catalogue. You may also wish to mark up the other Open classes in your section and possibly side classes too. As you get to know other cats and their owners you will probably wish to study their progress as well as your own.

The cats' numbers on the results slips are usually in the same order as in the catalogue, but occasionally they are not, so check this before writing the results down.

The judging
Judging in the United Kingdom is done by unpaid judges with the help of one or more stewards. The stewards find the cats which have to be judged in each class and let the judge examine each one, usually on a movable table, which is taken from pen to pen. The table is disinfected before each competitor, as are the hands of the stewards and judge. The judge makes notes in his or her book after examining each exhibit. He judges against a standard of points as laid down by the govern-

Above: Judging in progress. At this UK County Club Show the judges and stewards move from pen to pen, examining each cat in turn. The judge takes detailed notes.

Right: Judging at a UK National Cat Club Show. Notice the cat's show entry number disc (called the 'tally') tied around its neck.

ing body for each breed. Body shape, coat texture, coat colour, eye colour, etc., have a number of points allotted to them, adding up to 100. Most judges do not actually award points but put remarks in their judging books which enable them to assess the cat's standard. If they feel it is not high enough, the Challenge Certificate may be withheld.

The results will appear on an awards board showing each class with the cats entered marked 1st, 2nd, 3rd, etc. The letter CC mean Challenge Certificate, an award granted to the best cat in an Open class. In the United Kingdom, winning three Challenge Certificates at three shows under three different judges makes a cat

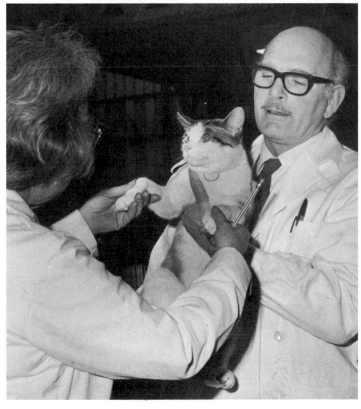

141

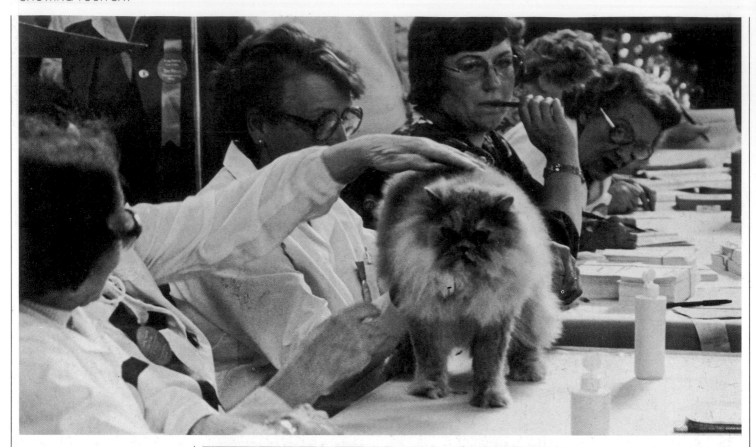

Above: Best in Show judging. Cats nominated from the winners of the breed classes are taken to a separate table and seen by a panel of experienced show judges.

eligible to apply for recognition as a Full Champion. Premier Certificates are awarded to the winners of the Open neuter classes for championship status breeds only if the judge deems the cat to be of sufficient merit. Three certificates must be won under three judges for a cat to be awarded Premier status.

Each judge nominates a best cat, kitten and neuter from the exhibits he or she has judged. A panel of judges, usually five of the most senior judges, see all the nominations, provided they have won their breed class, and vote secretly for the Best Cat, Best Kitten and Best Neuter. If the show is divided into sections, there will be a different panel for each section. They may ultimately, if there is such an award, choose the Best Exhibit in show from the Best Cat and Best Kitten. Neuters do not compete against full cats, but a Best Neuter will be chosen from other neuters nominated.

After the results are pinned up, the award cards are placed on the pens and sometimes the winners' rosettes as well. If your cat has won something, this is a very exciting time. It is a good idea to keep records of each cat's show wins, prize cards, dates of becoming a Champion and any other relevant information.

If judging has not finished when you are allowed to re-enter the hall, you must not talk to the judges while they are judging and you must not hang around your pen, indirectly telling a judge that

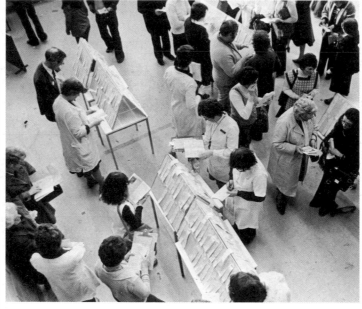

Above: Owners check on the progress of their cats as the results slips are attached to boards away from the judging area of the hall.

the cat is your exhibit. Nor must you obstruct the aisles while the judges are circulating. You must leave your cat on view to the public until the show closes, but for security reasons do not leave your cat alone towards the end of the day, and don't wait until people start dismantling the cages before you put your cat in its carrier: the animal could be upset by the noise. Lastly, do not leave your prize cards behind on the show cage!

After the show
After the show you and your cat will be tired. It is best to go straight home and rest. If several cats are

at home, isolate the show cat for two weeks if you can, in case it has caught and spreads an infection. All the show equipment must be disinfected. Your own clothes and shoes should also be sterilized.

There is a 14 day rule in the United Kingdom which means that a cat cannot enter two shows in under 14 days. This helps to curb infection and also prevents the cat being shown too often.

If you have won a cup or other prize, you may have to wait some weeks to receive it. Prize money is now paid out on the day at United Kingdom shows and must be collected on the day. It is refundable if later the exhibit is disqualified for some reason. If this is not done disciplinary action may be taken. If you have won cards or rosettes you can usually bring them home on show day,

and proudly display them at once. If you have not won a prize, do not get upset: somebody has to lose, and next time could be your lucky day.

If you and your cat have enjoyed your day, by all means go on exhibiting. Many cats plainly revel in show conditions. But if yours displayed nervous or bad-tempered behaviour, then it is kinder to leave it at home next time and go just for fun or taking another exhibit.

Perhaps you will come to enjoy shows enough to want to help with the organization. There are many jobs you could probably do—for example, stewarding for a judge, helping to enter results, fixing cards on the pens and placing result slips on the awards boards.

Becoming a steward
To become a steward in the United Kingdom you must ask a judge of the breed that interests you if you can act as his or her steward. If two stewards are required, you will probably first get the job as a second steward. In this capacity you would gain a great deal of experience. It is possible to work for your Steward Certificates.

It is the steward's job to make sure everything is ready for the judge to commence the judging, such as seeing that he or she has a judge's book; a Nomination for Best in Show form; a spray bottle with diluted disinfectant, paper towels and a cloth for wiping the table; a small table or trolley on which the judge can examine each cat; luncheon, coffee and tea vouchers, for both judge and stewards; badges for judge and stewards, which should be worn; and a pencil with a rubber on the

Above: A Seal Tabby-point Siamese with its splendid array of trophies, including Best in Show, awarded at the UK Supreme Show.

end. All of these items are supplied by the club running the show but it is the steward's job to make sure the judge has everything that is required. It is also the steward's job to get the cat out of the pen and to replace it in the pen after the judging. Consequently, it will be helpful if you are an expert cat handler, for cats are sometimes nervous at shows and take it out on the steward! It is important for everyone to clean his/her hands before handling another cat or the scent of one cat could upset the next, with dire results.

Once all the cats in one class have been judged, it is the steward's job to take the award slips to the awards table, having made sure that they are made out correctly. When all the classes have been judged, the steward takes all the equipment back to the show manager. Then comes the Best in Show judging and it is once again the steward who takes up to the table the cats that the judge has nominated for Best in Show. These are collected in their own carriers as there is often a long wait on the platform until each is called for. After judging, it is the steward's job to see that the cat is either placed in the Best show pen in front of the stage or taken back to its own pen.

Stewards are unpaid but the rewards for true cat lovers or young people aspiring to be a judge are manifold. You can learn a great deal. Stewards are not expected to offer their opinions on judging the various cats unless asked to do so by their judge. If you are known to be an expert by this time on a certain breed, you may be asked for your opinion. Otherwise listen and learn!

After many years of breeding and showing you may even consider becoming a judge or a show manager. Many famous judges are asked to judge at shows in other countries. Showing could open up for you a whole new exciting field with an international flavour. You may also have the opportunity to export cats with your prefix worldwide.

Showing in the USA

The United States has seven registering associations, each with its own standards and rules. The largest and most powerful is the Cat Fanciers' Association (CFA). Most of the smaller associations will accept a CFA registration without question, but the courtesy does not necessarily go both ways. In some ways, CFA is a conservative association, so it is beneficial to the cat fancier at large to have other associations where new breeds and colours can be registered and shown before achieving CFA acceptance. Additionally, some of the minority associations are strong in certain regions of the country and they give the public and the exhibitors the opportunity to participate in more shows than if there were just one association. It is not unusual for a cat to be registered with several associations and to hold titles in each. Since there are so many associations holding shows, it is possible, particularly on the East or West Coasts, to show your cats almost every weekend if you want to and can afford it.

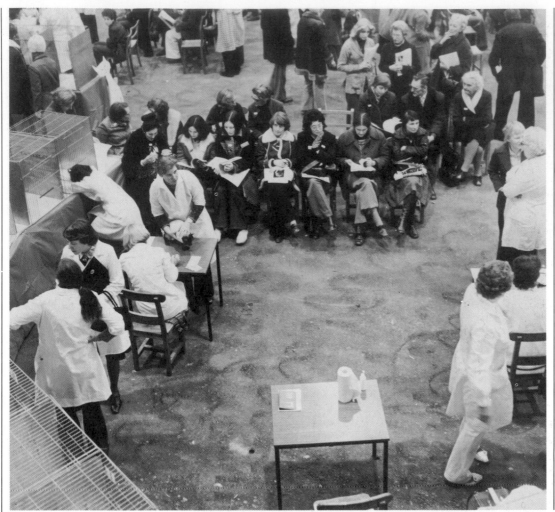

Above: A top judge at the Supreme Show checks the points awarded by previous judges before selecting from the cats in front of him those which will go forward for the Best Exhibit round of judging.

Left: The judging area at the Supreme Show. This follows the American layout with the judges grouped near a row of pens that open on two sides. The cats are put into the pens on the outer edge of the area and taken by the stewards from inside to the judges' tables. Cats are seen in batches.

Below: Steward and judge working as an efficient team at the Supreme Show, which is restricted to prize-winners from Championship shows.

Most American shows have roughly the same format, regardless of sponsoring association. The cats are brought to the show hall, which may be an auditorium or a banquet room in a large hotel. They are checked in by a clerk and assigned a cage that will be theirs for the duration of the show. All cats shown by the same person(s) are benched together regardless of breed. Exhibitors may request to be benched next to certain other exhibitors so that most of the Korats or most of the Manx may be in one part of the room.

The cages are decorated with fabric curtains, colour-matched litter pans, toys, and other paraphernalia which will flatter the cat and/or be compatible with the theme of the show. Most shows give prizes for the best decorated cages. Usually trophies and ribbons from other shows are not displayed.

Each cat has a number which corresponds to its listing in the show catalogue. The catalogue carries the name of the cat, the names of its parents, owner, exhibitor and breeder, and the cat's date of birth. It also shows the cat's show status in that particular association—Novice, Open, Champion, Grand Champion, Premier, Grand Premier. It is not unusual for an Open to be a Champion in another association and a Grand Champion in still another, but these other-association titles are not indicated in the catalogue.

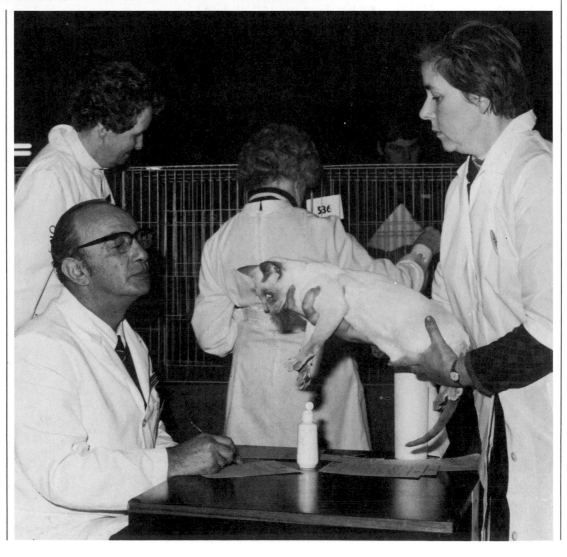

The judging

Judging tables are set up in a section of the room, or around the edges. Behind each table is a row of 10 cages; in front of the tables are rows of chairs for the spectators and exhibitors.

Show committees schedule the classes so that each cat will be evaluated by each judge. Most shows have four judges, but the larger, more prestigious shows may have as many as six or eight. In the past, two-day shows were common, but due to inflation and the increasing cost of transportation more and more shows are trying to get it all into one day.

Judging usually begins at about 10.00 a.m. and may last until 6.00 or 7.00 p.m. Cats are called by breed and colour, 10 at a time. A large class, such as the Burmese, for example, may take a very long time to judge. The judge takes each cat out of its judging cage, puts it on the show table, examines it from all angles and thoroughly assesses its merits before returning it to its cage. The judge then makes notes about the cat and sprays a sterilant on the judging table and his or her own hands before handling the next cat. This first handling tells the owner and the audience very little. It is only when the cat is called back to be compared to other outstanding cats that it becomes apparent that the cat is being seriously considered for meaningful awards.

This process of elimination is followed by each of the four judges, and the judges work independently, so although they are all following the same standard, it is not surprising when a cat does well under one judge and is not even noticed by another. That's show business! It takes a truly extraordinary cat to meet the standard *and* please the personal preferences of four experts.

The suspense of the day culminates in the judging of the Best of the Best. The 10 cats that have gained the most points during the course of the show are called for a final judging.

Points are collected for each Champion beaten. If a cat has no disqualifying faults, it is relatively easy to become a Champion at one show (unlike the UK), but when that status is achieved, the competition becomes more intense. In some of the smaller associations as few as 15 points may be required to become a Grand Champion, but in CFA most breeds must have 250 points to become Grand Champions.

Most US shows range between 200 and 500 entires. In a 300-cat show, 40 might be Household Pets (no points), another 60 might be Kittens, and the Premier (Alter/Neuter) class might be as large as 30-40. The whole (entire), adult purebreds are not competing with any of the above classes, so it is virtually impossible for a cat to Grand at a single CFA show. It can be done at some of

Above: An Abyssinian at the Supreme Show in a pen decorated for the Christmas season. Great care goes into decoration and at some shows prizes are awarded for the most attractive displays.

the large shows, but such winnings are rare. More likely, a good cat will be shown regularly for one or two seasons, gradually picking up points.

The luxury of time is not available to the Siamese and some of the Himalayan cats. All cats are shown as kittens until they are eight months old. Although the experience is good for them, they do not acquire any permanent points. Siamese and Himys are shown heavily between 8 and 12 months to get their Grand Championships before their coats start to darken. Since Himalayans do not get their full growth until they are three years old, there has been an effort to breed lighter coated cats and more Blue-points to gain a longer show career.

Other breeds that may have an awkward adolescence, such as Manx, are shown as kittens and then disappear from the show scene while they go through their rangy stage. When they start to look cobby again at two or three years, they are brought out again to compete for their adult honours.

Some cats are retired when they reach their Grand Championship to embark on a

breeding career, but many continue to be shown. These cats are going for Regional and National wins. Points continue to be gained just as they were before the cat became a Grand Champion. These points determine the top 10 or 20 cats in the entire country and in each section of the United States. With so many fine cats vying for these honours, campaigns are planned so that the cat is entered in one or two shows almost every weekend of the season. The cat may be shipped coast to coast and shown by other exhibitors called agents. It is estimated that the entry fees, shipping and travel expenses may total as much as $18,000 to $25,000 to get the title of Best Cat of the Year in America. If the cat is a well-adjusted male, he may offset some of his expenses by accepting stud dates in various cities he visits, but usually a cat in the show circuit is not a dependable sire, and the risk of exposing the cat to different females every weekend is very great. A scratch or a disease might end his show career.

Cats are campaigned for prestige and for increased value of future kittens, but not for immediate money. A few shows have been known to give silver dollars or foreign coins featuring cats, but these are tokens. There are no substantial money prizes at cat shows as there are in other types of livestock competition.

Instead, ribbons, rosettes and trophies are given. There has

been a trend in recent years toward non-trophy trophies. Conventional trophies are handsome to win, but are dust-catchers when you get them home, so show committees are leaning toward plaques, trays, silver, crystal and the like as prizes and these more useful, less space-consuming awards seem to be appreciated by exhibitors.

Household Pets

The most enjoyable prizes are often given in the Household Pet competition. Wine, cheese, chocolates for the owners and pillows, toys and catnip for the cats are typically given.

The Household Pet class at most shows is quite large. This is the entry level. This is where most people start showing. Often, after they have had the satisfaction of being rewarded for the good care they give their pets, they decide to buy a purebred and get into the mainstream of competition.

The criteria for Household Pets are condition and grooming. Cats may be of any age, size or description. In most associations they must be neutered (after eight months of age) and they must not be declawed. The class may be divided into longhairs or shorthairs, males or females for judging purposes. The Household Pets may or may not be judged by the same people who judge the purebreds.

A few associations have a separate class for pets that look

like purebreds but are obviously pet quality examples of their breed or do not have pedigrees. This category removes purebred look-alikes from the Household Pet competition, thereby eliminating possible prejudice for or against them from the judging.

New breeds

There is also a Provisional class for breeds that are being considered for Championship status. Representatives of these new breeds are handled and evaluated by the judges, but they are not really in competition. Some breeds spend as long as five years as a Provisional breed before becoming eligible for championship competition.

Cats that may be shown but are not handled by the judges are classed as For Exhibition Only and For Sale. Purely experimental cats that have not achieved Provisional status may be displayed to acquaint the public with them and to get the unofficial reaction of judges and other exhibitors.

Kittens over four months of age and cats that are For Sale are sometimes brought to shows because many spectators are looking for a cat to buy. More often, breeders put up signs and hand out cards to prospective buyers to protect their kittens from the stress and exposure of the show environment and to have a better opportunity to screen the would-be owners to make sure the cat will be getting a good home.

The cost of cat shows

Cat shows are designed to give people the opportunity to show their cats *and* to be revenue pro-ducing. Currently, the average entry fee is about $15.00 per cat, purebreds and Household Pets alike. Sometimes there is a small discount for people who enter several cats. Admission for spectators may be $1.50-$2.00. Additionally, areas around the show hall are rented to vendors who put up booths to sell cat supplies, cat art and artifacts, T-shirts, books, magazines and anything else that is cat related. Usually the sponsoring club has a food booth so that the show may go on uninterrupted rather than having people go out to lunch. Most shows also hold a raffle which raises money for the club. A show with 500 entries, 5,000 spectators, 20 vendors and a hungry crowd can be a real money maker. After the auditorium rental, judges' fees, trophy, advertising, printing and all other costs have been paid, the sponsoring club usually donates most or all of the profits to charities such as shelters or feline research projects.

Cat shows are the heart of the Cat Fancy in America. The millions of cats owned and the billions spent on them are widely publicized the world over. High density living coupled with clean-up-after-your-dog laws in major cities have made cats the Number

One pet in America. Only a small percentage of these are purebreds; fewer still are used for breeding. Breeders hope to cover the costs of keeping and showing their cats. Purebred cats are expensive—and so are feed bills, veterinary costs and show fees. Hardly anyone is making money with their cats, but through cat shows, money is made that helps support the Cat Fancy at large through contributions to shelters, neuter and spay clinics and advertising campaigns, and research programmes to improve the health and population control of all cats.

Cat shows generate media interest. Every article, every TV film clip about a cat show and the spectacular cats in attendance helps raise cat consciousness.

Very many spectators flock to the Household Pet judging because they love seeing cats just like the ones they have at home win prizes and get applause. They talk to exhibitors and learn how to give their cats better care. They find out that if they want to enter old Fluffy in the next cat show, they'd better get old Fluffy spayed and vaccinated.

Without the purebreds, there would be no cat shows, but the

Below: A Birman third prize winner at the Supreme Show. This com-petitor seems completely at home amidst the bustling show scene.

fall-out from the exhibition of these exotic beauties is of growing benefit to all cats.

Showing in other countries

Show procedure varies from country to country. Standards of points for different breeds also vary and vetting-in regulations in each country depend on the endemic diseases there. In New Zealand, Australia and South Africa it is basically similar to the British pattern.

New Zealand In New Zealand there is only one Cat Fancy comprising many clubs, each running shows. Judges must have bred cats of their section (Longhair or Shorthair) for at least five years in order to be eligible. Foreign judges are often invited to judge at the larger shows. Only Championship shows are held but there are usually classes for Household Pets.

The shows last one day only and as in the UK the cats are penned anonymously, grouped according to breed. In addition to the Open classes there are various Side classes including 'type classes' in which the cat is judged on type alone, coat colour and pattern being disregarded.

Sweepstake classes are also held, the winners each getting a percentage of the entry money. Challenge Certificates are awarded to Open class winners of sufficient merit and, as in the UK,

three Certificates under three different judges give the cat his Championship.

The hall is cleared for judging, which takes place from the pens. Stewards get the cats out for the judge and make notes for him. Judging usually finishes by 1 p.m. and the exhibitors are allowed back into the hall to see what their cats have won and to decorate their pens to make a splendid show for the public.

Australia There are seven states in Australia, each with at least one Cat Fancy, but these all co-operate with each other. They use judges from other fancies, recog-nize each other's registrations and exhibit at shows run by clubs belonging to other fancies.

Judges have to train hard and are not simply accepted on breeding and stewarding experience. As in the United Kingdom they are not paid and receive only their expenses.

All judging, including Best in Show, is done by the judge going to the cats in their pens. In all classes cats are judged only against others of their own breed, unless they are nominated for Best in Show, when they will compete against other breeds.

South Africa Shows are run similarly to those in the UK, the judge going from pen to pen. Two stewards get the cats out for the judge, who dictates his remarks on

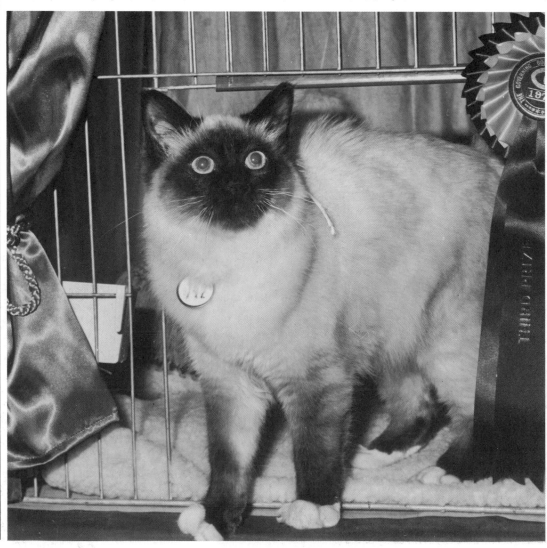

the cats to a note taker or scribe.

There is a sheet of paper for each cat, giving details of breed, sex, age, etc. (with the name to be filled in later by the judge), on which the judge makes a written report. These reports are later circulated to the exhibitors.

All the classes a cat may be entered in at any one show will be judged by the same person but Best of Breed or Best in Show is determined by a panel of judges. The panel sits in a roped off area to which the cats are brought by stewards.

Training to become a judge is very rigorous: clubs nominate suitable people, who then go through a course of lectures and demonstrations, at the end of which there is an examination. Judges are unpaid, receiving only their expenses.

Europe On the continent there are many Cat Fancies, some of which are linked together under the Fédération Internationale Féline d' Europe (FIFE), which has member organizations in 12 European countries. FIFE does not recognize registrations with other bodies in Europe, nor may a cat be registered with FIFE members as well as with others. FIFE members may not buy kittens from non-members, nor use their studs.

FIFE shows are all Championship shows and may last one, two or three days. Cats are judged on a points scale as follows:

Excellent 88 to 100 points
Very Good 76 to 87 points
Good 61 to 75 points
Fair 46 to 60 points

The major classes are:

International Champion for Longhair/Shorthair full International Champions.
International Premier for Longhair/Shorthair full International Premiers.
Champion for Full Champions, with classes for both sexes of each breed. A CACIB (Certificat d'Aptitude au Championnat International de Beauté) is awarded to the winner of each class if it gains at least 95 points.
Premier for full Premiers, with classes for each breed. A CAPIB (Certificat d' Aptitude de Premier International de Beauté) is awarded in the same way.
Open for cats 10 months and over, but not including Champions or International Champions with separate classes as before. A CAC (Certificat d' Aptitude au Championnat) is awarded to each class winner if it gains at least 93 points.
Neuter for neuters 10 months and over of each breed. A CAP (Certificat d' Aptitude de Premier) is awarded to winners gaining at least 93 points.
Kitten classes for 3 to 6 month kittens and 6 to 10 month kittens of each sex and breed.
Neuter Kitten classes as above.
Litters, 8 weeks to 3 months, with at least three in each litter.

Four places are given in each class, first, second, third and mentioned, and the judges' reports on each cat are given to the exhibitors at the show.

To become a Champion a cat must win three CACs under three different judges, and to gain its International Championship it must be awarded three CACIBs under three judges, at least one of these being won in a different European country.

In addition to the major classes there are classes for imported cats, progeny classes and novice classes in which unregistered cats may be entered. If the latter gain sufficient points they are registered.

The cats are penned in decorated pens with all the cats belonging to one owner grouped together. The hall itself is also beautifully decorated. Judging usually takes place in a separate room, to which the cats for each class are carried by stewards. They are then penned anonymously in plain pens. The International classes are judged first, followed by all the Champions, then Premiers, Opens, etc. Afterwards all the judges form a panel to select the Best Longhair cat, kitten and neuter, and Best Shorthair cat, kitten and neuter, and finally the Best in Show.

In addition to the shows run by members of FIFE there are also independent shows in most European countries.

Above: A hopeful entrant in a show for Household Pets organized by the UK Milk Marketing Board, a 'one-off' special event.

Below: Best Lilac-point Siamese kitten in Show, proudly held by the Show Manager, whose hard work has made the show possible.

10

TRAVEL AND BOARDING

Sometimes you are bound to want to take your cat on a journey— maybe to the veterinarian, a boarding cattery or a show. The most docile cat can become very lively, even uncontrollable, when frightened by unusual surroundings, smells or noises. For this reason never carry a cat any distance in your arms: it may go suddenly berserk and leap off, never to be seen again. This can also happen to an unconfined cat in a car when the door or window is opened.

A cat-proof container is, therefore, essential for travel. The ideal container is one that is light to carry and easy to clean, with plenty of ventilation all round, but above all escape-proof. The one pictured on this page is an example. If you are preparing for a journey of any length it is a good idea to confine the cat some hours beforehand so that you can be sure it is not missing at departure time. A clean litter tray presented before putting the cat in its box will usually have the desired effect of 'potting' the animal before take-off. Making calming noises to the cat during transit will help to reassure it, and many cats that would not do so at home will hold a conversation on a journey. They seem to need the constant assurance of the owner's presence.

Sedatives

Tranquillizers are sometimes prescribed for cats before a long journey. They may be excellent for dogs, but often seem to have the opposite effect on cats: some appear less controllable or more ferocious after taking sedatives than they were before. Most cats travel quite happily, if sometimes noisily, without them, so unless you find they make an otherwise

Above: Cats being taken anywhere must be in a cat-proof container. This one in polypropylene is hygienic and well ventilated.

Left: This cat is enjoying a holiday in a spacious boarding cattery with an individual run and high-level shelves for viewing and interest.

intractable animal easier to manage, it is wisest not to use them. It is doubtful whether sedatives help most cats, and possible that they cause considerable harm.

Short journeys

For really short journeys, such as a visit to the veterinarian, your container need hold no more than the cat's blanket, so that the cat is not entirely cut off from all that smells familiar. Prepare the carrier in advance and show it to the cat only inside a room with closed doors and windows, as some cats disappear at the sight of a container, knowing from experience that something strange is about to happen. Use the same procedure

for removal to a new home or to a boarding cattery if these trips are also short, but on such occasions include a toy or some other additional familiar or favourite object.

Long journeys

These may include going to a show, away to stud, or on holiday with the owner, or moving house— perhaps even to another country. If a show is held a long way from home, you may have to make a very early start or spend a night in a hotel. Either way do not use the show blanket for the journey, as it may get soiled; keep it for the show pen. Travelling long distances with a cat means taking a supply of food and water and making provision for calls of nature. If travelling by car, you can stop now and then. Make sure you close all doors and windows before letting the cat out of its carrier to perform in a litter tray. Put it back after it has stretched its legs, done some investigating, had a cuddle and been offered a drink of water. This last item is especially important on a hot day. This routine is not possible when you are travelling by bus, plane or train (though some have tried it in a closed compartment). For these occasions it is best to use a container large enough to take a small litter tray and with provision for D-shaped food and water dishes to hang inside. Dry food is preferable to wet food for a long journey as it does not attract flies.

If the journey is to another country it is essential to find out beforehand whether there are any quarantine restrictions at the point of entry. Cats coming to the United Kingdom, for instance, are required by law to pass six months in quarantine at a registered

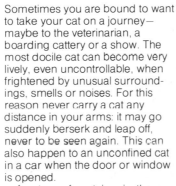

quarantine cattery. They must be met at the point of entry by a representative of that cattery and transported there under conditions laid down by the appropriate ministry from whom a permit must be obtained. This is because the United Kingdom is rabies free and wishes to remain so. There are strict penalties for trying to smuggle a cat into the country or otherwise contravening these regulations.

Holidays

Whether or not you take a cat on holiday depends on the cat and the situation involved. If you have two homes, you may find that your cat adjusts quite quickly to spending some time at each. But if you are visiting a place unfamiliar to the cat, it should be kept in a wire pen and taken for walks on a harness in dog-proof territory. It is never very satisfactory to tether a cat and most cats are great escapers.

Remember, too, that unlike many dogs, cats from one household do not mix readily with those from another, because cats have a strong sense of territorial rights and each feels threatened if a strange feline enters its territory. There are exceptions, but it is generally better for a cat to stay in its own home or to go to a boarding cattery than to accompany its owner to an unknown holiday home.

Right: A visit to a veterinarian has sometimes to be made and this see-thru carrier shows the cat off very well, but some cats prefer to be invisible when travelling.

Cat Containers and Cages

1 Plastic-coated wire carrier. Well ventilated and easy to clean.
2 Small breeding unit with two compartments, one private.
3 Solid cardboard carrier with air holes in the sides. Folds flat when not in use. Inexpensive; useful.
4 This vinyl Karri-Kat Holdall has a see-thru clear plastic viewing window. Easy to carry.
5 The Hi-Flyer was designed specifically for cats and can be used at home as two beds or for kittening in. The two halves nest and there is provision for a padlock. A small litter pan and parrot cups can be used for long journeys.
6 This is a smaller but heavier carrier in polyethylene.
7 See-thru containers are popular with owners who want the public to admire their cats. This one is sold in a box for self-assembly.
8 Fibreglass carriers have metal doors with locks. Good-quality, but somewhat expensive.
9 These fibreglass cages are ideal for one night at a boarding cattery, for use as an isolation unit or for recovery after an operation.
10 The large plastic-coated wire playpen and fibreglass base make an ideal combination to put kittens in whilst you are out, cooking or otherwise occupied.

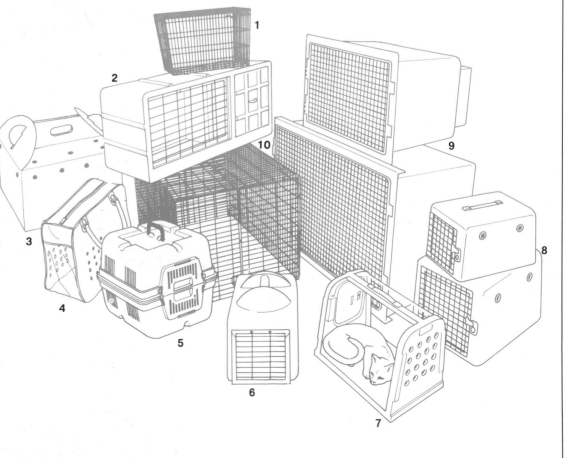

A cat can be left at home by itself for one night provided you leave water available and set a timed or other feeder to provide food when necessary. There are several types of such feeders available. If you are away for more than one night, it is necessary for someone, preferably familiar to the cat, to live in as a 'cat sitter' or at least to visit and feed the cat on a regular basis and change the litter tray. In this way the animal stays in its own familiar surroundings and enjoys human company each day.

The boarding cattery

If no responsible friend or neighbour can care for your cat while you are away, the cat must go to a boarding cattery. There are relatively few really good ones about, so when you have found one, book as soon as you know the dates of your absence from home. You might need to inspect several catteries first. If possible, pick one with an individual house and fresh-air run for each cat, where it can view the others, but not come into 'sneeze' contact. Keep your cat in for some hours before taking it to the cattery.

It is a good idea to invest in a packet of instant grass, sowing a batch one week before departure date and asking the cattery owner to sow a second batch on arrival. This will ensure a constant supply of grass for your cat to chew during the holiday. Another good idea is a flower pot planted with a root of catnip from the garden, or catnip plants grown especially in pots to be put in the boarding quarters. The cat will enjoy chewing the catnip and rolling in ecstasy round it! A favourite toy and a blanket the cat can recognize by smell will make it feel at home. Tell the boarding cattery of any food fads and fancies and about any medication that needs to be administered. Some catteries will groom longhaired cats for a small extra charge, and you can expect a good cattery to give a little individual time to each guest while feeding, watering, changing the litter tray or bed making.

Quarantine

Cats undergoing quarantine are effectively placed in a boarding cattery for a long stay: six weeks in some countries, six months on entering the United Kingdom. These cats need the same basic care as short-stay boarders, except that their grass needs replenishing weekly. But six months without seeing their owners would be a trial for most cats. Visiting once a month, or more often if distance permits, will renew friendship and keep a bond between the cat and its owner. If you are importing a new cat, your visits will help the cat and its owner to get to know each other. I suspect that people who never visit on the grounds that 'it would upset the cat' say that for their own convenience. Cats love having visitors who come along to make a fuss of them and to break the monotony. As visiting day comes round they get obviously

Above: An ideal boarding cattery has a house for each cat and a separate outdoor run. Only cats from the same household can be put together. These two Siamese watch other cats with interest.

Right: Two young owners bring their cat in for boarding and help it to settle in. Its own blanket and basket will help to make it feel at home. The owners can now really enjoy their own vacation.

excited on hearing their owner's reassuring voice.

Stud visits

A queen who is calling may be taken or sent unaccompanied to a male cat for stud service. At such times it is doubly important for the container to be cat-proof because a calling queen is an escaper extraordinary who will squeeze through the narrowest of openings. It is advisable not to open the container on arrival until the queen is inside the quarters she will occupy for the whole of her stay. A fight often ensues when the stud meets the queen, if the stud is ardent and the queen is not ready or has gone off call on the journey. (See the section on breeding, starting on page 121). A diet sheet is usually sent to the stud owner with the queen, explaining her particular likes and dislikes.

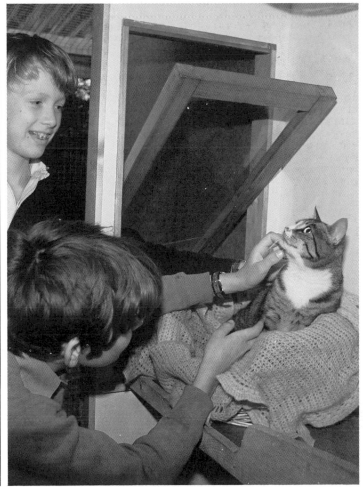

11

THE LAW AND YOUR CAT

Unlike dogs, cats are virtually outside the law, and because they are considered untrainable their owners are not held responsible for their actions—particularly if these merely express their nature as cats. But cats do have some legal rights, and acquiring a cat involves accepting legal as well as moral responsibility for its welfare.

Licences

Individually, cats are unlicensed, because ownership is difficult to prove and impossible to enforce. Similarly, in the United Kingdom, people do not need a licence specifically to breed cats or sell their offspring.

However, a pet shop must have a licence before it can sell livestock of any kind, including cats. The shop must have its quarters inspected regularly and satisfy the licensing authority that it has suitable accommodation for the species it wishes to sell; houses no more than the number of animals stipulated on the licence; offers a suitable and adequate supply of food and drink; and visits the animals at required intervals. The licence is for one year and must be renewed annually.

The pet shop must not sell animals under a certain age depending on the species (kittens 8 weeks) or to children under 12 years old. The shop must also take adequate precautions against disease and fire. Cats may not be kept in a cellar or near mice or other animals that would normally form their prey. Also they should be out of reach of the public. It is in the interests of all animal lovers if you report unsatisfactory pet shop conditions to the local authorities.

When a pet shop sells a non-pedigree cat, the responsibility lies with the buyer to purchase the kind of kitten that he or she wants. However, when selling a pedigree cat, the pet shop or breeder is responsible under the UK Trades Descriptions Act (1968) for selling exactly what is stated on the pedigree form (known as 'Papers' in the USA). Pet shops should also be careful to buy only from reputable sources or they may find themselves accused of 'receiving stolen property.'

In some states of Australia a licence is required for the sale of cats. In New Zealand licences to sell livestock are not required by pet shops unless there is a bylaw under the local authorities. Australian and New Zealand pet shops are visited and checked regularly by the RSPCA and SPCA Inspectors to check accommodation, cleanliness, over-stocking, supply of food and water and for any disease. All pet shops are required to take adequate precautions against disease, fire and other emergencies.

In the United Kingdom boarding catteries must also have licences. These establishments are obliged to provide suitable accommodation, food, drink, heat and light. They must undergo annual inspection by a veterinarian acting for the licensing authority, who may then revoke or renew the licence. (Incidentally anyone wishing to start a boarding cattery may also have to get planning permission for a purpose-built establishment.) Unfortunately it is left to each local authority to decide the precise meaning of terms such as 'adequate' space or ventilation or what constitutes 'suitable' accommodation. Ideally, legal minimum standards should be clearly specified on a national basis.

Licences are required in some states of Australia for people who board other people's cats. Licences are not required in New Zealand, but in both countries the local authority's permission is necessary for the operation of a boarding cattery and it must comply with town planning specifications. Boarding catteries are also inspected by RSPCA and SPCA Inspectors.

A third type of licence is that needed to quarantine imported animals.

Quarantine laws that apply to the United Kingdom

Animals that could transmit rabies must go into a quarantine establishment for six months on entering the United Kingdom. This includes *all* cats. Some other countries have a quarantine law but most countries will accept animals from the United Kingdom as rabies safe, providing they carry with them a health certificate to this effect. Rabies is such a frightful disease for people to contract that anyone bringing undeclared cats or dogs into the United Kingdom is liable to a large fine and imprisonment. It is only by the strict enforcement of quarantine laws that the United Kingdom remains rabies free. Strict quarantine measures have also kept Hawaii, Australia and New Zealand free of rabies.

Quarantine laws for Australia

Dogs and cats may be imported only from the following places: the United Kingdom (including the Channel Islands), Ireland, Hawaii, Fiji, Papua New Guinea, Norfolk Island and New Zealand. The animals must have been continuously in the country of export for six months previously. During that period they must not have been in an import quarantine kennel. They must arrive in Australia with the prescribed documents, and this includes a health certificate.

Dog and cat owners who want to take their pets overseas, other than to New Zealand, should realize that they may not be able to bring the animals back into Australia on their return.

All dogs and cats destined for Australia from the UK, Northern Ireland or Eire must have with them an import permit issued by the Counsellor (Health), Australia House, London, together with health certificates issued by the veterinary authorities of the country of origin. Owners should check whether a clearance certificate for leptospirosis is required within 14 days of shipment. Leptospirosis can be present without the dog or cat showing any signs of ill health and owners are wise to have a preliminary test carried out in the last 14 days before consignment. If a positive test is returned, the case will be assessed by veterinary authorities at the time.

Any cats being brought in from a country that is deemed by the government authorities to warrant quarantine must be vaccinated for cat flu. All dogs and cats from the UK and Ireland are subject to 90 days' quarantine when they arrive by air or 60 days if they arrive by sea.

If a seal around the animal's crate is found to be broken on arrival, the animal may be refused entry. If a ship calls at ports on the way to Australia, or is not a container ship, or if on a plane trip the animal's crate is removed, the quarantine period is extended to nine months. Sea travel by container ship is often best, as unscheduled unloading rarely occurs. The animal may be quarantined at Sydney, Melbourne, Perth or Adelaide.

Permission to import from Papua New Guinea, Hawaii and Norfolk Island must come from the Chief Quarantine Officer (Animals), Department of Primary Industries, William Street, Brisbane. Quarantine is available in Brisbane only.

Animals from Hawaii, Fiji and Papua New Guinea must be accompanied by special documents, including a declaration of residence by the exporter, a health certificate issued by the veterinary authority of the country of origin and a veterinary declaration that no rabies has occurred in the country of origin for the previous five years. Special certification is required for animals from Norfolk Island.

Import of dogs and cats from New Zealand does not require special permission. The animal must, however, have a health certificate showing it has been treated for tapeworm within a specified period before entering. Quarantine is not required.

Quarantine laws for New Zealand

All cats being imported must have one month's quarantine in New Zealand, with the exception of animals from Australia. It is necessary to have a licence to quarantine animals imported into New Zealand. Licences are issued by the Ministry of Agriculture, and establishments holding such a licence are inspected regularly by the Ministry.

All animals that may carry rabies must go into a quarantine establishment for three months on entering New Zealand. Persons transporting cats and dogs into New Zealand without declaring them are liable to a large fine and imprisonment. It is only by a strict enforcement of the quarantine laws in New Zealand that the country has always been rabies free.

Identity discs

In the UK, Australia and New Zealand there is no statutory requirement for cats to carry such identification. However, if your cat goes missing such a disc may help you to recover it. Have the disc engraved with your name, address and telephone number and attach it to an expandable elastic collar placed around the cat's neck. If the collar snags on a branch when the cat is climbing a tree, the animal will be able to slip out of the collar instead of being hanged by it. Do not include your cat's pet name on the disc; a would-be thief could entice the cat away by using it.

Stray cats

Indiscriminate breeding among non-pedigree cats means there are far more unwanted cats about than there ought to be. Cat owners should do their best to stop this situation by neutering their pets, but for no good reason countless people shirk this responsibility and so add to the world's many million stray cats, most half-starved and diseased. In some areas cats running wild form packs that live round garbage dumps, causing health hazards. Health, fire, police and other local services lose valuable time attending to problems created by the stray animal community. Eventually, unwanted animals found wandering in the streets are taken to a pound and kept briefly in the hope that someone will offer them a home. Then most are destroyed, for their numbers far exceed the homes available.

Most people would surely be horrified to learn that over 18,000,000 cats are put down in the USA alone each year, and that most of these are healthy but simply unwanted. In the UK almost 99,000 cats were put down by the RSPCA alone in 1980. (Although nearly 37,500 were found homes.)

A well-organized and successful education programme would not only stress the need to neuter but provide funds to cover the cost for owners who cannot afford it themselves. In fact the USA has schemes and campaigns for federally funded spay and neuter clinics and already some of the clinics of British animal charities will perform free altering operations in certain circumstances. Ideally every cat born should be a wanted cat.

Cat charities
These were started to combat cruelty to cats—deliberate, due to neglect, or caused by ignorance of the animals' requirements. Some cat charities are scores of years old, but still a very necessary part of the cat scene. The first reported cat charity in the British Isles was the Dublin Home for Starving and Forsaken Cats, founded in 1885. There are now many national and local cat charities, some with a membership fee to help with expenses; some also produce a magazine giving monthly or quarterly news of the animals in their care. It is arguably a moral offence not to report cruelty towards an animal to the nearest or most powerful charity in your vicinity. Most national charities supply the names of their local inspectors in the telephone directories.

If you are an animal lover with funds to spare, such charities would also welcome bequests and donations. Some cat charities have been left veritable fortunes by grateful clients, and even individual cats have received quite large sums of money to assure their comfort after the death of their owners. The record amount in the USA was $415,000 in San Diego in 1960; and the record in the United Kingdom was £22,000 in Sheffield in 1975.

Cats and property
There are some homes, notably flats or apartments, where it is forbidden to keep pets. People who own their own houses usually have no trouble in this respect. But in the UK the Animals

Act of 1971 lays down that the keeper of a cat is liable for damage caused by the animal unless the damage is the fault of the person suffering from it or that person has voluntarily accepted the risk. The keeper of the cat is either the person who owns it or the head of the household, if the owner is a household member under the age of 16.

A cat keeper may not be held responsible for acts which are ordinarily committed by a cat. These include fighting (unless there is a known history of fighting with vicious intent) or watching or catching birds including pigeons, pheasants and chickens. The owner is generally not responsible when a cat trespasses and does damage if it is merely following its own instincts, like digging up a neighbour's seed bed, when wishing to perform its natural functions! Cats may not be shot at merely for trespass: they must also be proved to have caused considerable commercial damage. It is an offence to cause suffering to an animal or to a neighbour's cat or even to threaten to do so! (UK Protection of Animals Act 1911.)

Transport
Cats are required to be properly constrained in order to travel in public transport. It is an offence to have a cat loose in a car, if there is only the driver present. As a cat easily panics in strange surroundings, it is as much in its own interest as society's not to carry it along the street in your arms but to keep it inside an escape-proof container at all times when it is away from home. Normally you would not take a cat into shops, but you are likely to visit the veterinarian, where the presence of other animals, particularly dogs, calls for secure restraint of this kind.

Cats' rights
Although the United Kingdom has no statutory laws dealing with cats, these have their rights under the Pet Animals Act (1951), Cruelty to Animals Act (1876), Protection of Animals Act (1911) and Abandonment of Animals Act (1960). They are not protected by the Road Traffic Act and there is no obligation to report a motor accident involving a cat, although it is legally an offence not to report a motor accident involving a dog. You must also report any motor accident involving a cat to the RSPCA, the SPCA or the Police in Australia. But if a cat has been injured, the person who has caused the injury must do something to relieve the animal's suffering or they can be accused of cruelty. Scientists in the UK have to apply to the Home Secretary for permission to experiment on animals.

In the United States cats are protected by the Federal Laboratory Animal Welfare Act (1966), though this deals more with the housing and transportation of laboratory

animals than with the actual experiments performed on them. Otherwise cats are protected against cruelty, injury, abandonment, theft and ill treatment. The Animal Welfare Act is overseen by the United States Department of Agriculture (USDA) and requires that the care and treatment of animals in research laboratories is humane. All research institutions have to register with USDA and report annually.

Hundreds of thousands of cats are used annually in scientific experiments worldwide. Scientists use fewer stray cats than before, as modern laboratories prefer cats with a known history, especially those bred specifically for research and known to be pathogen free. Such animals are costly to replace, which—as much as any legislation—may help to ensure that they are reasonably treated, though some experiments are unquestionably cruel.

Certain moralists may take the view that all animals should have a legal right to live; others would argue that uncontrolled breeding results in so much suffering that some sort of population control is essential. The only two kinds of control are lowering the birth rate and raising the death rate.

Most people will prefer the first option, but far more education and legislation concerning neutering is required worldwide to make this kind of population control effective. Incidentally, as far as euthanasia is concerned, the American Humane Association has satisfied itself that the best method is introducing nitrogen into a cabinet.

Veterinarians
These have to pass rigorous examinations before becoming qualified to practise. It is an offence for a veterinarian to neuter or otherwise operate on an animal without a general anaesthetic.

Most New Zealand SPCAs have found that the best method of euthanasia is by intravenous injection of a barbiturate, done by a veterinary surgeon. When an SPCA Inspector has to destroy a badly injured cat, this is done by using a mixture of chloroform and carbon tetrachloride in a special chamber.

The different states of Australia have differing methods of destruction.

Responsible ownership
Feeding a cat on your premises may constitute ownership and you can be held legally responsible for the animal if you go on holiday or move house without making proper provision for it in your absence: it is an offence to cause suffering by neglect. Ownership will continue to apply until another owner takes over, so once you have accepted ownership you cannot just opt out of it. In fact it is an offence to tease, torment, ill-use, beat, torture, infuriate or terrify an animal; to neglect giving medical care in illness or accident;

to keep a cat in insanitary or otherwise unsuitable conditions; or to let it starve.

You may not legally carry a cat in such a way as to cause it suffering; or adminster poisonous or injurious substances or drugs; or perform an operation without anaesthetic. Furthermore it is a moral offence not to protect a cat against dogs and other natural enemies; or against being stolen by thieves for vivisection or fur. It is an offence to steal a cat known to belong to somebody else (Theft Act 1968) or to receive a cat known to be stolen. It is also an offence to keep a cat in too small a cage or to give it insufficient nourishment, proved by its emaciated condition. Cruelty under the law is generally reckoned to be such as 'to appal an average decent person.'

If you really care what happens to your cat or cats on your death, you should make a request in your will for your chosen actions to be taken, and these will usually be honoured.

Cat carriers
Airlines, railways and other carriers are legally bound to feed and water animals in their care at regular stipulated intervals and are liable for any injury which occurs due to their neglect or default.

Principal Animal Charities

In the United Kingdom
The RSPCA (Royal Society for the Prevention of Cruelty to Animals)
The PDSA (People's Dispensary for Sick Animals)
The Cats' Protection League
The Central Fund for Feline Studies (Feline Advisory Bureau)
The Blue Cross (& Our Dumb Friends League)
The British Union for the Abolition of Vivisection
The Raystede Centre

In the United States
ASPCA (American Society for the Prevention of Cruelty to Animals)
AHA (American Humane Association)
API (Animal Protection Institute)
American Anti-Vivisection Society
Bide-a-Wee Home Association
California Humane Council
FOA (Friends of Animals)
Fund for Animals
HSUS (Humane Society of the United States)
Mercy Crusade Inc.
Morris Animal Foundation
National Anti-Vivisection Society
Pet Assistance Foundation Inc.
Pet Pride
Society for Animal Rights
United Action for Animals

In Australia
The RSPCA
The Animal Welfare League
The Cat Protection Society

In New Zealand
The SPCA
The New Zealand Humane Society
The Feline Cat Protection Society

FURTHER READING

Alcock, James *A Cat of Your Own*
Sheldon Press, London 1980

Ashford & Pond *Rex, Abyssinian & Turkish*
John Gifford Ltd, London 1972

Beadle, Muriel *The Cat History, Biology & Behaviour*
William Collins, Sons & Co Ltd Glasgow

Burgess, Grace *Cats & Common Sense*
Price Milburn, New Zealand 1973

Catac Publications *All About Shows & Showing*
Catac Publications, Bedford, England 1979 (Reprint)

Dunhill, Mary *Siamese Cat Owners Encyclopaedia*
Pelham Books Ltd, London 1978 (Reprint)

Epton, Nina *Cat Manners & Mysteries*
Michael Joseph, London 1973

Faler, Kate *This is the Abyssinian Cat*
TFH Publications Inc. N.J. USA 1981

Feline Advisory Bureau *Boarding Cattery Construction & Management*
Feline Advisory Bureau 1979 (Reprint)

Fireman, Judy *Cat Catalog*
Workman Publishing Co, New York, USA 1976

Greer, Milton *The Fabulous Feline*
Dial Press, New York, USA 1961

Henderson & Coffey *Cats & Cat Care*
David & Charles 1973

Joshua, Joan *Cat Owners Encyclopaedia Veterinary Medicine*
TFH Publications Inc, N.J. USA 1979

Jude, A.C. *Cat Genetics*
TFH Publications Inc, N.J. USA 1977 (Reprint)

Kirk, Hamilton *The Cat's Medical Dictionary*
Routledge & Kegan Paul 1956

Lauder, P. *The Siamese Cat*
B.T. Batsford Ltd, London 1978 (Reprint)

Linzey, Andrew *Animal Rights*
SCM Press Ltd 1976

Lippman, M *Cat Training (How To Do Tricks!)*
TFH Publications Inc, N.J. USA 1974

Loxton, Howard *Guide to the Cats of the World*
Elsevier Phaidon, Oxford, England 1975

MacBeth & Booth *The Book of Cats*
Secker & Warburg Ltd, London 1976

Manolson, Frank *C is for Cat*
Pan Books Ltd, London 1979 (Reprint)

Manolson, Frank *My Cat's in Love*
Pelham Books Ltd, London 1970

Manton, S.M. *Colourpoint, Longhair & Himalayan Cats*
Ferendue Books 1979 (Reprint)

McCoy J.J. *Complete Book of Cat Health & Care*
Herbert Jenkins Ltd, London 1969

McDonald Brearley, J. *All About Himalayan Cats*
TFH Publications Inc, N.J. USA 1976

McGinnis, Terrie *The Well Cat Book*
Wildwood House Ltd, London 1976

Meins & Floyd *Groom Your Cat*
TFH Publications Inc, N.J. USA 1972

Mery, Fernand *The Life, History & Magic of the Cat*
Paul Hamlyn, London 1967

Moyes, Penny *How To Talk To Your Cat*
Arthur Barker Ltd, London 1979 (Reprint)

Naples, Marge *This Is The Siamese Cat*
TFH Publications Inc, N.J. USA 1978 (Reprint)

Nelson Vera M. *Siamese Cat Book*
TFH Publications Inc, N.J. USA 1976 (Reprint)

Pond, Grace *The Cat (The Breeds, the Care & the Training)*
Orbis Publishing Ltd, London 1980 (Reprint)

Pond, Grace *Complete Cat Encyclopaedia*
W H Heinemann, London 1979 (Repeat)

Pond, Grace *Observers Book of Cats*
Frederick Warne (Publishers) Ltd 1979 (Reprint)

Pond, Grace *Pictorial Encyclopaedia of Cats*
Purnell Books, Maidenhead, Berks, England 1980

Pond & Raleigh, G & I *Standard Guide to Cat Breeds*
Macmillan London Ltd, London 1979

Pond & Sayer *Intelligent Cat*
Davis-Poynter Ltd, London 1977

Ramsdale, J. *Persian Cats & Other Longhairs*
TFH Publishing Inc, N.J. USA 1976 (Reprint)

Robinson, Roy *Genetics For Cat Breeders*
Pergamon Press Ltd, Oxford, England 1978 (Reprint)

Sayer, Angela *Encyclopaedia of the Cat*
Octopus Books Ltd, London 1979

Sheppard, K *The Treatment of Cats by Homoeopathy*
Health Science Press, Holsworthy, Devon 1960

Silkstone Richards, Pocock, Swift & Watson *The Burmese Cat*
B.T. Batsford Ltd, London 1979 (Reprint)

Silkstone Richards, D. *Pedigree Cat Breeding*
B.T. Batsford Ltd, London 1977

Smythe, R.H. *Cat Psychology*
TFH Publications Inc, N.J. USA

Soderberg, P.M. *A.B.C. Cat Diseases*
TFH Publications Inc, N.J. USA 1967

Thies, Dagmar *Cat Breeding*
TFH Publications Inc, N.J. USA 1980 (Reprint)

Thies, Dagmar *Cat Care*
TFH Publications Inc, N.J. USA 1980 (Reprint)

T.V. Vet *Cats Their Health & Care*
Farming Press Ltd, Suffolk, England 1977

Urcia, Ingeborg *All About Rex Cats*
TFH Publications Inc, N.J. USA 1981

Urcia, Ingeborg *This is the Russian Blue*
TFH Publications Inc, N.J. USA 1981

West, Geoffrey *All About Your Cat's Health*
Pelham Books Ltd, London 1980

Williams, Kathleen *Siamese Cats* (Foyles Handbook)
W & G Foyle Ltd, London 1980 (Reprint)

Wilson, Meredith D *Encyclopaedia of American Cat Breeds*
TFH Publications Inc, N.J. USA 1978

Wolfgang, Harriet *Short Haired Cats*
TFH Publications Inc, N.J. USA 1963

Wright & Walters, M & S *The Book of the Cat*
Pan Books Ltd, London 1980

Zimmerman, Ruth *Abyssinians*
TFH Publications Inc, N.J. USA 1980

GENERAL INDEX

Page references to illustrations are in *italics*.

INDEX OF BREEDS

Page references to illustrations are in *italics*. Main entries are in **bold** type.

CREDITS

Artists
Copyright of the artwork illustrations on the pages following the artists' names is the property of Salamander Books Ltd.

Colour artwork
John Francis (Linden Artists): Pages 10-79

Line artwork
John Francis (Linden Artists): 18-41, 44-79
Alan Hollingbery: 116, 128
Keller-Cross: 88, 90, 102, 109 (BL), 114
Gordon Riley: 117, 118
Clive Spong (Linden Artists): 89, 109 (T), 123, 125

Photographs:
The Publishers wish to thank the following photographers and agencies who have supplied photographs for this book. The photographs have been credited by page number and position on the page: (B) Bottom, (T) Top, (BL) Bottom left, etc.
Alice Su: 76(T), 134(B)
Animal Graphics: Title page, Copyright page, 16, 24, 26, 28, 46, 50, 74, 88(BL), 92, 94(B), 96(B), 97(TL, TR), 98(T), 102, 103(T), 104(B), 122, 123
Animal Photography Ltd: 80, 84, 86, 91(TR), 94(T)
Animals Unlimited: Half title page, 8, 20, 68, 70, 76(B), 126(T)
British Museum: 131
Catac: 88(BR), 89(B)
Creszentia: Contents page, 36, 38, 40, 42, 44, 54, 58, 60, 78, 130, 132(B), 133(B,TR), 134(T)
Anne Cumbers: Endpapers, 22, 48, 62, 72, 82, 83, 85, 87, 89(T), 90(T), 91(TL), 93, 95, 99, 104(T), 105, 112, 114(B), 120, 121, 124, 125, 126(B), 127, 128-9, 132(T), 133(TL), 135(L), 147(T)
Folkestone Herald: 133(BR)
Fox Photos Ltd: 101
Marc Henrie: 106-111, 113, 114(T),115(B), 116-119, 135(R), 136, 138-146, 147(B)
Roger Hyde (© Salamander Books Ltd.): 100, 103(B)
Kentfield Taylor: 90(B)
Panther Photographic International: 96(T), 97(B), 98(B), 115(T)
Hugh Smith: 137

Author's Acknowledgment
Dorothy Richards would like to thank the Governing Council of the Cat Fancy (UK) and the Cat Fanciers' Association (USA) for granting permission for extracts from the show standards to be quoted; also the many people in the USA and Norway who sent in material on new breeds. A word of thanks to Miss Pat Turner, who answered awkward questions on genetics and a final thank you to June Brown and Debra Smith, who did much of the typing.

Publishers' Acknowledgment
The Publishers would like to thank the following individuals and organizations for their help in the preparation of this book: Elizabeth Pegg of the Royal Veterinary College, London, for advice on cat parasites; Grace Pond for help with the showing section; Maureen Cartwright for copy-editing and proof-reading; David Lambert for sub-editing; Stuart Craik for preparing the index.

PRINTED IN BELGIUM BY
proost
INTERNATIONAL BOOK PRODUCTION